ONE PUNCH FROM THE
PROMISED LAND

One Punch from the Promised Land

Leon Spinks, Michael Spinks,
and the Myth of the Heavyweight Title

John Florio and Ouisie Shapiro

LYONS PRESS
Guilford, Connecticut
An imprint of Globe Pequot Press

Lyons Press is an imprint of Globe Pequot Press.

Layout artist: Sue Murray
Project editor: Ellen Urban

Library of Congress Cataloging-in-Publication Data is available on file.

ISBN 978-0-7627-8300-7

Printed in the United States of America

10 9 8 7 6 5 4 3 2 1

This one's for Bill, Grot, Phil, Slim, Rick, and all the other guys who gathered around the TV at Applegates on fight night.—JF

For Ken Hartnett, who taught me the ropes.—OS

Contents

A Note to the Reader

In an effort to present Leon and Michael's story objectively and accurately, we have relied on first-person interviews and archival material. Quotes from our interviews, which we conducted over a two-year period from 2011 to 2012, appear in present tense. When quoting from secondary sources such as books, newspapers, and magazines, we have provided attribution within the narrative.

1

It started at a dead end in St. Louis.

One block from the rats, roaches, and junkies roaming the Pruitt-Igoe housing project, dozens of kids exercised in a square one-story brick building with broken plumbing, finicky heat, and a makeshift boxing ring set up on a volleyball court. This was the DeSoto Rec Center, and a glance around the room revealed the usual faces: Jesse Davison skipping rope, Harold Petty smacking the speed bag, James Caldwell sparring in the ring. Another regular, an eighteen-year-old with a thick neck, strong back, and nose for mischief, was pummeling the heavy bag. He hammered it so ferociously that the rest of the kids wouldn't dare get in the ring with him. His brother, a lanky teen three years younger and an inch taller, quietly shadowboxed in the corner. He had the look of a young pony learning to take its first steps. Leon and Michael Spinks had come to the DeSoto for the same reason as the others: to learn how to defend themselves on the streets they called home.

Pruitt-Igoe was no ordinary housing disaster. It was *Mean Streets* and *New Jack City*, circa 1971. It was an urban-American *Lord of the Flies*. And from the day the ribbon was cut on the first twenty of its thirty-three towers in 1954, it had been a lie.

The complex was a mile from the Gateway Arch, the city's iconic centerpiece, and had come with a promise direct from the St. Louis Housing Authority: Pruitt-Igoe would mark the end of the urban slum.

The cluster of nearly identical eleven-story glass and concrete erections was supposed to replace the decrepit row houses that had become an eyesore. The hype machine was cranking. The ads for Pruitt-Igoe presented a community straight out of *Ozzie and Harriet* and interiors worthy of *Better Homes and Gardens* magazine.

"Bright new buildings with spacious grounds," the ads read. "Indoor plumbing, electric lights, fresh plastered walls, and other conveniences expected in the 20th century." It wasn't long before other major cities—Baltimore, Detroit, Chicago, Philadelphia, and Boston—were modeling their own urban-renewal projects on the Pruitt-Igoe prototype.

But the developers had been skimping on materials from the start. Pruitt-Igoe was falling apart before the tenants had a chance to move in.

Worse yet, racial conflict was pulling at the seams of St. Louis, and Pruitt-Igoe only heightened the tension. The project itself was segregated: Pruitt Apartments were meant for black residents, Igoe Apartments for whites. Only when the Missouri Federal District Court ordered the desegregation of St. Louis public housing in December 1955 did the city tear down the project's invisible walls. Faced with the prospect of living in an integrated complex, white tenants backed out en masse. Black tenants with any other option followed. Only the poorest of black families remained.

When President John F. Kennedy was assassinated in November 1963, two years and ten months into office, his successor Lyndon Johnson vowed to carry through Kennedy's social programs, which were designed to address the very issues plaguing Pruitt-Igoe.

President Johnson addressed Congress in March 1964: "I have called for a national war on poverty. Our objective: total victory . . . Because it is right, because it is wise, and because, for the first time in our history, it is possible to conquer poverty, I submit, for the consideration of the Congress and the country, the Economic Opportunity Act of 1964. The act does not merely expand old programs or improve what is already being done. It charts a new course. It strikes at the causes, not just the consequences of, poverty."

Johnson didn't stop there. His administration was behind the Civil Rights, Food Stamp, and Fair Housing Acts. It introduced local health-care centers and nationwide urban-renewal projects. And it pushed through an unprecedented amount of anti-poverty legislation, including Job Corps, VISTA (Volunteers Service to America), Upward Bound, Head Start, Legal Services, and the Neighborhood Youth Corps.

But none of these programs made it to Pruitt-Igoe. North St. Louis offered its residents only two significant employers: the Brown Shoe Company and a General Motors plant that turned out the Caprice, the Impala station wagon, and the Corvette. Both factories systemically shut black workers out of skilled trades and confined them to menial jobs such as porters, sweepers, and material handlers. As such, unemployment among blacks in north St. Louis hovered at 19 percent. The only tangible impact Johnson's dream of a Great Society had on Pruitt-Igoe residents was that they now had a new label: the hard-core poor.

By the late 1960s drug dealers commanded the street corners, desperate junkies habitually ripped copper pipes from the walls, and armed vandals controlled the common areas. Residents ran for their lives, leaving two-thirds of the apartments empty. Life in Pruitt-Igoe became so precarious that cops patrolling the area stopped answering emergency calls coming from the tenants. The gangs grew stronger and the murder rate in north St. Louis soared, soon doubling that of New York City and eclipsing that of the rest of the country. The press reported crime in Pruitt-Igoe as black versus black. A more accurate description may have been gangs versus anybody left.

Michael and Leon lived the way most everybody who was stuck there did: in fear. How bad was it? For starters, the original plan called for skip-stop elevators, so by design, the lifts stopped at every third floor. A cost-saving measure, it was billed as a way to encourage residents to congregate in communal spaces. But the foul, urine-stained elevators rarely worked, and the squalid common areas—especially the desolate stairways—became dangerous pockets of crime. For most residents, there was no safe way to get home, other than scaling the side of the building with a pick and a rope.

"Pruitt-Igoe was a terrible place to live," remembers DeSoto boxer Jesse Davison. "No guys would come to fix the elevators 'cause they were afraid. I lived on the eleventh floor, but I didn't ride the elevators. I walked up the steps. You'd ride in the elevator, the lights would be broken. If you got stuck, you'd try to climb out the top, but you didn't know what would be waiting. There'd be drug dealers on top of the elevator. You'd be afraid they'd shoot at you, urinate on you."

Fellow boxer James Caldwell still remembers the dangers of playing basketball in Pruitt-Igoe. "Some guy would walk up to a car and start shooting. We'd all scatter. As soon as the commotion was over, we'd go back out and start playing ball again."

John Crittenden, who grew up on the same block as the Spinks brothers, has his own memories. "There were car thefts. There were homicides. There were robberies, crimes against the mailman, the insurance man. The insurance guys had to be escorted by police when they came to collect the premiums. It was crazy. When the police were called, they would wait on the main street until the backup came, if any came. They were slow to respond to anything that happened in Pruitt-Igoe because they felt like victims themselves. They would be shot at. People would throw bottles down on their cars."

For many young men trying to stay alive long enough to get out, there seemed to be only two means of survival: join a gang or learn how to box.

"Leon was a quiet kid," says Crittenden. "He kept to himself. He was bullied a lot. I was a little guilty of [the bullying] myself. He wouldn't stick up for himself. He was just a little snotty-nosed kid. He shied away from everybody. We took his lunch. We slapped him upside the head. We really did bully him, and Michael also. They wouldn't fight back. They cried and ran away. That kind of stuff was going on. You were either with the gang or you weren't. It was just part of growing up in Pruitt-Igoe."

When Michael Spinks was sixteen, a friend got caught in a robbery. "It was the first time I really thought that could have been me," he told Sam Smith of the *Chicago Tribune*. "I figured I either do this for the rest of my life or stop now and lead a new life. That's when I started listening to my mom regularly, going to church, learning about Jesus Christ. And I fought temptation like it was a disease. It was like I had to get in the ring every day because it was out there. Every time temptation came, I fought it off with prayer. The gangs came and turned on me. A guy punched me in the face and said, 'Fight back.' But I said, 'I ain't fighting. I'm done.'"

By the time Leon and Michael had walked into the DeSoto in the late 1960s, word had gotten out that the boxing workouts were agonizing. The source of that agony was postal worker Kenny Loehr, a five-foot-seven, bulldog-jowled ex-Marine. Loehr was easy to spot: He had a military buzz cut, baby blue eyes, bulging neck veins, a clenched jaw, and white skin. He was an ex-boxer himself—he'd won the St. Louis regional Golden Gloves in 1948—and started training boxers after serving in Korea.

Having never quite caught on to lackadaisical civilian life, Loehr had an old-school work ethic that he foisted onto the kids at the

DeSoto. He pushed them hard, routinely calling them "chickenshits" and "freaks," and never let up until the workouts were over. He ran the five-year-olds as hard as he did the teenagers, and when one of his kids got knocked out, he'd send him back into the ring the next day, telling him it would toughen him up.

The day Harold Petty walked into the DeSoto to try boxing, Loehr was patrolling the place with a broken two-by-four in his hand. Petty, a ten-year-old pipsqueak who would go on to become a decorated bantamweight and, following that, Loehr's assistant coach, had never seen the trainer before.

Loehr strolled over to a boxer who was whacking the heavy bag.

"Get your hands up! Extra rounds!" he shouted, as he cracked him on the small of his back with the plank. *Wham.* Then he turned to face the wide-eyed Petty. "Whaddaya want?"

"I want to box," the terrified Petty said, feeling his palms moisten.

"Get a rope!" Loehr shouted.

Petty scurried to the equipment locker to do as he was told. He swears to this day it took three years before he got up the nerve to speak to Loehr again.

Every boxer who came up through the DeSoto has a similar story about Loehr. What they'll also tell you—but what Loehr will never admit—is that the trainer doled out much of the money he earned as a postman to the boys, buying them shoes, coats, and food. In many cases Loehr was the closest thing to a father these kids had.

"If we didn't have something we needed, he would front it himself," James Caldwell says about Loehr. "And it wasn't just equipment. There were times when he made sure that guys had coats and shoes. Let's say we were in a tournament and a guy didn't have a nice pair of tennis shoes. He would get the guy a pair so that he could feel good about going into the tournament."

Steve Holley, former president of the St. Louis Amateur Boxing Association and longtime friend of Loehr, was equally generous. "It wasn't uncommon for us to have well over a hundred amateur boxing shows a year," Holley says. "The majority of the kids came from the projects like Leon and Michael, and when they came to the shows, we gave them ten, fifteen, twenty dollars for dinner money, and that was a lot of money back then. A lot of times they would save the money and take it home so they would have a little bit of money to either share with their families or use when they got back."

Loehr often drove through Pruitt-Igoe in a beat-up green '57 Chevy station wagon inherited from his sister-in-law. He'd rally the boys for training camp or ice cream, or in one case, his parents' anniversary party. He was one of the few white outsiders to dare enter the projects. But Loehr had an ace in the hole. Any gang member who touched him would have to deal with the wrath of seventy angry boxers.

"Hey, Chickenshit!" he'd yell out the driver's window as he parked near the Spinkses' building. "Get out here, freaks."

He'd then repeat the process at the Davison, Caldwell, and Petty households. One day, heading to a boxing show, he piled seventeen kids into the dilapidated car, the vehicle's engine wheezing under the pressure.

"If you scream, I'll kill ya," he told the boys.

They didn't scream. They didn't dare.

"Pruitt-Igoe, that was a tough place," Loehr says now. "That was no life. I remember this one store burned down and all my kids put on five, ten pounds 'cause they were going over there and eating all the food they could. They never had any food. You'd be riding by with your arm out the window and some kid would take the watch right off of your hand. Well, but they never had nothin'."

What the boys didn't realize was that Loehr was slowly turning them into skilled boxers and transforming St. Louis into a top-ranked amateur-boxing town.

"Back in those days we had one of the strongest amateur programs in the country," Steve Holley says. "Budweiser sponsored us. When the boxers wore those black jackets that said 'Budweiser Golden Gloves,' it meant something. Around town people knew that 'Hey, these guys, they're doing the do.' It wasn't jealously as much as it was respect."

And if a young boxer won his local matches, the program provided a ticket to the outside world. "I saw that I could travel as long as I beat my opponent . . .," Leon told BoxingTalk.com. "It was my best escape. And it was my best [way to get] respect in the neighborhood I stayed in. So the guys knew that I boxed and how good I did at it. And the guys that would jump on me wouldn't jump on me no more."

Michael suffered at first due to Leon's reputation. "Leon would get in fights all over the projects and win. But me, I became the target," Michael told Earl Gustkey of the *Los Angeles Times*. "Guys Leon had beaten up, they'd put together gangs and come looking for me, to get even. It was always: 'Hey, you Leon's brother?' And then . . . pow!"

But Leon's new status in north St. Louis served as Michael's inspiration. "I adored Leon. I wanted to be just like him," Michael said in an interview with Robert Seltzer of the *Philadelphia Inquirer*. "He was boxing as an amateur before I got into it, and he was knocking out everyone around. He was gaining a lot of respect in the neighborhood."

So the younger Spinks—quiet, diligent, and determined—took on the one contact sport that seemed to suit his gangly frame and long reach. And while he struggled to become more like his big brother, he listened to what Kenny Loehr and the other trainers told him.

By their late teens both Spinks brothers had built fighter's reputations for themselves. Nobody messed with them on the streets of Pruitt-Igoe. And few outboxed them in St. Louis amateur tournaments.

~•~

2351 Biddle Street. That's where the bubbling, gregarious Kay Francis Spinks raised her seven children in a cramped apartment on the eighth floor, smack in the middle of Pruitt-Igoe.

She was twenty when she and Leon Sr. moved into the projects—grateful they could rescue two-year-old Leon and one-year-old Karen from the converted bathhouse they'd been living in. It was 1955. Michael came a year later.

Leon Sr. wasn't ready for parenthood. Waking up just a year removed from his teens with a wife, three children, and a job as a busboy in a downtown hotel overwhelmed him. He handled the situation much the way he had dealt with high school and the countless jobs that followed: He quit. He owned little more than the worn-out pants around his waist, so there was virtually nothing to fight over. The divorce became official in 1959.

Leon Sr. made cameo appearances in the lives of his children but did nothing to support them other than sending Kay a monthly check that amounted to five dollars for each child. Kay's only income was her monthly welfare check of $135. And squeezing her budget even more were four additional children—Kenneth, Leland, Eddie, and Evan—none of whom belonged to Leon Sr. With all eight family members living on Kay's $150 total monthly income, food became a luxury. Dinners usually consisted of corn bread and government-surplus peanut butter.

It was clear to anybody who crunched the numbers that Kay needed every possible penny. Apparently, the government didn't bother doing the math. The welfare rules as they applied to female residents were as clear as they were unfathomable: A woman's aid would be cut off if she were living with an able-bodied male. It would also be reduced if she were receiving assistance elsewhere, even if it was the paltry sum of fifteen dollars a month from an unreliable ex-husband.

So when government workers came to the door to inspect—which they were prone to do—Kay's children knew never to speak of Leon Sr. or his monthly contribution. The task came easily to young Leon, a scrawny kid battling low blood pressure, intermittent blackouts, and memories of his old man that any child would choose to forget. One such recollection involves being hung by his shirt from a nail in the wall, then beaten and ridiculed. "You'll never amount to anything," Leon Sr. reportedly told his eldest son while swatting him across the face with an electrical cord.

According to a 1978 interview with Leon Sr. in the *Miami News,* the incident never took place. The elder Spinks said that he gave his son "only two whippings": once when young Leon refused to fight back after being kicked by another boy, and a second time when Leon returned from a shopping trip having spent family funds on a pocketful of candy.

Regardless of what really happened, Leon grew up resenting his father. Even Charles Sleigh, one of his teachers at Vashon High School, could see the animosity the teenaged Leon harbored.

"I wouldn't mention his father's name for anything," Sleigh told Tom Boswell of the *Washington Post.* "I couldn't watch his face."

Even though her funds were meager, Kay Spinks asked for no help raising her children. When Leon Sr. left, she found her strength in Jesus Christ. A devout follower of Pentecostal Christianity, Kay became an ordained evangelist, spreading the word of God through preaching, teaching, and living example. And anybody who came within a half mile of her knew it.

Kenny Loehr has memories of driving up to the Spinkses' building to take the boys to a boxing match, and having to wait outside until Michael and Kay finished praying. Cozy Marks, the former principal of Vashon High School, received letters from Kay asking him to pray for her and her kids.

Luther Boyd, Leon's childhood friend, recalls going to Kay's apartment for Bible study classes when he was nine years old. "She read scripture—I'll always remember 'The Devil's Funeral.' She told us the devil wanted us but God wanted us more, so we had to bury the devil. She was teaching us good and evil, and we knew about evil because it was all around us.

"There were between fifteen and twenty people [in the apartment], mostly children and teenagers. We would sit in folding chairs and praise the Lord and receive the Holy Ghost. We would dance and sing. People were foaming at the mouth. I don't know if it was the cookies and the potato chips, but I kept going back."

For every story about Kay that includes religion, there is another that mentions discipline. If the Spinkses' apartment were a city, Kay Spinks was mayor. She laid down the law and earned the respect of her children. There were rules to live by—how to behave, when to be home, where to hang out—and the Spinks kids did their best to obey. Except for Kenneth. He succumbed to the lure of the streets and at age twenty began serving fifteen years for first-degree armed robbery with intent to kill. Prison seemed to have done little to rehabilitate him. Two years after his release, he went back, this time for five years on a burglary charge.

It was between Kenneth's two prison stints, sometime around 1995, when Luther Boyd returned from the Army. Coming out of a grocery store, Boyd ran into a panhandler with a familiar face.

"You got all that shopping?" the panhandler asked, motioning to the bags in Boyd's arms. In north St. Louis, affording food was a sign of deep pockets.

"Yeah," Boyd said.

The panhandler flashed a wide grin and the smile reminded Boyd of his childhood friend.

"Look at you," Boyd said. "You're looking just like Michael Spinks."

"That's my brother," the panhandler said. "I'm Kenneth Spinks."

Stunned, Boyd reached into his pocket and plunked some coins into Kenneth's empty hand. As Boyd walked home, he couldn't help but wonder how a mother's teachings could land so squarely on some of her children and miss entirely on others.

The name above the entrance said Vashon High School. But the huge industrial windows, austere brick walls, and heavy metal doors gave it the look of a factory. And by the time Leon and Michael arrived, the hulking mass was on life support.

The late '60s had been as tough on Vashon as they'd been on Pruitt-Igoe. Originally located on Laclede Avenue, about a mile and a half from the projects, Vashon had been housed in a neighborhood systematically torn apart to make room for a spreading business district. During the decades-long transition, families moved away, teachers relocated, and enrollment dropped precipitously.

Few officials stood up for Vashon, the city's second all-black high school, which had turned out world welterweight champion Henry Armstrong, New York Yankee All-Star catcher Elston Howard, and US Congresswoman Maxine Waters. Why was Vashon overlooked? The answer is undocumented, but the evidence points to a deeply entrenched system of racism in the St. Louis public schools. After *Brown v. Board of Education*, Vashon should have been desegregated along with the rest of the nation's public educational institutions. Its neighborhood boundaries were supposed to be broadened to include white families, but those dividing lines never shifted. The school remained segregated and, like Pruitt-Igoe, was largely ignored and left to rot.

By the time Leon and Michael were ready for high school, Vashon had moved a couple of miles away to Bell Avenue. The hallways and classrooms were still bleak, but the school's curriculum offered its undernourished student body a range of courses that came with the promise of a living wage—auto mechanics, dry cleaning, shoe repair.

For Leon and Michael, it was too late. The dehumanizing conditions at Pruitt-Igoe had sabotaged any chance they'd had at academic success. They had too much to unlearn, and they weren't alone. According to the St. Louis Housing Authority, in 1972 the median number of school years completed by students who came from Pruitt-Igoe was 8.6, one of the lowest figures in the city.

Although Michael is remembered at Vashon as having a keen intelligence, a positive attitude, and a flair for boxing, he was too anxious about his mother's financial plight to concentrate on schoolwork.

Leon was never an attentive student but he had learned that only the strong survive. It was certainly true at Pruitt-Igoe, and it seemed to be the case outside the projects as well. Look at Muhammad Ali and Joe Frazier. No diplomas there, just strong, well-timed punches.

Looking back, John Crittenden says his classmate was "not a bright guy at all. We had seventh and eighth grade together and he was way below the level of the eighth grade. I can remember him writing his name on the blackboard and he had the *e* in Leon backward."

Principal Cozy Marks acknowledges that "Leon might have been slow, but I never noticed dyslexia or anything. [He had learned about life] in the community where he was from—had to be the tough guy, and that sort of thing.

"He had a discipline problem with one of the teachers. The problem was disrespect. Leon spoke out of turn, or he didn't respond the way the teacher thought he should have. One thing that was in my favor was that I was taller than Leon and I had about thirty pounds over him. He was on the verge of being suspended more than once. He had a hard time following directions, maybe because of his lack of concentration. No teachers, it seemed, were able to find a way to motivate him."

Kay Spinks often showed up at the principal's office on Leon's behalf. According to Marks, she never blamed the institution for her son's troubles. "'I know my boy doesn't always follow the rules,' she would say. 'I try to make a good world for him at home. And you do the same here. But in between we have to turn him over to that other world.'"

Marks knew that other world was no cakewalk. It may have been a little easier on Leon and Michael, who stuck to a small clique and protected each other. Still, the simple truth was that students at Vashon had the odds stacked against them when they left the classroom for the real world.

—◦—

March 16, 1972. A crowd of Pruitt-Igoe residents gathered to watch the fireworks. The Dore Wrecking Company of Kawkawlin, Michigan, had jammed dynamite charges into the western half of the building at 2207 O'Fallon Street and would be pushing the plunger when the clock struck three. In an act of final surrender, the St. Louis Housing Authority was scraping the fifty-seven-acre melanoma from the city's landscape.

Only days earlier the Health and Welfare Council of Metropolitan St. Louis issued a report stating that those who remained at Pruitt-Igoe were living in a "state of siege." The morning of the implosion, the police drove through the project instructing residents to close their windows lest the dusty fallout invade their apartments.

The tower on O'Fallon was going now. A second tower, on Dickson, was next.

The onlookers wore the grim faces of family members at an execution. Like so many on death row, Pruitt-Igoe could be blamed for its own wrongdoings, but it could also be seen as the victim of abuse and neglect. Regardless, it had become a worldwide symbol of failed public housing.

Jesse Davison was on hand. Luther Boyd stood at the window of his tenth-story apartment. James Caldwell peered out from his schoolroom, where the class watched the city euthanize its ill-conceived dream.

When the plunger fell, one-half of 2207 O'Fallon dropped to the ground like a pair of empty trousers, collapsing into 20,000 tons of industrial rubble. The crowd cheered as the dynamite went off, but they turned somber when a mushroom cloud of dust and pulverized mortar filled the air where the tower had once stood.

Jesse Davison felt mixed emotions at the prospect of his neighborhood vanishing one explosion at a time. "I stood and cried. We cherished that place. Don't get me wrong, it was bad. But we made our fun and we boxed there. That was our glory."

With their eyes smarting from the thick yellowish plumes of smoke, those on hand slowly returned to their homes.

The rest of Pruitt-Igoe was brought down by 1976.

2

THE YEAR WAS 1973 AND THE MARINES WERE LOOKING FOR A FEW good men. Desperately.

Unlike previous generations, teenagers in the late 1960s and 1970s weren't shielded from the images of war by the rose-colored lens of Hollywood's propaganda machine. The Vietnam War had played out in America's living rooms courtesy of network news cameras, and educated young men had turned their backs on the armed forces.

The United States had abolished the draft and begun withdrawing its troops from South Vietnam early in the year. To keep its ranks full and morale high, the Marines turned to Madison Avenue and the legendary advertising agency J. Walter Thompson to craft a new recruiting message. The result was a campaign of television commercials and magazine ads designed to seduce uneducated young men into the Marines by promising they'd become "one of the few." The message reached Leon who, at the age of 19, was drifting aimlessly.

Not surprisingly, the boxers at the DeSoto laughed when Leon said he planned to join the Marines. They figured he lacked the smarts to get into the armed forces and that he was too incorrigible to make it out. But Leon was smart enough to see that prosperity was not coming to north St. Louis any time soon.

One more glance at the advertisements was all it took. Leon walked into a recruitment office and found the Marines willing to accommodate him. Perhaps too willing. In those days, if an enlistee hadn't been sentenced to the armed forces by a judge, he had to hold a high school diploma or a GED. But Leon had neither.

Tony Santana, a bony twenty-year-old kid from the projects in Brooklyn, New York, was watching the same TV commercials. A featherweight who would go on to win the world military championship at 126 pounds, Santana had a shock of black hair and shoulder blades as angular as chicken wings. He was looking to build himself up, and the ads told him what he wanted to hear: He'd go into the Marines a boy and come out a man. Bingo. He enlisted and would soon pal around with Leon, killing time by sharing stories about their parallel lives in poverty, housing projects, and boxing rings.

Unlike Santana, Leon's love of the fight game landed him in trouble as soon as he arrived at Parris Island, South Carolina, for what was supposed to be twelve weeks of boot camp. His pals back at the DeSoto were right—Leon was ready to take on anybody at any time, regardless of his rank or position. Drill instructors were one of his favorite targets.

"Those drill instructors were terrible," says Leon's friend and fellow Marine Roger Stafford. "They would do anything, beat you down, call you names, talk about your mother, your brother, your father. When they talked about Leon's mother, Leon knocked two drill instructors out. They put him in the hole—he stayed there for like three months or longer. He was in Parris Island for six months until he was discharged."

The incidents surrounding Leon's rebelliousness could fill a training manual. One popular story, perhaps apocryphal, places him later on with a group of privates at Camp Lejeune when a gunnery sergeant walked out of a building and spit on the sidewalk. The sergeant hadn't looked where he was aiming and his gob landed a little too close to Leon.

"How 'bout an 'excuse me'?" Leon reportedly said.

The story ended as many others did—with a superior officer on the ground and Leon in hot water.

"I was a wise guy off the street," Leon told *Sports Illustrated*'s Pat Putnam. "It was difficult for me to adjust to somebody telling me what to do and what not to do. So I fought it. But I learned. I straightened myself out because I learned it was not so bad to live the life of a Marine."

However convincing Leon sounded, there's little proof that he did straighten out. By all accounts his greatest success as a Marine came after he left Parris Island for Jacksonville, North Carolina, a low-lying town of military barracks, crumbling retail outlets, and empty dirt lots. It was in Jacksonville—between tobacco fields, sweet potato farms, and the Atlantic Ocean—that the military had built Camp Lejeune back in 1941. It was to Lejeune that Leon was assigned, and where he donned his first pair of military boxing gloves.

At that time the All-Marine boxing team, long a source of pride to the Corps, was in the hands of Art Redden. A handsome black man in his early thirties, Redden presided over the gym in a fisherman's cap even though he'd never picked up a reel in his life. The day Leon walked into the gym, Redden was conducting varsity tryouts with Gunnery Sergeant John Davis. Redden had fought on the 1968 Olympic team that included George Foreman; Davis had brought six fighters to the '72 Games in Munich. The two men knew talent when they saw it, or, in the case of Leon, heard it.

In the midst of tryouts, Redden and Davis stopped dead in their tracks when the sound of a speed bag reverberated across the gym. There was one problem: The camp didn't have a speed bag. The two men made their way to the other side of the gym and discovered the source of the ruckus: nineteen-year-old Leon Spinks wailing away at the heavy bag with a fervor they'd never seen before.

Redden and Davis tested Leon's mettle by putting him in the ring. They didn't tell him he was in there with the All-Marine champ; they simply put extra-padded sparring gloves on both fighters and clanged the bell. Within thirty seconds the champ was stretched out on the canvas, knocked out cold by the troublemaking private from north St. Louis.

There was no doubt that Leon would fare better in a boxing ring than on a battleground. The Marines assigned him to special services—the boxing team—and in doing so, swapped the duties he'd had trouble meeting with those he'd been handling since his days at the DeSoto. Leon now had a structured routine he could follow: roadwork in the morning, boxing in the afternoon, and representing the Marines in the ring. Perfect.

Teammate Ron DiNicola saw firsthand how boxing trainer Art Redden did what no drill sergeant could. "Redden was able to marshal all of Leon's skill," he says. "Leon was a tough, tough kid. The toughness of Pruitt-Igoe never left him. He was a ferocious fighter. He was born to be a fighter; he loved the ring. Redden was about the same size as Leon and he knew how a big man should fight. He was a good tactician, delivering punches from one end to the other. And Leon was extraordinarily good at cutting angles on a dime and throwing combinations. For Leon, Redden was the right guy at the right time. He was a critical part of Leon's transition to the big time."

Years later Leon told BoxingTalk.com, "I'm a boxer puncher. Steady puncher. I don't stop. Most guys fight for a little while and then stop and hug each other. But the military taught me to punch all the time and stay busy."

Private Spinks was funny, loud, and friendly. Members of the team—one of the toughest and most successful collections of boxers ever assembled onto a single Marine squad—agree that Leon was the dominant personality of the group. Leon used words, gyrations, and body language to express himself with no regard for what people thought of his unrefined language and sandpapery voice. Sure, he was the butt of some jokes, but he didn't care. He was in his element—the gym—and enjoying himself. Informally, he was the team leader—a position he'd achieved with more than brute strength. He would urge on his teammates—yelling words of encouragement from ringside—and always remained positive.

Tony Santana, the wide-eyed kid from the Brooklyn projects, soon became Leon's roommate. "Everybody wanted to be like Leon," he says, recalling the years they boxed together. "He had the character and the heart and the attitude that a boxer needed. Leon took me under his wing. He came to my corner every time I fought. And he always invited me to go running with him. He talked to all the team members and always kept them up. We had the best boxing team and Leon gave us that. He was the leader of the team."

Teammate Buster Drayton remembers Leon as having the role of de facto coach. "When I signed up to join the team, [the guys] said you can't make the team unless Leon approves it. You have to box Leon and if he wants you to stay, you can stay. I said, 'What?!' They said, 'That's the way it is.' So he approved me. He's the one who said I could make the team."

It was 1975, and after a couple of years in the Marines, Leon had finally found what had eluded him for twenty years in the ghetto. For the first time in his life, he was proud of himself.

—◦—

Boxers are dumb. That's what Michael Spinks told himself as he walked out of Vashon High School with no intention of returning.

He was proud to be a boxer but not so proud that he'd lost sight of what the sport took from those who pursued it. He knew all about the vultures that picked the pockets of the poor souls who risked their lives in the ring. Look at what had happened to Joe Louis. His story was reason enough to avoid the sport.

No, Michael didn't quit high school to box. He left Vashon because he had little interest in academics—and an admirable itch to help his mother pay the bills. The Spinks clan had been relocated into a two-bedroom apartment in the Darst-Webbe projects south of downtown. The new housing situation was no more than a replay of the one at Pruitt-Igoe. Kay still needed all the financial help she could get.

"My mom couldn't support me," Michael told Tom Wheatley of the *St. Louis Post-Dispatch* years later. "I knew I should be contributing to the home instead of taking away. So all my guys, we'd kind of meet up down on Market Street and Olive, somewhere down there, at this labor pool."

At six o'clock in the morning, Michael would take the bus downtown and line up with the winos and derelicts hoping to get picked for eight hours of off-the-books labor.

"The best job I had there was at a salt factory, a rock-salt factory," Michael said to the *Post-Dispatch*. "It was a good-paying job. Yeah, it was a nice-paying job. The rock salt was the kind they put on roads. We'd cover the salt mounds up for the winter. We had to put, like, a canvas tarp over the mounds. I just so happened to have some Boy Scout work when I was younger. And I knew how to tie knots, slip-knots and all that. I was always happy to have a job. I was grateful for it. My attitude was, 'Hey, work me. I'm here to work.'"

It wasn't just talk. Michael put in long hours, getting to the job early in the morning, leaving at six, and working out at the gym later that night. But in the projects, tragedy could strike anyone at any time, as it did to one of Michael's close friends.

"That was a very terrible day in my life . . . ," Michael said. "It was like a dark cloud over the building I lived in. He got shot in the head.

He was in a dice game, a crap game. They got arguing, and it turned into a fight, and two people got shot, actually."

Michael was doing his best at seventeen years old to build a life away from the projects. When word got out that the Holiday Inn, twenty miles away, was looking for a dishwasher, he didn't think twice. He traded in his boxing gloves for a pair of Rubbermaids.

In an interview with Mark Kriegel of the New York *Daily News*, Michael said, "I was already happy. I had my mom and best friend, Kay Francis Spinks. I had my lord and savior, Jesus Christ. And I had a job, potwasher at the Holiday Inn, made $100 every two weeks. They promoted me from dishwasher."

But despite his new title, Michael couldn't quite shake the sport that he loved—and that loved him back. His strong punch and awkward style were leaving opponents on their backs, baffled by the riddle named Michael Spinks. He'd quickly risen to the top of the St. Louis amateur circuit: In 1974 he won a Golden Gloves title; in 1975 he made it to the AAU finals and took the silver medal.

"Michael was a slickster," says DeSoto teammate Mike Cross. "You couldn't tell where his strength came from. Out of the two brothers, I think Mike was the better fighter, but he didn't like boxing as much as Leon. In those days Leon was a fighter, a killer. Leon loved to fight. Michael didn't."

Michael was convinced the public had little regard for boxers. The evidence was all around him in St. Louis, which showered accolades on baseball heroes like Lou Brock and Bob Gibson but did no such thing for boxing champions. From what Michael could see, the international stage at the Olympics leveled the playing field, commanding a respect that wasn't gained by simply slugging your way out of the sweat-stained DeSoto. So with his résumé of Golden Gloves and AAU accomplishments inspiring self-confidence, Michael devoted himself to making the 1976 US team, vowing to leave the game afterward, whether or not his bid was successful.

He stepped up his training at the DeSoto. When he wasn't at the gym, he thought about his opponents. He thought about his punches. He thought about everything. He continued training with Kenny Loehr and also worked with Charles Hamm, a part-time trainer, full-time plumber, and around-the-clock guardian to the fatherless kids in the area.

"I thought Michael would go further than Leon because he was disciplined," Hamm says now. "When Michael came to the gym, he came to work. And if he didn't come to the gym, he wasn't gonna fight. You couldn't get him no fight if he wasn't training. Leon never trained, and he'd fight anyway. Michael would be real cautious about who he'd fight. He wouldn't get into the ring against someone he didn't think he could beat."

When Leon left for the Marines, Michael became tighter with their childhood friend Jesse Davison. Looking back, Davison can still picture Michael showing up at the gym late at night after work, lugging a boom box. Michael would wait for the gym to empty out—then he'd crank up the music, lace up his boots, and slip on his gloves.

Even though the place was deserted, he never felt as if he were going it alone.

"He always had a Bible in his hand," Davison says. "When we'd go fight out of town, to New York, to California, to Boston, he always got us in the room and read the Bible to us. And he'd say, 'Let's pray.' We were eighteen, nineteen, we thought it was funny. We thought it was *weird*. But I think that Bible took him a long way. It gave him courage, faith. And Michael wouldn't date girls. Wouldn't hang out with me sometimes. He just stayed with his boxing. I said, 'Mike, turn pro. You might make it.'"

But Michael had only one goal—making the Olympic team—and he focused obsessively on it. When working out with his friends, he was usually part of a group being pushed and prodded by Kenny Loehr. One story puts the boys in the DeSoto Center on a frigid day in January. The gym's heating system had broken again; this time the pipes burst. The floor was a sheet of ice.

"Keep jumping that rope," Loehr ordered them.

"Kenny, the floor's frozen," Davison pleaded. "It's too cold in here to work out."

"Are you kidding, you little chickenshit?" Loehr said. He had a twinkle in his eye, but there was no budging him. "Keep on jumping."

The boys trusted Loehr, so they followed orders, dutifully jumping rope on the ice, hitting the bags on the ice, and sparring on the ice.

"We're gonna tell our mamas," Davison said.

Loehr pushed them even harder. And when the workout was over, he took them all for pizza.

Michael got more than free dinners from Loehr. He plowed through the amateur ranks like a finely tuned battering ram, knocking down any hopeful that stood in his path.

In March of 1976 Michael found himself at the Golden Gloves in Miami competing to make the Olympic team in the 165-pound weight class. The qualifying match paired him with Lamont Kirkland, a promising amateur who would eventually post a solid pro career. Watching Michael overpower Kirkland, the TV commentators praised Michael's raw ability—especially his powerful overhand right—the punch that would later become known as the Spinks Jinx.

"Be careful of that right hand," the announcers shouted for the world to hear.

Kirkland wasn't listening. Michael landed his right hand at will. The good news for Kirkland's corner was that their fighter walked out of the ring with barely a mark on him. The bad news was that he walked out before the fight was over. He quit in the second round, giving Michael the fight, and in the process, handing him the middleweight title.

Jim Howell, a longtime coach and trainer in and around St. Louis amateur boxing, worked Michael's corner for the fight. "Michael was totally dominating everybody he fought," he says. "He clearly won every fight. He showed tremendous confidence and was so sure he was going to win it. So were all of us. When you go to a national tournament, you're fighting five times in one week. So you better be in shape. And Michael was in tip-top shape."

By winning the Golden Gloves, Michael qualified for the Olympic trials. He had three months to get ready. And he'd need all of it—the competition was about to get a whole lot stiffer.

— ᴖ ᴗ —

Art Redden wouldn't tolerate drugs or tobacco, but Marine Private Leon Spinks didn't seem to care. Leon often missed workouts—preferring to cruise the dive bars off base in Jacksonville. Few teammates accompanied him—not one of them could drink, dance, and party through the night and still show up for roadwork in the morning the way Leon did. But the parties didn't seem to compromise his talent or his enthusiasm for the ring.

"A lot of times he didn't come to the gym," recalls Tony Santana. "We were in the Marines. I don't know how he did it. He'd make little excuses. Leon was Leon. Once a month we had field day; you had to wear your uniform. I don't remember him coming with his uniform. He was so good they made excuses for him. He did it his way. He was Leon Spinks. He didn't care. *This is who I am, a straight-up guy. This is me, I'm not gonna change.* That was his attitude. And he never made weight. When we were fighting in the nationals, he would jump rope to make weight, then he would win the fight. Then he would jump rope to make weight for the next fight, and then he'd win again.

"Every time we went to another state, first thing he'd do, he'd take off. When he came back he knew all the spots, the people, where everything was at. He would find the clubs, meet a woman, then he would take us."

While at Camp Lejeune, Leon could usually be found on Court Street hanging out on "the strip," a civilian wasteland of abandoned buildings, strip clubs, pawnshops, tattoo parlors, and bars. The strip had so many drinking establishments that Leon's teammates took to calling the bus that got them there the Vomit Comet.

As sheriff of Onslow County, North Carolina, Ed Brown had seen it all. "[The Marines] would come off the bus and the white [guys] would go on one side of the tracks and the blacks would go on the other side," Brown remembers. "In those days you had marijuana, PCP, mescaline, LSD.

"First night on the beat, I've never seen anything like it in my life and never seen anything like it since. Knives, straight razors, Saturday night specials, old thirty-eight revolvers. You had a military base filled with young men with a lot of energy. You could rest assured there'd be three or four fights a night. And then topless dancing came in. When these military people were brought into town, from about eight o'clock in the evening to about two o'clock in the morning, especially on Friday and Saturday, it was so impacted that you couldn't even drive down the street. Me being a country boy who'd never been to town, I said, 'Lord, if you allow me to live to be thirty years old, I will have seen as much as the average man will have seen in a lifetime.'"

Marine Captain Bill Darrow, now retired, was largely responsible for putting together the boxing team at Camp Lejeune. "There was a black bar that was infamous, [Shaw's Café]. It was surrounded by empty lots," he says. "That street was dark, not a lot of streetlights. If you didn't know what you were doing, you were taking your life in your hands [just walking into the place]."

Leon was drawn to underground holes-in-the-wall. Shaw's was one. Another was the Bunkhouse, a forgettable establishment on the corner of Court Street and Chaney Avenue. Alma Gibson worked the bar.

"Leon was not one of my favorite people," she says now. "He used to hang around with one of my girlfriends who was very much into drugs. She was doing heroin. I can't say that he was, but he was always with her. He used to get drunk and [dance], and on a couple of occasions, I'm almost certain [the cops] took into consideration [that he was on the Marine boxing team] and let him slide with petty stuff."

Roger Stafford talks about the time he and Leon donned civilian clothes and went to the strip for a bite to eat. Stafford ordered a hot dog and waited almost a half hour for the food to arrive.

"The guy in the restaurant was white and he was giving me a hard time 'cause I was black," Stafford says.

By the time the counterman brought the hot dog, Stafford and Leon were out the door. The counterman called the police, and within minutes three local, white cops were grilling the two Marines. The cops ordered Stafford to pay for the hot dog.

"We were off the base," Stafford says, "and those were Jacksonville police officers. But Leon didn't care."

Stafford tried to stop the scene from escalating. "C'mon, Leon, don't worry about it," he said. "Leave it alone. C'mon, let's go."

It was too late.

"[Leon] got to fighting and he was knocking them down. He was so strong. It took all three police and they still couldn't handcuff

Leon. He was something else with his hands. He kept on fighting. I was screaming, 'No, no, stop, stop! Please, Leon, stop!' He wouldn't stop and they put him in the paddy wagon."

Sheriff Brown doesn't recall the incident but questions Stafford's memory of it, nonetheless. "Leon may have been a good fighter, but it wouldn't have taken three officers to put him down. We were country boys and just as tough. We didn't have the boxing skills that Leon might have had, but we came up from the old bare-fist fighting. So I won't say that he doesn't have it right, but I don't see Leon Spinks decking three police officers. But I'll let the gentleman have his story."

According to Stafford, when the police found out that Leon was a Marine, they let him walk. Leon would have been off the hook entirely had the cops not followed up with a phone call to the base. When Coach Redden got word of the incident, he doled out his own brand of punishment.

"The coach made Leon spar with everybody on the team," Stafford remembers, "starting with the lightest fighter, 106 pounds, all the way up to heavyweight. It was supposed to tire Leon out, but Leon was so ferocious he wouldn't get tired. He held nothing back. It was crazy. The little guy, he ran and ran around the ring to get away from Leon. When I got in the ring with him, I said, 'Oh, god.' He sparred with me like he was trying to kill me. I said, 'Leon, I was with you!' It didn't make no difference. He fought everybody as if they were an opponent. I was jabbin' him and moving around the ring, practically running, and he was chasing me down, swinging like a wild man, and he swung a left hook. I screamed 'Coach! Coach!' Everybody got whupped that day."

Leon whupped more than his teammates. As an amateur, he went 178–7 with 133 knockouts. He had taken on the moniker "The Wild Bull of Camp Lejeune" and collected nearly every boxing title the military had to offer.

"I was in the gym, and when I heard my brother won the national Golden Gloves, I said, 'What's better than that?' And they said the AAU [Amateur Athletic Union], so I won the AAU," Leon told BoxingTalk.com.

Actually, Leon won the AAU light heavyweight championship three times—in 1974, '75, and '76. He also won an inter-services title, a bronze medal at the World Games in Cuba, and a silver medal at the Pan American games.

According to a Marine legend and picked up by Thomas Boswell of the *Washington Post*, the only thing Leon lost in a military ring was his smile. Supposedly, his two front teeth came loose during a fight with Army boxer Tommy Johnson—an off-night for the "Wild Bull," which he later avenged three times. But this story has been discounted, revised, or refuted by virtually everybody involved.

In an interview with Ed Pope of the *Miami Herald*, Leon himself gave an alternate story. He claimed he lost one tooth in a sparring session and a second in a boxing match—both while in the Marines. A third, he said, was later pulled by a dentist. But Leon's account has many doubters, including Alan Richman of the *Boston Globe*, who reported that at least one of Leon's teeth was extracted when Leon's wife, Nova, sat on Leon's chest as her son pulled it out with a string.

Most evidence, including reports from those who knew Leon best, seems to point to Leon's losing his upper incisors as a young child.

Luther Boyd, Leon's childhood friend, says, "Michael and Leon had the same smile. But Leon didn't have any teeth. I don't remember Leon *ever* having any front teeth."

Tony Santana remembers Leon showing up at Camp Lejeune with a gap in his smile. According to Santana, Leon would plug the hole by "sucking his thumb right before a fight or when we traveled."

One thing was certain, though: With or without his front teeth, Leon was a lady's man. And of the ladies surrounding him during his military years, the most significant wasn't in North Carolina but in Des Moines, Iowa. Leon had met Noble Bush, a twenty-three-year-old single mother, through his Marine buddy J. C. Wade. It was right around Christmas 1973 when Wade shoved a live phone in Leon's hand and told him there was someone on the line he might want to meet.

"We cursed each other for ten minutes," Leon told *Jet* magazine. "Then we started laughing. We actually started going together over the telephone."

Noble lived 1,225 miles away, so the two lovebirds didn't lay eyes on each other for months. Through frequent phone calls and letters, Leon was able to find out all about Noble. She came from only slightly better circumstances than he did, she was the eldest of nine children, and she carried the weight of knowing that her mother had served eight months in prison for stabbing her father to death.

Leon finally met Noble face-to-face in the spring of 1974. She was hardly in as good shape as Leon—who was?—but she did stand taller than his six-foot-one stature, if you included her bleached Afro. Leon was smitten.

By then Noble had changed her name to Nova ("It represents not the car, but a new star," she told *Jet* magazine). On May 21, 1974, she changed it again—this time to Nova Spinks—when the bride and groom exchanged their vows in Des Moines.

Leon was visibly shaking. He was obviously more nervous than he'd ever been stepping into a boxing ring.

The preacher turned to Leon. "What do you have to give this woman?"

Leon hesitated. "My life," he said.

Nova elbowed him in the side. "The ring, Lee. The ring."

Leon then delivered on both counts: He handed Nova a ring and his life.

Within weeks Leon, Nova, and Nova's six-year-old son, Charles, moved into Tarawa Terrace, a housing complex on the base. The marriage was anything but smooth. Nova was convinced the Spinks family didn't like her because she wore too much makeup. It's nearly impossible to substantiate or refute her claim, but it's noteworthy that, years later, Nova made similar accusations about Top Rank, the company that promoted Leon's early fights. "[They] told me I looked whorish and warned me that white people don't take to black people with blonde hair," she told *People* magazine. "They all make me think negatively about myself."

Leon may have been Nova's husband but he wasn't around often enough to boost her confidence. He continued to spend time at the bar or in a boxing ring, leaving Nova at home with Charles.

This was old hat to Leon. He had already fathered two sons—Little Leon and Darrell—who were back in St. Louis with their mother, Zadie Mae Calvin. Just as the eldest Leon had been a teenage father and largely absent from his children's lives, so too was Leon.

Yet when the Olympic trials started, Nova gave Leon what he wasn't able to give to her or to Zadie Mae: a voice of encouragement. She repeatedly built Leon up and was persistent enough to drown out the echo of Leon's father telling him he'd never amount to much.

"You can be anything you want to be," she told Leon. And she was right. She just never realized he wanted to be a champion, not a husband.

3

THE MID-1970S WERE THE GLORY DAYS OF AMATEUR BOXING.
Picture a band of hopefuls with names like Thomas Hearns, Sugar
Ray Leonard, Michael Dokes, and Aaron Pryor traveling the globe
in hopes of winning Olympic gold.

How did America's talent pool get so deep? One theory could
be called the Muhammad Ali effect. The champion's ring style was
so infectious that mini-Alis cropped up in YMCAs and rec centers
from Bed-Stuy to East L.A. AAU and Golden Gloves tournaments
were flooded with Ali look-alikes, dance-alikes, and brag-alikes in
every weight class.

Award-winning sports journalist Robert Lipsyte says, "By the
time that Michael and Leon are heading toward the Olympics, Ali
is at the absolute crest of his popularity. He was by all means *the*
boxing role model, the last great heavyweight champion. I don't
mean strictly as a boxer. I mean, with all the role model accolades
of what that really once meant. It must have been an enormously
exciting time for the Spinks boys. Ali had won a gold medal in the
Olympics as a light heavyweight. In a sense, they were following
in his footsteps."

Some ring insiders believe America's newfound grit wasn't
found in its larger-than-life champion, but in the unassuming figure
of Rolly Schwartz, a retired Army major who'd become a prominent fixture on the amateur boxing scene. Schwartz had officiated
at the 1968 and 1972 Olympics and at six Pan Am Games, and was

credited with bringing about new international rules, including one that required amateur boxers to wear protective headgear. Schwartz was tired of seeing the Americans come out on the losing end. In the previous three Olympics, the United States had won only four gold medals, half as many as the Soviet Union, which was considered the world's amateur powerhouse. When recruiting talent for the 1976 team, Schwartz set up matches in Eastern Europe to expose inexperienced American boxers to international styles.

Three-time All Army champion Charles Mooney remembers traveling where other US amateur teams had rarely ventured. "I guess parts of Russia hadn't seen that many black people. And especially with Michael Spinks wearing that big cowboy hat, they couldn't take their eyes off him. We went downtown to look for some gifts and stuff, and a little boy came up to me and touched my hair. In the lobby the whole front window would be filled with people looking at this black boxing team."

In March of 1976 Leon and Michael arrived at the Olympic trials in Cincinnati, Ohio. They were among eighty-eight boxers competing for eleven spots on the US team. Michael, six-two and fighting as a middleweight, was in peak form and sailed through the early rounds. In the finals he outpointed four-time All Navy champion Keith Broom to win a lopsided decision and capture the middleweight spot. Leon, fighting as a light-heavyweight, advanced with three straight knockouts before squeaking by John Davis in the final qualifying bout.

Boasting what Rolly Schwartz called "chins of granite," Leon and Michael became the first pair of brothers to make the US Olympic team since the trials began in 1904.

The other slots on the team would be filled by light flyweight Louis Curtis, flyweight Leo Randolph, bantamweight Charles Mooney, featherweight Davey Armstrong, lightweight Howard Davis, light welterweight Sugar Ray Leonard, welterweight Clint Jackson, light middleweight Chuck Walker, and heavyweight John Tate.

However, given Olympic protocol, none of the eleven fighters would officially become Olympians until they confirmed their spots on the team by winning a double-elimination box-off, which was to be held in Burlington, Vermont. The rules of the box-off were simple: Each winner of the Olympic trials had to defeat his runner-up one more time. He'd be given two chances; if he failed, he'd forfeit his slot on the team.

Schwartz's rules were equally straightforward: "No smoking. No booze. No babes." The idea was to instill in his young fighters discipline, hard work, and commitment—and to convince them that they could win. Schwartz himself had high hopes, declaring to the press gathered at the team's training camp at the University of Vermont, "We have a minimum of four men who, with a good draw and fair decision, could go all the way."

Leon was not counted among them.

Schwartz later told United Press International (UPI), "Leon had some personal discipline weaknesses at our Olympic training camp. Michael was the first up in the morning doing roadwork and the last out of the gym at night. But not Leon. He was the type of fellow you had to push and push hard. We were continually on Leon to get himself ready."

According to Charles Mooney, Schwartz was putting it mildly. "Team coach Pat Nappi was gonna send him home," he says. "But there was a big [discussion] about that because it was the first time two brothers had been in the Olympics together. So that didn't happen."

Most of the boxers shared sleeping quarters, so they got to know one another's idiosyncrasies. "We had fourteen of us in one huge room," teammate Howard Davis says. "I happened to be laying down in a cot next to Michael and Leon. They shared a bunk: Leon was on the top, Michael was on the bottom. They would watch TV until the wee hours of the morning. And I liked going to bed early because I got up at 5:30 to do my roadwork. So this one particular night, they were watching a movie and they were laughing and I kept tossing and turning. After about fifteen, twenty minutes I said, 'You guys, man, you're incredible. You're at the Olympics, not many guys make it here.' And Leon says, 'Shut up, you little lightweight.' And I said, *He's right, I am a lightweight.* So just based upon poundage, I shut up. Ray Leonard was the captain of the team and he had his own room. I eventually ended up there because I couldn't take Leon and Michael laughing and talking all night long."

The Spinkses' antics extended from bedroom to bathroom. "To go to the bathroom, you had to go down to the basement from our dorms," Davis says. "I'm at the urinal and I see Leon come in. I'm from Glen Cove, Long Island, a really honest kid and sort of naive, and I'm looking at him and he's putting water all over his sweat suit and his face, and then it dawned on me: He's coming in from being out all night and wants to make the coach think he just got in from running.

"There was definitely some destructive behavior on Leon's part that didn't fit in with boxing. You can't drink, you can't party, or shouldn't, because it's bound to catch up. I can't remember anyone else on the team doing it. Leon loved to fight, but he didn't enjoy the rigors of training. One night he came in around one or two and I asked him where he'd come from. And he said, 'I was at a discotheque.' He was incredible. I don't know how he could muster up the strength to fight. But he was one of those rare individuals that had that I-don't-care attitude, I'm gonna fight no matter what. I truly believe if you put him in a cage to fight a lion, he would actually fight that lion."

"Even after he did all that [partying], you couldn't tell when he got into the ring," teammate Leo Randolph says. "It was a whole different person come about. That killer instinct that they say develops in a boxer, he had it. He'd get into the ring and just start wailing on the guy."

Despite his penchant for extracurricular activities, Leon scored a decisive victory against John Davis in the box-off. Michael lost a 4–1 decision to Keith Broom in their first box-off competition but survived the second with a first-round TKO.

When the team broke training camp on July 10, all eleven trials winners had preserved their slots on the Olympic team.

Next stop, Montreal.

— ·· —

On July 17, 1976, the Summer Olympics kicked off with its opening spectacle. Under the gaze of Queen Elizabeth II, the parade of athletes and team officials—nearly nine thousand representing ninety-three countries—went off without a hitch. But in the days to follow, twenty-eight African nations, and a few additional countries, boycotted the Games in protest of New Zealand's inclusion. The issue had arisen earlier in the year when New Zealand's rugby team toured South Africa, which had been banned from the Olympics since 1964.

The diminished competition did little to raise hopes for the American boxing team. Most experts agreed that the United States was no match for the Russians or the Cubans.

"We knew that we were up against maturity and experience," Olympic coach Pat Nappi told *Sports Illustrated* at the time. "Our kids would be out-experienced ten to one. When a man becomes a champion in an Iron Curtain country, you can bet he's good. Look at Russia. The last time I was there, in 1971, they had 480,000 amateur fighters. We had ten thousand."

To give their kids a fighting chance, Nappi and Schwartz studied their opponents and searched for their weaknesses. They analyzed films of previous bouts and assembled a playbook to combat the more experienced Eastern Europeans, who routinely trained eleven months a year. As Schwartz told the press, "Our guys have to use a little strategy, a little pizzazz. That's the only way to beat them."

"We had different styles, so we played different [training] games," Charles Mooney says. "Pat Nappi would have us open the gap and close the gap. He would show us how to move and punch. And then if we were aggressive, we had to know how to cut the ring off."

The team—eleven fighters and three supervisors—was housed in a small apartment at Olympic Village. Schwartz felt that living with his team in cramped quarters enabled him to key in on what made his fighters tick. The arrangement also made for a tight-knit unit wherein the guys formed close friendships, watched one another's bouts, and cheered one another on.

The strategies and accommodations seemed to work, because the team looked strong right from the opening bell. Nine of the eleven fighters blew through the first round. When it was Leon's turn, he chased Morocco's Abdellatif Fatihi around the ring, putting on a fireworks show that thrilled the 6,400 fans packed into Maurice Richard Arena. He overwhelmed Fatihi from the start and finished him with one second left in the first round. After the bout Leon was chased by so many autograph seekers that it took him and Michael nearly twenty minutes to walk the short distance from the arena to their apartment.

Michael had benefited from a bye in the first round and a walkover in the second as a result of the boycott. When he finally got into the ring, in the quarterfinals, he barely broke a sweat—demolishing Poland's Ryszard Pasiewicz with the biggest lopsided decision in the first eleven days of competition.

In Leon's quarterfinal match, "The Wild Bull of Camp Lejeune" knocked down East Germany's Ottomar Sachse shortly after the opening bell and then pelted him with a hailstorm of rights and lefts for the remainder of the fight. The only hiccup came when the Tunisian referee took a point away from Leon for talking back on a caution. When Leon came back out for the announcement of the decision, he was wearing a red and white Scottish cap. The referee promptly pulled it off his head and threw it into Leon's corner, which only made Leon more of a crowd favorite.

By the time the semifinals came around, Louis Curtis, Davey Armstrong, Clint Jackson, and Chuck Walker were spectators. The Americans' biggest surprise happened when twenty-one-year-old truck driver "Big" John Tate defeated his first two opponents. But his luck came to an end when, in the semis, he was kissed by a picture-perfect right hand attached to the arm of Cuba's invincible Teófilo Stevenson.

Also in the semis, Michael won by walkover when Romania's Alec Nastac failed his prefight physical; he then watched as Leon easily defeated Poland's Janusz Gortat.

Six Americans—Randolph, Mooney, Davis, Leonard, and Leon and Michael—had reached the finals, giving the US boxing team its best Olympic showing since 1904.

After the semis team captain Sugar Ray Leonard spoke to UPI: "[This] shouldn't be a surprise to anyone. It's really beautiful. Every boxer on the team deserves it . . . the simple reason is we stick together, we train hard, we sacrifice a lot, and we're the most beautiful people in the world."

Nobody was more in tune with the merits of Schwartz's team than ABC boxing announcer Howard Cosell. Throughout the Games, he'd been urging Roone Arledge, the head of ABC Sports, to pay more attention to America's upstart boxers.

Terry Jastrow, Cosell's producer at the Olympics, was caught in the middle. "[Howard's] talking on a headset to me and I'm in the mobile unit underneath the arena with Roone Arledge," he recalls. "Roone was busy with gymnastics and track-and-field and there Howard was in the arena screaming at me, 'Tell Arledge that nobody gives a shit about gymnastics. The story is the American boxing team. Have him come immediately to the Maurice Richard Arena!' After a day or two, he would say, 'Put me on with Roone, I want to talk to Roone.'

"Roone would say, 'Howard is myopic. The boxing team may be great, but it's only one story and at any one moment there's twelve interesting stories.' And [fourteen-year-old Romanian gymnast] Nadia Comaneci was capturing the heart of the Americans up close and personal.

"Finally, Roone sort of capitulated. It was a combination of Howard's pressure and the fact that the Americans were undeniably winning round after round in all the weight categories that boxing got a disproportionate amount of coverage. [Howard] considered this team his boys. When they won, he won. It was personal to him. I was his producer for fifteen, eighteen years, and I never saw him happier. It was a quiet, happy, personal satisfaction, personal joy."

Cosell used his airtime to captivate viewers around the world with stories of the fighters' personal lives. No story was more compelling than that of Howard Davis, the twenty-year-old from Long Island who had been schooled in the ring by his father, a former boxer, and who'd beaten Thomas Hearns and Aaron Pryor on his way to Montreal. Two days before the opening ceremonies, Davis's thirty-seven-year-old mother, Catherine, died of a sudden heart attack. A grieving Davis was ready to give up his Olympic dream and fly home to be with his family, but Howard Davis Sr. and the team's assistant coach, Sarge Johnson, convinced him to stay and fight to honor his mother's memory.

What Davis's story had in pathos, Sugar Ray Leonard's had in sizzle. The twenty-year-old Leonard was a ready-made media darling: He was handsome, talented, and arrived in Montreal complete with a catchy nickname. Television viewers heard of the love poems he wrote to his girlfriend, Juanita, and of the good-luck charm he had taped to his sock: a photo of Juanita and their three-year-old son Ray Leonard Jr. America pulled for the wholesome fighter who dreamt of attending college after the Olympics.

Cosell also talked up eighteen-year-old Leo Randolph, the youngest and smallest member of the team. A devout Christian, Randolph had come up through the Boys Club in Tacoma, Washington. Until Cosell shared it on the air, nobody knew that he and Davey Armstrong had been sneaking food out of the Olympic Village cafeteria and bringing it to their coach, Joe Clough, who'd hitchhiked 2,700 miles to Montreal and was camped out in a local church.

At age twenty-five Charles Mooney was the team's senior citizen. An Army sergeant with a wife and young son, Mooney had come to Montreal from his station in Fort Bragg, North Carolina. Mooney had become his own brand of Cinderella. With a mere thirty-two amateur bouts under his belt, the inexperienced fighter was now within striking distance of a gold medal.

Next to these Olympians stood Leon and Michael, the two street kids who'd fought their way out of the war zone that was Pruitt-Igoe.

"Howard, above all else, was a champion of the underdog," Terry Jastrow says. "And so he loved the Spinks brothers. He even loved to say their name. Michael and Leon Spinks. [He imitates Cosell by emphasizing the *Sp* in *Spinks*.] He loved their backstory. Michael and Leon were shy, not particularly intelligent or articulate, but there was a soulfulness about them. There was a humanity about them. They were the kind of athletes that Howard loved—this whole idea of them coming where they came from in St. Louis and what they had to encounter and what they had to overcome to make the Olympic team."

Cosell praised "The Wild Bull of Camp Lejeune" and spoke often of Kay Spinks, who wanted to see her Olympic sons become preachers. And America heard about the anonymous donor in St. Louis who'd read in the local paper that Kay was watching her sons on a borrowed television set and sprung for her trip to Montreal.

In a story worthy of Hollywood, the donor told James Rogal in the *Post-Dispatch,* "I've played sports all my life and so have my kids. I can't think of anything better than going to see my kid win a gold medal in the Olympics."

"God bless him," Kay said. "This is just like getting a diamond ring. I'm just so happy, I can't believe it."

When asked how he greeted his mother upon her arrival in Montreal, Michael said, "'Hello, Mama.' That's all you ever say. After that, it's 'Uh huh and yes, ma'am.' She can rap."

It was Kay's first airplane trip and it brought her to Montreal just in time. She arrived Friday night and would see her sons and four of their teammates compete in the most important matches of their lives on the following day.

Michael was scheduled to take on Rufat Riskiev, the same fighter who'd bested him in the Soviet Union eight months earlier.

Leon was to fight Cuba's Sixto Soria, a tremendous right-hand puncher touted by the media as the odds-on favorite to take home the gold.

The Americans were underdogs. The Spinks brothers were long shots.

Ray Sons, writing in the *Chicago Daily News,* was convinced that no member of the US team was in the same class as their opponents. "American boxers will step into the lion's cage with a whip and a chair tonight in the Montreal Forum. They'll depend on tactics and skill to win Olympic gold medals, because the big claws and teeth are on the other side."

Flyweight Leo Randolph went first, squaring off against the reigning Pan Am champion, Cuba's Ramon Duvalon. Randolph earned the heavy side of a 3–2 split decision, and after receiving his gold medal, endeared himself to the television audience by telling the press he'd be home for church in the morning.

Next up was Charles Mooney, who was due to battle North Korea's Yong-Jo Gu. Unfortunately, Mooney was battling a case of diarrhea that left him weak and dehydrated. Still, when the final bell rang, he thought he had taken the fight from the Korean. The judges disagreed. He lost 5–0 and had to settle for the silver.

"I felt bad that I didn't win the gold," Mooney says. "I already had it practiced what I was gonna do. I was gonna snap a salute as soon as the American flag came up. But I just looked at that American flag while they played the Korean music. It was a hard moment to take."

Next in line was Howard Davis, who seemed to channel his grief and anger into his fists. Firing his arsenal at two-time European champion Simion Cutov, Davis outboxed the Romanian so deftly that the pundits began referring to him as a miniature Ali. Davis later received the Val Barker Award as the tournament's outstanding boxer, but he wasn't there to accept the honor. After slipping the medal around his neck and declaring that the gold was for his mother, he left Montreal and drove home to Long Island to be with his family.

Coming off unexpected victories by Randolph and Davis, America's hopes for a third boxing gold medal rested with Sugar

Ray Leonard. His opponent, Cuba's Andrés Aldama, had reached the finals with five straight knockouts.

In preparation for his match, Leonard had studied footage of Aldama. He told the Syracuse *Post-Standard:* "I'm sitting in this dark room watching the guy fight and I heard someone else in the room say, 'Damn, that guy's going to kill Sugar Ray.'"

But Leonard felt he and his teammates had found the secret to winning, which was to keep their opponents off-balance. He followed the plan beautifully, dropping Aldama with a left to the head at 1:10 of the second round and spending the rest of the fight cruising to a unanimous decision. After the bout, as the country embraced Leonard's plans to attend college, Sugar Ray bid one of the Olympics's most famous farewells when he declared, "My journey has ended. My dream is fulfilled."

Back in St. Louis, James Caldwell was at home watching the Games. He and his buddies anxiously waited for their childhood friends to enter the ring. Michael was first.

"Leon was a buzz saw," Caldwell remembers. "We knew he was going to do well. We were more concerned with Michael. We were on pins and needles for his final. Will he generate enough energy?"

Mike Tyson was a ten-year-old kid in Brownsville, Brooklyn, when he watched Michael fight for the gold.

"The Russian guy had beaten him in the fight before," he says. "You know what that must have felt like, going into that fight in front of all those people? This guy beat you, and normally when a Russian or a Cuban beats you, they're gonna beat you again. When they got your number, they got your number."

Michael Spinks couldn't wait to get at Riskiev. He told reporters he had done extra training in preparation. At the opening bell he uncorked laser-like two-fisted combinations, dazing Riskiev in the first round, decking him in the second, and finishing him with a cannon-shot to the gut in the third.

"Even though I had the reach on him, he was strong—exceptionally strong," Michael told UPI. "So I kept inside and worked on the body. I was catching him with flurries of punches every now and then and it was adding up."

Riskiev complained that the third-round body punch was a low blow, but his accusation went unheeded. When he couldn't go on, it was official: Michael had won the gold and pulled off the biggest upset of the night.

Leon was the last American to fight. Despite a spectacular performance throughout the Games, he was a huge underdog against Sixto Soria, and judging by the left hook he absorbed in the opening round of the gold-medal bout, the odds weren't steep enough. But on this night it would take more than a mustard-packed haymaker to drop Leon. As he had vowed after losing the finals in the previous year's Pan Am Games, "If I have to die in the ring to win the gold medal, then I'll die." He might well have meant it. After taking the left hook, Leon smashed the Cuban to the canvas with a succession of right hands and dropped him again in the third round. The fight was stopped.

"Oh, man, it was phenomenal how he just dominated the fight," teammate Leo Randolph says. "That Cuban guy was supposed to be one of the best in the world. And it was kind of comical how Leon did it. The adrenaline kicked in. The guy hit [Leon] and [Leon] said, 'Wait a minute, this isn't right,' and he ran over to the guy and pounded on him."

Kenny Loehr, who had paid his own way to Montreal and served as Leon and Michael's unofficial coach, recalls, "I was rubbing Leon down at ten in the morning the day he fought in the finals and he had enough alcohol coming out of his pores to knock me out. [Then] when this Cuban kid hit him, he just growled. He *growled*. The kid hit him with his best shot, and Leon just kept coming at him and knocked the kid out."

Charles Mooney knew that growl. He had heard it in an inter-services match when Leon absorbed a vicious punch that, by all rights, should have floored him. "But Leon stepped back and cleared his nose and started to fight," he says. "That was his call sign. He would growl, and you better get out of the ring."

Howard Cosell was at the microphone. "[Soria] is still punching and his hands are quick. You can see it. He's coming on! He staggered and hurt Spinks! Spinks is without boxing skills. Remarkable to see the way the Cuban is coming back. What a fight! Don't talk to me about proficiency. *Oh, the right!* A sudden turn and punch! The right punched Soria flush in the face. Down he went!"

George Foreman, ABC's color commentator, weighed in, "Spinks isn't a boxer, but he's the best street fighter I've ever seen."

As the Games wrapped up and the crowds filed out of Olympic Stadium, the US boxing team had done itself proud, winning thirty-five of its forty-one matches and capturing five gold medals. Only the 1952 US team had won as much gold. As for the other stand-outs of the Games, Nadia Comaneci took three gold medals back to Romania; and Americans Edwin Moses and Bruce Jenner each captured a gold medal and a world record.

"Standing on the podium after winning was the greatest feeling you could have in the whole world," Leo Randolph says. "You do all this preparation, you go through all these traumas of going into the valleys and tripping and falling, and you finally reach the top of the mountain. You see the flag waving and your hands go up. Hey, I did it! All the trauma and the hurt and the pain, it was all worth it."

Having lost out on that experience, Charles Mooney remembers the '76 Games differently. "I was feelin' real low. During the closing ceremonies, Leon and Michael swooped me up and we went to their coach's hotel. I did some cryin' and they popped me a beer and I cried some more. And they cried. Then we laughed and joked and they consoled me and it was over. I'll never forget that. They took time out from their glory to make me feel better."

For Gerald Early, professor and author of *The Culture of Bruising*, the Games were a watershed moment. "The 1976 Olympics was huge," he says. "That's when the Spinks brothers emerged in the public consciousness. Every guy who came out of that Olympics was a household name, at least among inner-city black people. Howard Davis, Sugar Ray Leonard, they became huge, huge names. They were super-famous. You had this class of unbelievably talented African-American fighters who were so disciplined and serious about the craft."

Douglas Hartmann, author of *Race, Culture and the Revolt of the Black Athlete,* points specifically to Leon and Michael. "When I think about the Spinks brothers, the '76 Olympics is what defines them, what makes them the interesting figures that they are. [That Olympics] was the last gasp of the old black athlete's story, which was out of the ghetto and showing that America was a great country and that you could overcome racism."

In 1976 Jim Lampley was a feature reporter for ABC Sports. The day after Leon won the gold medal, Lampley combed Olympic Village looking for the young light-heavyweight star.

"My assignment was to interview at least six or eight American medal winners," he says. "We wanted to roll these interviews into the closing ceremony before leaving the air, and one of the names on the list was Leon. And I ran around the Olympic Village with my camera crew, and I got everybody else within a two- or three-hour period. I kept coming back to his room and checking through the press attaché, and we couldn't find Leon. And finally I was just ready to bundle out and I saw him come walking around the corner. He was wearing a shirt that was completely unbuttoned and the tail was out. He had, in each hand, an open bottle of Cold Duck; you could've smelled it from two blocks away. I walked up to him and I began to utter my spiel, 'Leon, I'm here because I need to blah-blah-blah,' and I got about seven or eight words out and I looked at him and I said, 'I never saw you.' And he said, 'Fine.'"

The day after the closing ceremonies, Michael flew back to St. Louis with his mother, and when the plane landed at Lambert Field, hordes of relatives and friends—along with boxing and city officials—came to greet them. Michael wore an oversize sombrero, a gift from Kenny Loehr, and Kay showed off her son's gold medal by hanging it around her neck. As the police escorted mother and son into the city, Michael sat on the top of the backseat of a Cadillac convertible with younger brothers Evan and Eddie beneath each arm. In interviews that followed, Michael thanked the people of St. Louis who'd landed him in that motorcade, most notably Loehr and Vashon principal Cozy Marks. His gift to his old trainer was a pair of miniature leather boxing gloves that have hung in Loehr's car ever since.

Leon was celebrating in his own style, which meant that nobody knew where he was. He was supposed to be at Camp Lejeune, but according to the administrative officer at Headquarters Company, S. J. Stockhausen (now known as Suzanne Wheatley), he was AWOL.

"My CO [commanding officer] told us to hurry up and make leave papers for [Leon], so we could pretend he was on leave until we could find him," she says. "Then someone made the unbelievably dumb mistake of sending him unescorted up to Washington, DC, to see the Commandant of the Marine Corps [General Louis H. Wilson]. When my CO found out, he started yelling, 'What idiot was in charge of this? Why would anybody let him try to find the way to DC by himself?'

"He was frolicking about someplace and not back at the base, and we were extending leave papers, probably doing things that weren't exactly on the up-and-up, all to keep his name and the Marine Corps' name untarnished."

Leon resurfaced on August 4 at Kiener Plaza in downtown St. Louis. Two thousand people had come out for "Michael and Leon Spinks Day." A local drum corps, the Hornets, played marching music as the two Olympic heroes paraded into the staged area.

Jesse Davison took off work to attend. "We were shocked at how big the parade was, that they threw a parade for [guys from Pruitt-Igoe]. I most remember seeing them on the podium holding up their medals. Their mom was with them. It was overwhelming when I saw how many people were at the parade to celebrate these two guys, guys I knew and hung with."

In an unprecedented act of generosity, but a predictable act of public relations, the city of St. Louis bestowed gifts upon the Spinks family. Hamilton Jewelers presented Kay with a diamond ring. Local officials gave Michael and Leon keys to the city.

A grateful Michael addressed the crowd with typical reticence: "I want all of you to know I appreciate this."

Leon added, "I really enjoyed coming back to St. Louis to see my buddies and my partners, to see what's happenin'."

John F. Bass, the city's comptroller, addressed the crowd too. "We are proud because they not only bring home two gold medals, but more important to us, they are statesmen," he said. "They have gone out among men and have distinguished themselves as men who care about their country and as men who care about people. It's not where you came from but it's where you're going. You can rest assured these champions are going places."

Bass never mentioned where he thought Leon and Michael were going, probably because he had no idea. Nobody did.

Jesse Davison spent the night celebrating with Michael. "Mike came to my house, he got the key to the city, and he said, 'Let's go have fun.' I was the only one with a car, so we got in my car and rode all over St. Louis that night. Everything was free. We were drinkin' for free. Got into everyplace free. We don't drink but we was drinking that night. We got home about four, five o'clock in the morning."

Following the celebration, Bob Broeg, sports editor of the *St. Louis Post-Dispatch,* suggested that Michael might have benefited from more than a key to the city, that perhaps a more useful gift would have been the key to a job. "[Michael] needs something more substantial full-time than the outside chance to make good in professional pugilism, a field that offers more heartbreak than hope, more disappointments than surprises, more disillusionment than dough," he wrote.

John Holaus, president of the Ozark AAU, went even further in his attempts to improve Michael's prospects. Holaus solicited city hall for work on behalf of the local hero but received nothing more than a cold shoulder.

Leon, who'd begun a new celebration with unknown friends at an undisclosed location, showed up at Camp Lejeune a week after the parade. He memorialized his arrival by crashing his car into the welcome sign outside the base.

"The rumor was that he was driving drunk, but I have no evidence of that," says Administrative Officer Wheatley. "But that was what everyone was saying, and it was being hushed up."

Instead of reprimanding the young Leon, the Marines rewarded him, throwing him a party and milking it for every drop of public relations they could gain.

First Leon was handed a telegram from President Gerald Ford. Next he received a phone call from Marine Commandant Wilson. Then he was summoned to the Goettge Field House, the gymnasium where he had trained for three years.

The announcement came over the public address system: "Will Corporal Leon Spinks please report to the ring."

Three thousand people—Marines and civilians—cheered as the band played "St. Louis Blues" and Leon marched into the ring wearing his Marine uniform and newly minted gold medal. Major General Herman Poggemeyer, the commanding general of Camp Lejeune, joined Leon in the ring and congratulated "The Wild Bull of Camp Lejeune."

In the blink of an eye, Private Leon had been elevated to Corporal Spinks. Retired Captain Bill Darrow had recommended Leon for the promotion. "I looked at his pro and con marks," he says. "If he has good marks and he's doing his job, he gets promoted. He wasn't what we call a brig rat, someone that gets drunk and is sent to the brig a lot. Leon was promoted because he was a good Marine. Anything else he did brought honor to the Corps and to himself."

According to Suzanne Wheatley, "None of us knew who [Leon] was until the Olympics. He was a private first class. His rank was so unimpressive that we promoted him to corporal because of the Olympics."

Leon may have been promoted, but he also wanted out. He had a year of service left, and even though he didn't qualify, he applied for a hardship discharge. Wheatley voted against it. So did Kay Spinks.

"His mother was very much against him getting out of the Corps," Wheatley says. "He used to use the phone on my desk and talk to his mother; he'd plead with her to send us some kind of statement that she would like him out of the Marine Corps so that he could make more money and take care of her and his siblings. I distinctly remember him saying, 'Mama! But Mama!' He was a gold-medal boxer but she was the one that wore the pants in the family. He could barely get a word in edgewise. His only comments were: 'But Mama!'

"I was the recorder for the board, which meant I presented the government's case. I had to show whether Leon qualified to get out. The government wanted him out, but their guidelines did not support that. There were six or seven officers on the board, and they sat there like a bunch of puppets. They all had the word that he was supposed to get this discharge. I pointed out that he didn't qualify, but they all voted for it.

"I had the only dissenting vote. I recorded that and wrote a dissenting opinion. I had my company clerks type it up, because I knew the board would change it if they [could]. Then I got everybody on the board to sign it, and I turned it in. A few days later the board called me up to see a new copy they had typed up. It didn't lie, but it didn't mention my dissenting vote.

"My superiors wanted to get him out before he became an embarrassment to the Marine Corps."

Once Leon's discharge papers came through, he was free, and eager, to start making money in the ring. His timing was perfect, because gold-medal fever had swept the country.

And sports promoters were anything but immune.

4

THE SPINKSES' PROFESSIONAL CAREERS WEREN'T LAUNCHED IN Montreal—they were ignited by a man from the township of Ridley, Pennsylvania, a suburb of Philadelphia. That was where John L. Lewis, a local businessman and one of Joe Frazier's original investors, sold used cars. It was also where Frazier bought his Cadillacs, and where the ex-champ befriended the owner's son, Ronald "Butch" Lewis.

Butch was a quick-thinking, fast-talking profit machine whose business schooling had been confined to street hustles and small-time grifts. For the flashy five-foot-seven chain smoker, selling used cars was as boring as tallying ledger columns.

Butch Lewis explained it this way to Phil Berger of the *New York Times:* "I [grew up relying on] my wits. I had a friend of mine who worked in a jewelry store on Market Street [in Philadelphia]. And I would gather maybe twenty rings—buy 'em in volume for a buck-and-a-quarter apiece—and I'd be out on Market Street telling people these rings were worth three, four, five hundred bucks and all I wanted was fifty dollars. I'd say, 'Look, you want to appraise it? Go ahead. Take it and have it appraised.' The guy would go into the jewelry store, where my man was, right? My man puts the eyeglass on and looks at the ring, then says it's worth fifteen hundred dollars. The other guy comes hurrying out of the store, and he's happy to give me fifty bucks for a ring that's worth a dollar and twenty-five cents."

John L. Lewis put an end to his son's flimflamming by setting him up with a job. Before long, Butch was the lot's top salesman—bringing in more than $75,000 a year—but the job wasn't enough to stoke his fire. He was far more interested in his friend Joe Frazier's sweet science than he was in popular mechanics, so he took to flying around the world and attending Smokin' Joe's fights.

The young Lewis often told a story that put him in Kuala Lumpur. There, a group of German businessmen approached the misplaced American and asked if he was a boxing promoter. Lewis was smart enough not to say yes, but too savvy to say no. He simply said nothing. Before he left the country, he had an offer in his breast pocket: three million dollars to bring the winner of Ali-Frazier III to Munich to fight Richard Dunn.

Lewis seemed to have everything a promoter would need to make the fight: financial backing, a silver tongue, and an uncanny knack for making money. But he was missing the one thing he needed most: a fighter. Could he deliver either Ali or Frazier?

Getting the green light from Frazier wound up being easy enough—all it took was a phone call. Landing Ali, however, seemed impossible. The champion wanted no part of a promoter who'd never promoted a thing in his life.

So on October 1, 1975, when the bell rang to start Ali-Frazier III—now known as "The Thrilla in Manila"—Lewis was pulling for Frazier like no other fan on the planet. But any hope of making a Frazier-Dunn fight went out the window when Frazier couldn't answer the bell to start the fifteenth round.

Lewis had no choice but to pursue Ali in the hopes of making Ali-Dunn. He withdrew his life's savings to trail the champion, a chase that began in Manila and had no end in sight. It was a comedy worthy of a Blake Edwards film: Lewis being fed Ali's itinerary by Ali's secretary, then zigzagging across the country in hot pursuit. Ali dismissed Lewis, swearing that he'd take the fight only if his business manager, Herbert Muhammad, agreed.

Lewis got his hands on Muhammad's unlisted phone number and called him daily. He also showed up wherever Muhammad happened to be.

Those who knew Lewis weren't surprised. Robert L. Johnson, then a lobbyist for the National Cable Television Association and the eventual founder of Black Entertainment Television (BET), developed a close friendship with Lewis years after "The Thrilla in Manila." His friend's exploits, he says, were beyond a sane man's comprehension.

"Butch was always willing to go to the ends of the earth to try and put together a deal," Johnson says. "He was the guy who would go in selling a grand vision and he would be amazed if people didn't see the deal the way he saw it. He would ingratiate himself, or impose himself—however you looked at it—on people in a way that they couldn't deny his huge, huge charisma and dynamic charm. You had to react to him one way or another."

To land Ali, even the energetic Lewis had to kick into overdrive. He told the story to the *New York Amsterdam News* this way: "Herbert told me to get lost, to go take a hike. But Ali said I could wear him down. Every single morning, Monday to Sunday, every day, *every* day, I don't care where I was, I called Herbert. I had telephone bills of, like, $1,700, $2,000 a month. He would wake up to my voice. And Herbert would say, 'If you call me again, I'll do this and that. Don't ever call me again.' And every single morning, I'd call him. He'd change his number, and I'd call him. He didn't know how I got his number.

"Herbert finally told me, 'Too many people around the world have my phone number. I can't have it changed [again]. So I'm telling you this for the last time—just don't call me no more!' At seven o'clock the next morning, you guessed it. Herbert screamed, 'Look, if Ali wants you to promote him, you got it. Now leave me alone!'"

Lewis hopped on a plane to Chicago, found Ali at home, and relayed Muhammad's message. Ali made good on his promise, and the two men shook hands. But Lewis's celebration was short-lived. He knew he needed more experience, particularly of the logistical variety, if he planned to stage an event of this magnitude.

He pitched veteran boxing promoter Bob Arum on the Ali-Dunn fight, which was a slam-dunk, being that Lewis had Ali in his pocket. Lewis and Arum struck a deal, and the duo promoted the event through Arum's company, Top Rank. But instead of making money, the newly formed partnership wound up in a cash crunch, mainly because the Germans had come up short but also because ticket sales were lagging. They would have been sunk had Ali not saved the day.

Lewis told Greg Logan of *Newsday*, "Ali cut his purse by $300,000, and told Herbert [Muhammad] his end would still be the same. He said, 'I'm not going to let Butch fail.' Tears came to my eyes, and then he wrote a check for $100,000 worth of tickets and told me to give them free to the American soldiers in Munich and Frankfurt. I was blessed never to look back."

Lewis moved up to vice president at Top Rank and got busy. His first order of business was to visit Montreal and ingratiate himself with the five potential paydays sporting shiny new gold around their necks. Of course, he wasn't the only one with the idea. A swarm of promoters had already descended on the Olympic champions—and many had left empty-handed. Sugar Ray Leonard had signed with a group of Maryland investors. Howard Davis had wriggled off the hook when he struck a deal with two Long Island real estate executives. And Leo Randolph had chosen to finish high school before going pro. That left two fighters in the promoters' crosshairs: Leon and Michael. Lewis wasn't about to let them get away. He invited both brothers to the Ali-Norton fight as his personal guests.

As it turned out, Leon was an easy sell. He had wanted to turn pro so badly, the day after he won the gold, he'd signed a two-page management contract with a muscle-bound truck driver named Millard Barnes, who went by the name Mitt. Barnes was an organizer for Teamster Union Local 600 in St. Louis; he also ran a small gym in the basement of the downtown Railroad YMCA Hotel. At sixteen Leon had wandered into the YMCA looking for a place to sleep because he was tired of having to share a bed at home. Barnes gave him a cot and a key to the gym, and on occasion, put some money in his pocket. All he asked in return was 30 percent of Leon's earnings through 1979. In fairness to Barnes, that's a standard managerial contract. In fairness to Leon, many states don't require that fighters have managers, so in those states it's an unnecessary siphoning of funds. Regardless, Leon signed with Barnes and soon found that he also needed a promoter. Managers represent fighters, he learned, but it's the promoters who put together fights. Without the latter, Leon's feet would never touch the canvas of a professional boxing ring. So one month after the Ali-Norton fight, Leon inked a three-year promotional deal with Top Rank.

That left one unsigned medalist: Michael.

"I knew [Leon] could turn pro right away," Bob Arum says now. "He had enormous talent. I didn't think as highly of Michael. But some very astute boxing guys told me that, in their opinion, Michael was better than Leon at that point—that Michael had the real ability, more so than Leon."

Lewis told Mark Kriegel of the New York *Daily News*, "Most of the guys sitting around the coffee shop scouting the Olympics had Michael as the dude least likely to succeed. They said he's clumsy. They said he's lucky. But I'm saying to myself, 'If he's so lucky, then how come he's always beating the favorite?' When I seen him buckle that Russian, I knew. That wasn't no luck."

It's ironic that Lewis's interest in Michael had peaked when Michael knocked out Riskiev, because that's exactly when Michael's interest in boxing had ended. Michael had no desire to fight beyond the Olympics—he was proud of having a job, and besides, he still had the voice of Kenny Loehr in the back of his head. Although Loehr was a key player in the St. Louis amateur boxing scene, he had little use for the professional side of the sport. He'd even been quoted in the *Riverfront Times* as saying, "Them guys in the pros are so, what's the word, corrupt. They'll put you in the ring when you ain't ready, just so they can make a payday." Loehr had always advised his young fighters to avoid the pros and get a "real job."

Michael had taken Loehr's advice. He'd gone back to his job at the Holiday Inn, and his boss had paid him for the days he'd missed while in Montreal. Then he showed his gold medal to his co-workers and they xeroxed copies for themselves. He was where he wanted to be.

But Lewis was relentless. He kept calling, wooing Michael with talk of the money and the fame that came with professional boxing. Lewis tried every trick in his book, with the exception of selling Michael a discounted ring on Market Street.

"And, I mean, I'm hitting Mike with everything just to get him to sign with me," Lewis told the New York *Daily News.* I'm telling him this, telling him that. I'm telling him, 'Boy, you gonna miss out on what you been blessed to do.'"

Lewis wasn't the only one knocking, however. Nick Miranda, a former Pruitt-Igoe neighbor who had become a theatrical agent, had also tried to sign Michael. But Miranda found out what Lewis was just learning: Michael was determined to avoid a boxer's life, which in his mind meant becoming a palooka and handing his money over to a bunch of sharply dressed, double-talking charlatans.

Michael's longtime friends knew the score. "After the Olympics Michael wasn't interested in turning pro," James Caldwell remembers. "I think he was helping Leon, so Leon wasn't out there by himself, 'cause there was so many people making offers to Leon. [Michael] wanted to sit back and watch how the game goes."

In the end it was Michael's pursuit of conventional employment that helped Lewis get his man. The switch came after Michael left the Holiday Inn for what he considered an "office job"—cleaning the offices at the Monsanto Chemical Plant.

Michael told Earl Gustkey of the *Los Angeles Times*, "[At Monsanto], I was bringing home $550 every two weeks. Then they transferred me to [another] building to clean bathrooms, where the chemicals were, and I started breathing those fumes. I took this as a demotion, seeing as how I'd had an office job before.

"One night, I laid down on a cot in the women's restroom and fell asleep. Well, my supervisor walked in, wakes me up and called me every name under the sun. I'm sitting there, thinking that no way do I want to spend the rest of my life listening to this stuff. I was probably dying sucking in those chemicals anyway. So I said, 'Sir, I'm going to do you a favor and rid yourself of me.' I walked out. The next time Butch called, I said, 'Yeah, Butch, I'm ready.'"

But Michael's consent came with a no-bullshit clause. "Right off, I told Butch not to talk about big numbers and give me the lie," he explained to *Sports Illustrated*'s Pat Putnam. "I told [Butch] I had been lied to all my life, so he could skip all that and just tell me it like it was. I was going in for me, but mainly I was going in to be with Leon, to help Leon. He's my brother. He's very weak in some points. He has a tendency to trust people he shouldn't. All those smiling faces and shaking hands, and he just trusts. He should check people out. As for me, if I get messed up, I want to do it myself, then I can blame only myself. I don't want any help. If I fail, I want to fail on my own."

Now that both Spinks brothers were in his stable, Lewis walked into the office of Barry Frank, president of CBS Sports, and sold him on airing Leon's first professional fight in Las Vegas, on January 15, 1977. To Lewis's delight, Leon was getting his discharge from the Marines and would now be free to take the fight. But Leon went off to celebrate and never returned.

"I saw right away when we started promoting Leon as a professional what he was," Lewis's Top Rank partner Bob Arum says. "Leon didn't have a mean bone in his body, but he was totally and completely irresponsible. I mean, he was almost childlike. He certainly wasn't a rocket scientist."

Lewis called Mitt Barnes, but Barnes had no idea where Leon had gone. So Lewis called CBS and offered Earnie Shavers as a substitute, but CBS insisted on the young Olympian. By chance, Lewis spotted a small article in a local newspaper that said Leon had been given a traffic ticket for driving with a suspended license in Des Moines, Iowa. It was the holiday season, but Lewis wasn't about to sit idle and watch his deal with CBS disintegrate.

Lewis told Pat Putnam of *Sports Illustrated*, "Here it is, New Year's Eve, and I'm the only guy on a plane flying to Des Moines. I didn't know where Leon was in Des Moines. Hell, I wasn't even sure he was there."

Lewis rented a car at the airport, drove to the black neighborhood, and asked the kids hanging out on the corners if they'd seen the young fighter who'd just won a gold medal in Montreal. Eventually, someone directed Lewis to a house nearby. Sure enough, when Lewis knocked on the door, Leon was inside—but Leon said he didn't want to fight, that he needed some time for himself. Lewis managed to drag his fighter back to Delaware, promising an easy payday. Leon's opponent was "Lightning" Bob Smith, a butcher's helper from Brooklyn, New York, who had compiled an unelectric 7–7–1 record.

"Leon had trained for only eleven days," Lewis told *Sports Illustrated*. "I was scared to death he was going to run out of gas."

Leon, now fighting as a heavyweight, had enough in his tank to last five rounds, which is when he knocked Smith out. His next bout was in Liverpool, England, where he knocked out Peter Freeman with a right to the jaw midway through the first round. Two weeks later he kayoed Jerry McIntyre, also in the first.

Boxing writer Ron Olver reported on the Freeman fight in *Boxing News*. "Leon sure can punch but he wasn't around long enough to show if he can box, too."

For his fourth pro bout, Leon took a hometown fight with a much tougher opponent, Pedro Agosto, and he gave the Puerto Rican much the same treatment he'd given Freeman and McIntyre. With Kay and Michael watching from ringside, Leon traded blows with Agosto and sent him crashing to the canvas in the first round. Agosto hung on to the ropes and then struggled to his knees, but that was as far as he would get. The referee counted him out at 1:55.

The following month Leon kayoed Bruce Scott in three rounds, and after five pro fights in four months, he was 5–0 with five knockouts. According to Butch Lewis, Leon was also richer by $65,000, "give or take a few."

Phil Berger of the *New York Times* wrote, "Lewis was a kind of Svengali who chided and guided Leon, and even delivered rousing pre-bout orations that conjured terrible visions of Leon's St. Louis ghetto as the fate that awaited Leon should he lose. . . . Leon often had Lewis tracking him like a bloodhound to dingy bars and to hideaways where Leon would meet female friends."

Michael tried to help, and he said as much to Pat Putnam in *Sport Illustrated*. "I saw that Butch needed me to get to Leon. I was the key. Leon did a lot of running off on his own. I'd get Leon back and we'd talk. We'd argue, then he'd be okay. Most of the time, it was very confusing to us. Everything was moving so much. We never were allowed the time together we needed to get our heads straight.

As each fight took place, I noticed a lot of shaky things happening. Like we discovered friends of Butch's selling Spinks T-shirts at one fight. When we asked about the royalties, nobody knew where the money was going. Leon was upset. There was a lot of neglect, a lot of disinterest. We were looking good to the world but going nowhere. And he was having family problems with Nova. He was having so many problems my heart went out to him. You can't lay too many things on Leon at one time. So I went home and talked it over with mama. She tried to call Leon. She told me she tried to call him through the Top Rank office in New York a lot, and that she got turned away a lot."

Michael, now a light-heavyweight, made his pro debut three months after Leon's. On April 17, 1977, he knocked out Eddie Benson in the first round; within four months he'd outpointed Luis Rodriguez and kayoed Joe Borden and Jasper Brisbane. Over that short span he earned forty thousand dollars, and since he'd never signed with a manager, he kept everything he earned. Leon was still forking over 30 percent to Barnes.

"I guess [Leon started questioning his manager] the first time they came in together to get paid. Mike got a hundred percent of his money," Butch Lewis told *Sports Illustrated*. "But when we paid Leon, Barnes's thirty percent had been deducted. He looked at Mike's pile, and then he looked at his pile, and then he said, 'Why the hell am I giving this guy all my money? He doesn't do anything.'"

Michael did eventually need a manager, though. His fifth fight was in Los Angeles; his sixth and seventh were in Las Vegas. Both California and Nevada required fighters to have managerial representation. Michael hired his old friend the theatrical agent Nick Miranda, and the two struck an agreement—their business relationship would dissolve after the fights were made and Michael would continue to handle his own career.

Nobody, however, was looking after Leon's career—not even Leon. The little money that he'd kept after Top Rank and Mitt Barnes took their cuts was either poured straight into a highball glass or piled onto a coke spoon. Not a penny went to fund a savings account or training camp. The bad habits were blossoming, and Leon's biggest paydays were right around the corner.

5

February 1978. Leon didn't stand a chance. This wasn't Sixto Soria. This was the world heavyweight championship. This was Muhammad Ali.

By now Ali had done it all. In 1964 he'd freed boxing from the clenches of the mob by beating the last connected titleholder, Sonny Liston, and used the heavyweight title as a stage from which to champion the Black Power movement. He joined the Nation of Islam, gained followers worldwide, and changed his name from the one listed on his birth record, Cassius Clay, to the one emblematic of his new religion. In 1967 he had polarized much of white America by refusing induction into the US Army, a news-quaking act of rebellion that resulted in his exile from boxing.

According to Douglas Hartmann, author of *Race, Culture and the Revolt of the Black Athlete*, "At that period Ali was especially influential for coming-of-age black athletes. That was the story of athlete consciousness in the sixties: that they needed to be more than athletes to take pride in their accomplishments, to represent their race. A lot of people really hated [Ali] because he was trying to call attention to discrimination and prejudice on racial and religious grounds, and Americans weren't ready to hear that."

Ali had returned to the national stage in 1971 after a three-and-a-half-year exile and took on the new champ, Joe Frazier. The event, billed as "The Fight of the Century," was the Holy Grail: It marked the first time two undefeated world champions were meeting in the ring. After fifteen mesmerizing rounds Frazier retained the title with a unanimous decision, dealing Ali the first loss of his career. Ali regained the title in 1974 by knocking out George Foreman in Zaire, and successfully defended it the following year against Frazier in Manila. By 1978 America had changed and Ali was one of the biggest benefactors of its newly revised history. The new generation didn't see him as an arrogant draft-dodger, but as a visionary who had guts enough to stand up for his beliefs.

In his second reign as champion, Ali had achieved nearly god-like status. He had come to be an ambassador of sorts—bringing title fights to countries around the world and meeting with foreign heads of state. He had become the voice of a generation—Leon's generation. And like others before him, he had used the heavyweight title to vault himself into nobility.

Leon was the first to say he had spent his life worshipping at the altar of Ali. Back in Pruitt-Igoe he and his friends would watch the champ fight on *Wide World of Sports* and then spend hours in the gym imitating his moves.

"Ali was the guy we always talked about," James Caldwell remembers. "We wished we could be him. It was amazing that a guy his size was so fast and could do the shuffle. He was fast enough to hit a guy, do the shuffle, and hit him again. That's a bad son of a gun."

Luther Boyd recalls, "Ali was the man. He was a beautiful man. He didn't look like a boxer. He ran his mouth but he could back up his words. What we loved about him most was he told the government where to go in so many words. He stood up for what he believed in and it paid off."

To this day sportswriter Robert Lipsyte sees in Ali an athlete of supreme conviction. "Ali sacrificed for his principles. He was the most important person in sports who ever did that," Lipsyte says. "He sacrificed money, influence, and prestige for his religion. To white kids of that era, he said you're not a coward or a faggot, no matter what people call you, for refusing to fight in this war. For blacks, he was the man who told the establishment to go to hell."

According to Ali biographer Thomas Hauser, "Ali at that point was almost universally beloved in this country. He had gone through his rehabilitation. Gerald Ford invited him to the White House. He was the king. He was royalty."

Michael Conforti, clinical psychologist and pop culture analyst, views Ali as an athlete who rose above his circumstances. "Ali incorporated aspects of a much bigger world, and he wasn't a thug. He was elegant, well-dressed in Armani suits, praying, religious," he says.

Professor and boxing writer Gerald Early echoes the others' sentiments. "At his height Ali was not just the most famous boxer of his time, he was the most famous boxer in history. He was the most famous American athlete on the planet. Because of Ali, people were interested in boxing."

Culturally, Leon was the antithesis of Ali. He wasn't pretty; he didn't care that he'd lost his front teeth. He wasn't articulate, and he hadn't shown any awareness of political or social issues. His service in the Marines scored him some points with old-timers, but the armed forces had become a nonissue to the younger generation. Leon was seen simply as an opponent, a payday, a wide-eyed ghetto kid walking into the lion's cage with nothing in his pocket but a slingshot.

———

The Ali-Spinks fight defied all sense of fair play. At the age of twenty-four, Leon had amassed all of seven professional fights. Standing six-one, he weighed only 197½ pounds—barely a heavyweight. Ali outweighed him by twenty-seven pounds and held a four-inch advantage in reach. The Vegas casinos had the odds at 10–1, but most bookmakers wouldn't even take the bet.

Even Ali had thought the match was a crazy idea.

"I can't fight this kid," he told Butch Lewis when Top Rank had first suggested putting the fight together. "It would make me the laughingstock of the world."

But Ali realized he needed a laugher. His recent fights had taken their toll on his thirty-six-year-old body. After dispatching Richard Dunn in five rounds, he'd met Japanese wrestling star Antonio Inoki in a mixed-martial-arts exhibition. The farcical event took place in Tokyo in June 1976 and was so overhyped that wrestling promoter Vince McMahon Sr. was able to sell 32,000 ten-dollar tickets to a closed-circuit telecast at Shea Stadium.

The contest had near-tragic results. Because the agreed-upon rules had outlawed basic wrestling moves, Inoki spent the entire fight on the floor, kicking at Ali's shins, ultimately sending him to the hospital with blood clots in his legs. Ali's personal physician, Ferdie Pacheco, insisted that Ali's mobility never fully recovered.

Bob Arum, who promoted the match, called the encounter "terrible" and "embarrassing," and years later described it to TheSweetScience.com this way: "Ali is bleeding from the legs. He gets an infection in his legs; almost has to have an amputation. Ali could've been a cripple for the rest of his life."

In September 1976, three months after the Inoki fiasco, the exhausted champion was back on his battered feet, eking out a decision against Ken Norton. He then sleepwalked to a unanimous decision against Alfredo "The Spanish Omelet" Evangelista, followed by fifteen bone-crushing rounds with Earnie Shavers. So when the champion saw that Leon could only muster up a draw against the mediocre Scott LeDoux, his wheels started turning. Fighting Leon would be the rough equivalent of taking a weeklong vacation in Vegas—Ali just needed a way to justify the bout. After weeks of deliberation, he found his answer hanging around Leon's neck: Olympic gold. Ali, a gold medalist in 1960, had beaten Olympic stars Floyd Patterson, Joe Frazier, and George Foreman. With a little salesmanship, he could pitch Leon as the next in line. Should anybody accuse him of handpicking the ripest tomato can in trunks, he had a precedent. In 1957 Floyd Patterson's manager, Cus D'Amato, had agreed to give the previous year's Olympic gold medalist Pete Rademacher a title shot against Patterson in his first pro fight. Rademacher hit the deck seven times before the fight was stopped in the sixth round.

Ali got Lewis on the phone. "Butch, I want him," he said. "I want your boy bad."

To Lewis and Arum, Top Rank's contracts made the fight a win-win. If Ali kept the title, Top Rank would retain control over the world's most popular athlete. If Leon somehow came out the winner, Top Rank would have contractual rights to Leon's first three defenses, with an option for the next three.

The only glitch was a World Boxing Council (WBC) rule requiring the challenger to be a top-ten contender—a practice presumably adopted to stop champions from wreaking havoc on untested opponents. Leon hadn't yet cracked the top ten—he hadn't cracked the ratings system at all—so Lewis and Arum held a closed-door meeting with WBC president Jose Sulaiman. When the door reopened, Leon had his shot. He would fight Italian heavyweight champion Alfio Righetti and the winner would then challenge Ali. Nobody questioned that Righetti wasn't ranked any higher than Leon (although his name did magically pop up as the number-nine contender after the Sulaiman meeting). Righetti was so obviously handpicked that if anybody had bothered digging, they might well have found Arum's fingerprints all over the WBC files. Righetti, a traffic cop in Rimini, Italy, had not been defeated in twenty-seven bouts, but those opponents had a collective record of 444–283, which averages out to 16–10. Not exactly world-class contenders.

Lewis later recalled in Thomas Hauser's *Muhammad Ali: His Life and Times*, "Leon beat Righetti in a [10-round decision]; they both looked awful. But I figured Leon, if he trained right, would be respectable against Ali, because Ali was slipping; he was slipping a lot."

Slipping enough to lose to Leon? Leon's own mother was skeptical.

"You're small potatoes compared with Ali," Kay had warned her son. "You're crazy, Leon. You'll get wiped out."

Nobody disagreed. Not even Leon.

—⁓—

Leon sat a few rows back of ringside. He was shrouded inside a hooded sweatshirt and yelling up at Michael, who was trading blows with Tom "The Bomb" Bethea, a meaty slugger from New York.

"Wiggle!" Leon yelled, urging his kid brother to move his head. "Wiggle!"

Michael wiggled on cue.

Leon jumped and shouted for all eight rounds of the fight, whooping especially loud when Michael rested his lethal right hand and pelted Bethea with left hooks.

Once the decision was announced and Michael had claimed his seventh victory in as many fights, Leon scampered back to his dressing room. It was time to have his hands wrapped for the biggest fight of his young career.

—⁓—

At the Hilton Pavilion the chants had been sparking all evening. When Leon crossed the ropes to the Marine Corps anthem "Semper Fi" they spread like a forest fire.

"Ali! Ali! Ali!"

In the ring Leon shadowboxed on the balls of his feet, letting off enough nervous energy to power the overhead lights. Of the 5,298 spectators surrounding the ring, at least three were pulling for Leon: his mother Kay, who clutched the worn leather-bound red Bible that sat on her lap; his brother Michael, who sat near Leon's corner; and his wife, Nova, who claimed that the ABC producers, much like the Spinks family and Top Rank, shunned her because she was over six feet tall, had a bleached blonde Afro, and tipped the scales at two hundred pounds.

The music switched to "Pomp and Circumstance" and the crowd roared, knowing it was about to see the self-proclaimed "Greatest."

Ali emerged from his dressing room surrounded by a parade of cornermen, hangers-on, and sidekicks. He made his way to the ring, a somber face peeking out from behind a white hooded robe. The noise inside the Pavilion reached fever pitch as spectators rose to their feet, cheering, shouting, clapping, chanting. Even Leon applauded as the champion crossed the ropes and entered the ring.

Leading up to the fight, the major dailies had already begun running stories on how Ali had gone from invincible champion to aging fighter. Ferdie Pacheco had quit Ali's corner a year earlier, insisting that the champ was risking neurological damage by continuing to take punches to the head. According to Pacheco, Ali should have called it quits after defeating Frazier in Manila three years earlier. While many fight fans were arguing whether the sport should let Leon into the ring with Ali, Pacheco was convinced it shouldn't have let Ali into the ring at all.

While the champ had been diagnosing himself fit to fight, Leon had been in the Catskills following his usual training regimen of hard work and harder partying. Michael had joined him in camp and buoyed his spirits, but there was little he could do to keep his brother in check.

"Leon was a problem right from the beginning because he was so undisciplined," Bob Arum says now. "We started making fights for Leon and he would get drunk before the fights. So we knew that he didn't have a very long life as a top heavyweight because of how he was abusing himself."

Nobody was more frustrated than Sam Solomon, Leon's sixty-two-year-old trainer, who had worked with the likes of Sonny Liston, Ernie Terrell, and, for a short time, Ali. Solomon was a disciplined, punctual man, a streetwise cornerman who'd spent the 1930s and 1940s barnstorming in tents and local social clubs as an amateur and semipro welterweight. He'd also spent a few seasons as a catcher in the Negro National League, pocketing $7.50 a game.

Solomon told *Sports Illustrated*'s Pat Putnam, "To get [Leon] to the gym, I have to wake him at noon to get him there by three. For roadwork, I gotta get up at five to get him running by eight. He has no conception of time. And sleep? Man, does that boy sleep. He'll fall asleep just sitting on the edge of the bed with his head in his hands. Or he'll walk in circles for a while and then sit down and fall asleep. When he goes to the bathroom and he don't come out after a while, you know he's fallen asleep. But when he does get awake, there's no stopping him. Out all night. Loves to dance. Jumping from one thing to another. Even when he trains he goes overboard. Can't get him to quit."

Roger Stafford, Leon's Marine Corps buddy, remembers that nobody was able to stop Leon from being Leon. "Alcohol, marijuana, cocaine. You name it, Leon did it."

And, according to Stafford, Leon indulged right up until the bell rang.

"I was the only one besides his brother that knew what Leon would do," Stafford says. "But Michael couldn't hold him back. I tried to keep him in line before the fight against Ali. These pimps in Las Vegas had these houses and lots of girls and a lot of drugs. They told Leon they were having a get-together and they invited him. I pleaded with him not to go.

"Leon couldn't pass the drugs by. He said, 'If you ain't going with me, I'm going by myself.' So I had to go with him to watch out for him, to watch they wouldn't steal nothing from him. And Leon got tore up, he was so intoxicated, and this was two days before he fought Ali. He didn't get hooked up with no women. All he was thinking about was getting drunk and full of drugs. I was just sitting there watching him and they were fixing drugs on him.

"It was early in the morning when we got back to the Hilton. It was time for us to put on our sweats and run. Leon was in the best shape of his life. This guy could run, I swear. He was an animal. That's what they called him. Butch Lewis called him Leon the Lion."

The stories surrounding Leon's exploits prior to the Ali fight don't end there. As Ali was leaving the hotel to do his roadwork at four in the morning, Leon was coming in from an all-nighter, and, according to Ali's business manager Gene Kilroy, was dressed to the nines right down to his "playboy alligator shoes."

"Hey, Muhammad Ali!" Leon called out. "Heavyweight champion of the world!"

Ali didn't answer, but instead of taking to the road, he went into the coffee shop, turned to Kilroy, and said, "What am I doing here? I'm the heavyweight champion of the world and this kid is nothing."

So when the bell rang, Leon the Lion, high from a party that had started in Pruitt-Igoe and still showed no signs of slowing down, ran to the center of the ring and met up with "The Greatest."

Leon went after Ali with a vengeance in round one, hitting the champ with everything but a two-by-four. This was not a surprise. Leon's reputation preceded him.

It was more surprising that Ali was out of shape—noticeably so. His punches were sloppy and lacked zip. He willingly handed Leon the first three rounds by relying on his self-styled "rope-a-dope," which he had used so effectively against Norton, Shavers, and, most famously, Foreman. But Ali's strategy of covering up against the ropes was quickly looking as worn out as the champion himself. Designed to exhaust Leon by seducing him into letting loose with relentless, energy-sucking punches, the "rope-a-dope" wound up doing the opposite: It weakened Ali. Leon's cornermen deserved the credit. Solomon and assistant trainer George Benton, whom Butch Lewis had brought in before the Alfio Righetti fight, figured that Leon's youthful body had a far deeper gas tank than any of Ali's previous opponents. They instructed Leon to target his assault at Ali's biceps, thereby tiring the champ's aging arms, slowing his jab, and forcing his hands to drop.

Throughout the first six rounds, the plan seemed to be working. But either due to battle fatigue or a cocaine hangover, Leon tired in the seventh. Running out of steam, he reverted to his old habit of standing straight up, which made him an easier target.

Angelo Dundee, Ali's longtime trainer, had spent the night exhorting his fighter to get off the ropes. Now he saw Leon sucking in gallons of air through his open mouth. Before the bell rang to start the eighth, Dundee urged Ali to finish off the young challenger. Leon had made Dundee nervous ever since the night Dundee saw him do away with Pedro Agosto at Kiel Auditorium in St. Louis.

In his memoir, *My View from the Corner*, Dundee recalled spotting Leon at five o'clock on the morning of the Agosto fight. "I caught Leon getting out of a cab, kissing his lady friend of the evening, or morning, or whenever, goodbye, and then taking a swig out of a bottle—no glass, mind you, that would have wasted a step, just straight out of the bottle. That night he went into the ring and cold-cocked his opponent, Pedro Agosto, in one round. Now that's tough."

Dundee shouted at Ali before the bell. "He's starting to stand up, this kid. That's his style, you'll nail him."

Ali responded by staying light on his feet throughout the eighth, stinging Leon with laser-like jabs. The thousands of fans who had paid a total of $756,300 to pass through the Hilton Pavilion turnstiles were now on their feet, whooping and bellowing.

But Leon had a reserve of energy and weathered the storm. When the bell rang for the ninth round, he glanced over at Michael for reassurance and then returned to his electric bob-and-weave agenda. Ali leaned against the corner post and covered up as Leon fired a seventeen-punch salvo of hooks, crosses, and uppercuts. He didn't slow down until the final seconds of the round, when Ali let loose with a combination that staggered Leon. But that didn't stop Leon from giving Ali an affectionate pat on the butt as the bell clanged and Leon headed back to his corner.

Ali's handlers were encouraged by the champion's late burst. Bundini Brown, Ali's ever-present sidekick, was one of them.

"Beautiful," Brown said as Ali slumped down on his stool, trying to regain his breath.

"He's ready, he's ready," Dundee told Ali. "Let's go to work. Bury him. The left will take him out."

But Ali couldn't bury Leon. The best the champ could do was back him up and bombard him with combinations. Ali took the tenth and eleventh but Leon was still pumping in the twelfth. For every punch Ali threw, Leon retaliated with at least one of his own. Neither fighter gave an inch. At the end of the twelfth, the bout was even: Judge Harold Buck had it 114–114; Judge Lou Tabat had it 115–113 for Leon; and Judge Art Lurie had it 116–112 for Ali.

It all came down to the final three rounds. Ali knew his way around this part of a match; he had taken bouts from the likes of Frazier, Norton, and Shavers in the so-called championship rounds. For his part, Leon had never gone more than ten.

It's no wonder the Hilton crowd was stunned when, in the thirteenth, Leon blew in like a tornado. The spectators weren't privy to the exchange in Leon's corner before the bell sounded. Neither were the viewers at home, since CBS had cut to a commercial while keeping its cameras rolling. After the fight, replays of the raw footage revealed a curious scene.

"You're doing it, baby! You're doing it!" the balding, moon-faced Solomon could be heard shouting at Leon. "But I want you to keep that left hand going." Then, while holding an unmarked brown bottle, he told Leon to spit out his water so "I can give [you] some juice."

Nobody will ever know for certain what was in that bottle—although it's reasonable to assume it was more refreshing than lemonade. Leon's pals from the DeSoto suspected it might have been honey water, an innocuous mix of sugar water and mint used by Kenny Loehr to relax his fighters' stomachs during a fight. Veteran trainer Emanuel Steward watched the fight and had no idea what was in the bottle, although he'd heard of cornermen juicing their fighters with a home brew of orange juice, honey, and cocaine. Years after the fight, Milt Bailey, the legendary cutman who worked Leon's corner that night, admitted to mixing some quasi-legal concoctions for his fighters, one of which was a mixture of ammonia, water, and peppermint schnapps.

While the exact contents of the bottle remain a mystery, there's no doubt that Leon's punches in the thirteenth and fourteenth regained the potency they'd been missing in the middle rounds. Leon threw sharp combinations and took it to Ali.

With three minutes left, Dundee tried desperately to wake up his fighter.

"This is the ballgame," he implored Ali. "You got to go out and win this round big, real big. Look at him over there; he's out on his feet; he's shot his bolt. Hit him and he'll go."

Across the ring Solomon was in his fighter's ear, pumping him with words of encouragement. He was sure Leon could take the title if he ended the night on his feet.

"Don't get careless now, understand?" Solomon shouted at Leon, his voice smothered by thunderous cheering.

Leon nodded, sweat drenching his face, neck, and shoulders. *Don't get careless. Stay off the ropes. Wiggle.* Had Solomon stepped aside—and maybe he knew not to—Leon may have lowered his guard at the sight of Ali slumped on his stool, an almost lifeless figure succumbing to the forces of gravity.

Solomon wasn't the only one to sense an upset. The crowd, fearing the end of Ali's mythic reign, was on its feet trying to will its hero to victory.

"Ali! Ali! Ali!"

Millions of television viewers were doing the same in their living rooms. By now CBS's share of home viewers had risen to 71 percent in New York, 62 percent in Chicago, and 60 percent in Los Angeles. Before the fight a CBS executive had approached Ali and asked him to let the fight go a few rounds so the prime-time audience would have something to watch. The network had been billing Leon as the real-life Rocky Balboa. Word was out that it might be true.

Solomon's advice didn't stick with Leon for long. From the moment the bell rang to start the fifteenth, he and Ali were both swinging for knockouts. Some called the round a phenomenal display of heart;

others called it a street brawl. For Leon, it was risky. He didn't seem to care that he was battling an experienced champion. He had only two speeds—turbo and sleep—and he opened the throttle. He was "The Wild Bull of Camp Lejeune."

The Bull landed cutting blows—all of them zeroing in on Ali's head—but the champ unloaded vicious combinations of his own. Leon stumbled from an Ali right, but quickly recovered his footing and snapped back with a two-fisted assault. The energy in the ring amped up as quickly as the clock wound down. Ali tried to put Leon away, to pummel him back into obscurity. But Leon seemed to gather strength as he and the champ slugged their way deeper into the round.

More chants of "Ali! Ali! Ali!"

No doubt, Ali saw the openings. But some insidious, invisible opponent—most likely age but possibly Solomon's brown bottle—made penetrating those openings an uphill battle.

Leon launched haymaker after haymaker. A hard left staggered the tired champion. Ali looked as if he might tumble to the canvas, but he righted himself and came back with a perfectly executed combination. A minute later Leon connected with a left uppercut that stopped Ali, but again the champ retaliated with a flurry of his own.

When the bell rang, Ali patted Leon on the shoulder and then trudged back to his corner and collapsed on his stool, a far more humble man than the godlike figure that had entered the arena sixty minutes earlier.

Leon's handlers rushed to congratulate their fighter. Michael tore through the ropes, joining in the celebration. Leon's circle was obviously convinced the decision would go their way. This was quite an assumption. No contender had taken the heavyweight title by decision since 1935, when James J. Braddock dethroned Max Baer.

Not to mention that Ali's fights had become notorious for questionable outcomes, usually favoring the champ.

The frenzy died down when ring announcer Chuck Hull stepped to the microphone.

"Ladies and gentlemen, we have a split decision."

A spike of moans and boos bit into the air but then quickly melted away.

"Judge Art Lurie scores 143–142, Ali."

A few cheers rang out but then the arena grew anxiously silent again as Hull read the two remaining scores.

"Judge Lou Tabat scores 145–140, Spinks."

Again, the crowd let out with a smattering of cheers and boos.

"Judge Harold Buck scores 144–141." Hull then paused before declaring, "The *new* heavyweight champion of the world, Leon Spinks."

Screams rang out, arms shot up in the air, tears gushed. Leon had pulled off the impossible. He'd been given nothing in life other than a pair of fists and he'd used them to pummel his way out of Hell and into the Promised Land.

Cornermen, insiders, and newfound friends piled onto their hero like a swarm of ants on a breadcrumb. They hoisted the new champion onto their shoulders; in midair Leon thrust his still-wrapped hands to the sky and turned his face to the heavens, his black hole of a mouth stretched open, his eyes squeezed shut as if in rapturous prayer. His sculpted body glistened under the blinding lights, a diamond bouncing on a blanket of red velvet sweat suits.

Boos and catcalls rang out from Ali fans, but they were merely background noise to the real party going on.

In post-fight interviews Ali's team came up with a litany of excuses: The champ hadn't trained, he had spent too much time on the ropes, he'd been robbed by the judges. In a few hours they would also cry foul about Solomon's magic bottle.

Ali, though, took the defeat with class. As he made his way through the crush of Leon's well-wishers, he congratulated the new champ.

"You upset the world tonight," he said to Leon in the center of the ring.

"Just like you used to," Leon said. "Thanks for the shot."

Leon meant every word. After the fight he went to the ex-champ's dressing room, kissed him on the cheek, and told him "good fight."

Then he headed back to his hotel room, only to find seventy-five reporters and celebrity seekers squeezed into the modest two-bedroom suite.

Hiding his swollen eyes behind a pair of oversized sunglasses, Leon lacked the bravado usually associated with champions in the testosterone-driven sport. About Ali he said, "He's still the greatest. I'm just the latest."

Then he answered questions as best he could, but he had never been good with words and wasn't about to change simply because he'd won the title. *I want to be the best. He didn't think I was as strong as I was. I want to retire while I'm young.* Clichés, sentence fragments, rambling thoughts. It wasn't what the world expected from the heavyweight champion. Then again, the world had gotten used to Ali.

Still, boxing's rainmakers happily embraced Leon as the new champion. CBS executive Robert J. Wussler had big plans for him, figuring that Leon's refreshing candor, crude brawling style, and up-from-the-ghetto success story would make him more of a people's champ than Ali had ever been. But to get at Leon, Wussler would have had to cut through a thicket of shysters and charlatans that had already encircled him. As one sports columnist put it, Leon arrived in Vegas alone, but left "surrounded by smiling thieves." Michael was painfully aware of the predators that instantaneously descended on his brother. Years later, he would recall how the "bad things" started the minute the fight ended.

Those bad things surely included a festering power struggle in Leon's corner. Veteran sportswriter Jerry Izenberg, who'd just finished covering the fight for the Newark *Star-Ledger*, ran into George Benton at the Hilton coffee shop. There he heard the extent of the infighting.

"It's about one o'clock in the morning," Izenberg recalls. "George is sitting alone having a sandwich. So I walked over and sat down, and we were talking about the fight. George said, 'It was a fuckin' miracle. The other guy didn't try very hard tonight and I was able to help Leon a little bit. But you know what I had to do to [duck Solomon and] help Leon? I took him into the bathroom of Caesars Palace [the day before the fight] and showed him how I wanted him to throw a jab. And we stood there and I'd say to Leon, 'Now you do it.' So whatever help Leon got to win the world heavyweight championship came in the bathroom with George Benton."

As for the new champ, he was in his hotel room strapping the WBC and WBA belts across his waist, the way champs do when they pose in *Ring* magazine. He stood in front of the mirror and repeated the words whose meaning he may never have fully grasped: *I'm the heavyweight champion of the world.*

6

On February 16, 1978, when the morning edition landed on doorsteps around the world, Leon Spinks was as famous as President Jimmy Carter. Maybe more so.

The New York Times: Spinks Defeats Ali to Capture Title

The Montreal Gazette: Ali Loses Title; Boxing World Is Stunned

The London Times, below an oversize picture of Leon raising his fists in triumph: New World Champion

Leon had taken the WBC and WBA belts from Ali; he'd also become the twenty-fifth fighter since John L. Sullivan to win the lineal title, or as boxing fans would say, he "beat the man who beat the man." As history shows, it took a certain personality to thrive under the spotlight—and not every champion had it.

In the 1930s Joe Louis had become an American icon. He was willing to play the part of a humble black man who knew his "place" in society. He was willing to adhere to a code of conduct furnished by his handlers, and the strategy paid dividends. Throughout America he was a role model to blacks *and* whites. It didn't hurt that he stayed in peak fighting shape and held the belt for twelve years. In 1938 he won a symbolic victory over Nazism by beating Germany's Max Schmeling. When America entered World War II, Louis joined the Army, raised money for war bonds, and recruited for the armed forces. He shilled for Republican presidential nominee Wendell Willkie, endorsed Chesterfield cigarettes, and kept himself relevant in popular culture. The public drank Joe Louis punch and Joe Louis bourbon, swung Joe Louis boxing gloves, and wore Joe Louis hair pomade. By the end of the war, the whitewashed Joe Louis had become the face of America.

Decades earlier Jack Johnson had confronted a far different set of circumstances. When he beat Tommy Burns in 1908 to become the first black heavyweight champion, celebrations were cast aside in favor of race riots; and boxing promoters scoured farms, factories, prisons, and coal mines for a white challenger who could beat him. The best they could come up with was ex-champion James J. Jeffries, who had swelled to 330 pounds and had retired to his alfalfa farm. Jeffries lost a hundred pounds to face Johnson in the first "Fight of the Century." But shedding extra poundage didn't turn back the clock: the "Great White Hope" was TKOed in the fifteenth round.

Following Johnson's victory, the revised lyrics of an old Negro spiritual were circulated throughout black communities:

Amazin' Grace, how sweet it sounds,
Jack Johnson knocked Jim Jeffries down.
Jim Jeffries jumped up an' hit Jack on the chin,
An' then Jack knocked him down agin.
The Yankees hold the play,
The white man pulls the trigger,
But it make no difference what the white man say,
The world champion's still a nigger.

Unlike Louis, Johnson relished stoking the white man's fire. Refusing to play lackey to white America, he took on the role of devil. One of the most well-known men on the planet, Johnson wore swanky clothes, married white women, flashed a set of gold front teeth, and flaunted his considerable wealth. Legend has it that when pulled over for a fifty-dollar speeding ticket, Johnson gave the cop a hundred-dollar bill and told him to keep the change, that he'd be coming back at the same speed. Eventually, the government ran Johnson out of the country on a trumped-up charge that he was transporting white women across state lines for the purposes of prostitution.

"Why was it such a big deal that Jack Johnson *not* be heavyweight champion of the world?" sportswriter Robert Lipsyte asks. "Because [the champion] really was this powerful role model. Why else would you care if this guy could beat up white men and fuck white women and taunt opponents and do everything he wanted except for the fact that this title has enormous significance?"

According to BET founder Robert L. Johnson, "The heavyweight division was a visible sign of escaping some of the indignities of being a black man. If you go back and look at the heavyweight championship, it gave, in the case of black Americans, pride that a black man—when put into a ring where the rules were pretty transparent—could stand up and defeat a white man. That was something you could not even think about in your regular day-to-day job. You'd get lynched or beaten up or whatever. So when you see Jack Johnson, then Joe Louis, and of course, Muhammad Ali, you see black pride being carried on inside those gloves."

Leon didn't represent black pride, but he did find himself in a similar predicament to Johnson's. The "Galveston Giant" had had the nerve to take the title from a white man; Leon had had the nerve to take it from Ali. It was straight out of Faust. In beating the unbeatable, Leon was left with an even greater challenge: Replace the irreplaceable. To fill Ali's shoes, he would have to become the voice for all that he represented: Pruitt-Igoe, the Olympics, the Marines, the blacks, and the have-nots. This was no easy feat for an inarticulate kid from the projects who had little guidance, an eye for the ladies, and a sweet tooth for cocaine.

The public was waiting. And the spotlight wasn't going to shine long on an empty stage.

Jackpot. Leon had just earned $300,000—less Mitt Barnes's 30 percent—and his next fight would bring him more than ten times as much. And that didn't include endorsement deals. Butch Lewis was already fielding calls from the US Dairy Association, Coca-Cola, 7Up, and Prudential Life Insurance, and he hadn't even warmed up yet. If Leon invested wisely, he'd be set for life.

To his credit, Leon often said the right things, telling the world he was just Leon, a product of north St. Louis—living proof that the American dream was possible.

"When I came out of the Marines and turned pro, it was life and death for me," he told Pat Putnam of *Sports Illustrated*. "If I didn't make it, I knew what I had to go back to, what was waiting for me. I came from poorness and I don't want to go back to poorness."

Spoken like a true champion, only it rang hollow. Within days of winning the title, Leon had assembled a full-blown entourage. Unlike other fighters who hired friends and relatives to accompany them around town—a practice started by Sugar Ray Robinson in the late 1940s—Leon barely knew his entourage. His payroll included two press agents, four trainers, three lawyers, a manager, an accountant, a valet, a personal physician, two promoters, a sparring partner, and a 247-pound bodyguard with a shaved head named Lawrence Tureaud, who preferred to be called Mr. T.

The spending didn't stop there. It didn't stop anywhere. Leon shelled out $45,000 on a white six-door Lincoln Continental limousine complete with color TV, bar, phone, and stereo; $18,000 on a Cadillac Seville to go along with the two-and-a-half-carat diamond ring he'd given Nova; $75,000 on a house in Detroit for him and

Nova; and an undisclosed sum on a home in Des Moines for his mother-in-law. He also outfitted himself with a new wardrobe that included a pair of black and white mink coats, each with a matching mink hat.

It was evident that Leon had no plans to become any kind of role model. Maybe he didn't know how. Or maybe he didn't want the responsibility. More likely, he never even considered it. The one thing that's certain is that ghetto culture had attached itself to his DNA.

Emanuel Steward was no stranger to poverty himself, having grown up the son of a coal miner. He was also no stranger to the plight of boxers.

"[Leon] moved across the street from where I live in Detroit," Steward told the authors in 2011 (Steward died unexpectedly the following year.). "He hooked up with Ed Bell, a flamboyant lawyer. And so Bell enticed him to move to Detroit, where he could have more control over him. So [Leon] gets a beautiful house in a neighborhood called Rosedale Park, and a friend of mine invites me to go there for a party. I open up the door, it was just, to say it was off the hook was an understatement. They were doing some kind of train, everybody's going through the whole house. Leon had his cowboy hat on, and a couple of guys are yelling, 'C'mon, Coach, get on!' So I get on with 'em. I see a football player from Pittsburgh, and he's got a game the next day. It was unbelievable.

"That was the first time I got to see Leon personally. The whole house was rocking. When he would have parties, everybody's house on the block would be moving. You'd call him and tell him to turn the music down. [He'd ask,] 'Is it loud?'

"You gotta remember where he came from: the projects. He got started there early and it became part of his genetic makeup. Smoking weed, drinking beer. Some people outgrow it and are able to control it. He was never able to control it. He never did feel comfortable in a nice environment. He's comfortable in a ghetto, low-income-type place. He has a low image of himself."

Michael Conforti, clinical psychologist and pop culture analyst, sees Leon's transition from poor man to rich man as understandably difficult. "You're gonna take somebody like a Leon Spinks and all that they've been through—the ghetto, the wars, the fights, the family stuff—and ask him to live like a rich man? It's insane. And it's really cruel. You're saying to him, 'Hey, here's the keys to your Maserati. Here's the keys to your beautiful home. Enjoy the good life, the rich life, the cultured life.' Of course his response would be, 'Hey, you fuckin' with me? This is not my world. I got a big house, I can have more pimps, I can have more prostitutes, more dope and all that stuff.' Like Pig-Pen you carry your field with you."

Professor and boxing writer Gerald Early says, "It takes a certain kind of mentality to be able to maintain yourself as champion and to be able to control your entourage—and control yourself. And Leon never seemed like he was in control of himself. In some respects, he got a genie and didn't know how to deal with it.

"Leon represented the kind of uncouth black guy from the ghetto. He brought to the fore the whole set of so-called pathological behaviors typically associated with inner-city black males. Leon couldn't have been what white America wanted in a heavyweight champion even if they wanted Ali to be defeated."

According to Carlo Rotella, author of *Cut Time: An Education at the Fights*, "In the Seventies there were tons of models of black masculinity from the ghetto. If you look at popular culture, there's *Shaft*, *Superfly*. There are a million versions of this character but Spinks, I think, embarrassed everybody. He was not Ali. He was emphatically not Ali. And he didn't fit any of the other handy, available slots. And the one slot available was embarrassing to everybody."

Ali biographer Thomas Hauser says, "[Leon] didn't know any better. He didn't really understand what society thinks of as the responsibilities that come with being heavyweight champion of the world. Even if he understood those responsibilities, I'm not sure that he had the personal resources to carry them out."

In an interview with the *Washington Post* in 1978, Bob Arum said that Leon was the "distasteful product of a ghetto environment. He has all those ghetto speech patterns and there's a lack of discipline about him. He sleeps late. He's not too concerned with keeping appointments. He's not all that quick when he talks. Whites are uneasy with him and so are middle-class blacks. They look at him—the champion—and all they see is a ghetto black that they've learned to shun, to fear."

According to Douglas Hartmann, author of *Race, Culture and the Revolt of the Black Athlete,* "In a lot of ways Leon was the stereotype that a lot of educated, more self-conscious black athletes were the most afraid of. [They were] trying to run from that. He wasn't a figure that many people really wanted to associate with anymore—the almost cartoonish character who had no place in society outside of black culture, for sure not in mainstream white America.

"Before the Sixties, simply being a great athlete [like Joe Louis or Jackie Robinson] was seen as a real contribution to the civil rights movement, the struggle for black justice and equality. But that wasn't the case anymore. The Spinks brothers gave the [pre-Sixties] narrative, or that was the narrative that was constructed around them."

Bruce Newman wrote in July 1978 in *Sports Illustrated,* "Last month, while Leon Spinks was dancing in a discotheque with quarters jammed in his ears, Ali was in Moscow, deep in conversation with Leonid Brezhnev at the Kremlin."

Leon told Newman, "People may be disappointed because I'm not Ali, but times change and the world changes. Now I'm the champion. People want the heavyweight champion to fit a certain image, and they're afraid I'm nothing but a dumb nigger. But I'm just Leon."

Leon's being Leon meant that he was an accident waiting to happen. And each accident was a publicist's nightmare.

Three weeks after winning the title, Leon took a ride down to Camp Lejeune to visit his old Marine Corps buddies.

Tony Santana remembers the day. "I'm on the third floor and he calls my name out, 'Saaaantaaaaana! Saaaantaaaaana!' I look out the window. 'Hey, Leon!' Then he yells to Hosea Sprewell and the three of us get in his new car and we go downtown. We're walking down the strip, and this guy across the street says, 'You didn't beat Muhammad Ali. You ain't nothing.' We had to hold Leon back because he was gonna go after him. Here he is, the champion of the world, and he's ready to fight this guy.

"And then we went to this chicken shack and this old lady says to him, 'Are you Leon Spinks, champion of the world?' He says, 'Yeah, I'm Leon Spinks, champion of the world.' And he's sucking his thumb. He's sucking his thumb! He's the champion of the world and he's sucking his thumb!"

The guys continued to cruise the strip until the police stopped them for a minor traffic offense. When Leon failed to produce the car registration, the cops escorted him to the local precinct.

"Me and Sprewell go to the precinct, but Leon wasn't there," says Santana. "He must've bailed himself out or they knew who he was [and let him go]. But we knew where to find him. We could always find him across the tracks."

In the seven months after taking the title, Leon was arrested five times—once taken away in handcuffs after driving the wrong way on a one-way street. He was stopped for smashing up his Lincoln Continental in Detroit, crashing his Corvette through a fence in

Ohio, speeding in North Carolina, and possessing one-hundredth of a gram of cocaine in St. Louis. The coke had a street value of $1.50, yet it landed a photo of a handcuffed Leon on the front page of nearly every major daily. Goodbye, endorsements. Hello, laughingstock.

Johnny Carson on *The Tonight Show:* "The American Dental Association chose its poster boy today: Leon Spinks."

Garrett Morris on *Saturday Night Live*, portraying Leon in a caricature uncomfortably close to the lazy and slow-witted roles of black actor Stepin Fetchit: "I'm world heavyweight champion now and that be a psychological advantage."

Comedian Richard Pryor in concert: "Bad luck be tipping up on Brother Leon. That's what gives him such heart to fight. Leon's saying, 'I ain't got nothing to lose—I ain't got no money, I ain't got no teefus, and I definitely ain't got no driver's license. So what the fuck can you do to me?'"

In the same breath that Pryor used to ridicule the new champ, he also exposed the heavyweight title for the myth that it was. "Only thing, I don't like to hear when white people be saying, 'He dumb, ain't he?' And niggers be agreeing with him. That's what tickled me. Be happy for any nigger doing anything. 'Cause nobody ever said the heavyweight champion had to be no anthropologist anyway.

"I say, 'Leon, what do you do?'

"'I knock motherfuckers out.'"

Butch Lewis told *Sports Illustrated*'s Calvin Fussman, "People would come up to [Michael] and make fun of Leon. Everybody had a Leon Spinks joke. [Michael] would want to punch those people in the mouth. He was confused. He wasn't sure if that's what happened when you became champion or if Leon was bringing it on himself."

Michael met with sportswriter Jerry Izenberg in Detroit soon after Leon's victory and voiced his concerns about his brother.

When the ribbon was cut in 1954, Pruitt-Igoe was hailed as the answer to the nation's urban development woes. But for the Spinkses and thousands of other poor families, it was an abject failure. AP IMAGES

The western half of 2207 O'Fallon St. came down in 1972. Demolition of the remaining 32 buildings was completed by 1976. The site where Pruitt-Igoe once stood is now an empty lot. FROM THE COLLECTIONS OF THE ST. LOUIS MERCANTILE LIBRARY AT THE UNIVERSITY OF MISSOURI–ST. LOUIS.

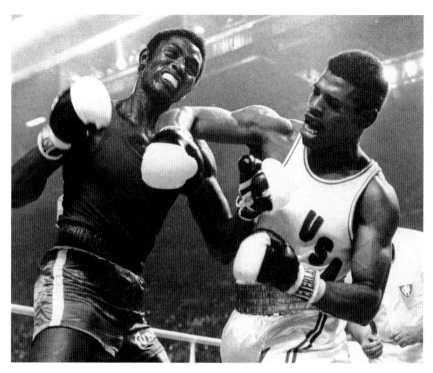

A 23-year-old Leon connects against Sixto Soria on his way to the gold in the 1976 Olympics. The morning of the fight, Leon "had enough alcohol coming out of his pores to knock me out," recalls trainer Kenny Loehr. AP IMAGES

Leon (center) and Michael (right) were the first brothers to win gold medals in the same sport in the same Olympics. Here, they are awarded the key to the city from St. Louis Mayor James Mason. AP IMAGES

Michael gets a kiss from his mother, Kay, upon their return from the Olympics in Montreal. Kay's strong religious beliefs rubbed off on Michael, who referred to her as "my mom and best friend." FROM THE COLLECTIONS OF THE ST. LOUIS MERCANTILE LIBRARY AT THE UNIVERSITY OF MISSOURI–ST. LOUIS.

Leon often told reporters that he was beaten by his father, Leon Spinks Sr. (pictured here). Leon Sr. denied the accusations. FROM THE COLLECTIONS OF THE ST. LOUIS MERCANTILE LIBRARY AT THE UNIVERSITY OF MISSOURI– ST. LOUIS.

On April 16, 1977, in his pro debut, Michael knocked out Eddie Benson. Benson went down from an overhand right—a punch that would later be known as the "Spinks Jinx." AP IMAGES

Leon watches Michael defeat Tom "The Bomb" Bethea, hours before taking on Muhammad Ali for the heavyweight crown. It would be Leon's eighth pro fight. AP IMAGES

Leon is lifted on the shoulders of his handlers after taking the title from Ali on February 15, 1978. The celebration never stopped. AP IMAGES

After winning the title, Leon bought a white six-door Lincoln Continental limo, a Cadillac Seville, and a house in Detroit's Rosedale Park. Here, the champ and his first wife, Nova, visit New York in matching mink coats. AP IMAGES

The champ chats with the press the day before his first title defense—a rematch against Ali. Leon's personal bodyguard, Mr. T, keeps a close watch. AP IMAGES

Leon and Ali ignore each other as they wait to be interviewed on network TV. Their rematch, a week away, would draw more than 90 million viewers. AP IMAGES

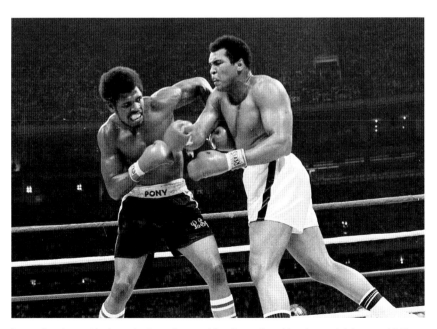

Leon drank, partied, and whored away his championship days, right up until the hours before the Ali rematch. Here, an ill-prepared Leon exchanges punches with "The Greatest" at the Superdome in New Orleans. AP IMAGES

Sam Solomon (lower left) tends to Leon in the champ's only title defense. Milt Bailey (center) was Leon's cutman for both Ali fights. He supplied the mysterious brown bottle the night Leon took the belt. AP IMAGES

Leon, now an ex-champion, lifts Michael's arm in victory after Michael wins his eighth pro fight—a fourth-round KO over Eddie Phillips. AP IMAGES

According to Izenberg, "[Michael] said he was gonna have a few fights and then stop fighting. He said, 'I have to go with Leon. Leon has some problems,' which I took to mean he was retarded.

"And I said, 'You mean you're gonna put your career on hold?'

"He said, 'Yeah, well, I want to be with him. I want to take care of him and make sure he gets his money. You know, I'm not the smartest guy in the world but I can count. And Leon can't.'"

Bob Arum remembers the brothers in much the same way. "Michael always seemed so logical compared to Leon," he says. "It seemed to me that Michael had some sense. Leon never had any sense. He was just not very smart. And he was irresponsible. You could've had Einstein advising him and it wouldn't have mattered."

But Leon had no intention of shutting down the party. The only problem was that he had a title to defend. And the more he partied, the farther he drifted from training camp.

—

The big money was in a rematch with Ali. The public knew it, the promoters knew it, and Leon's handlers knew it. All of which posed the question: Who exactly *were* Leon's handlers?

Bob Arum and Butch Lewis said Leon was "their boy."

Mitt Barnes claimed he was Leon's manager and accused Arum and Lewis of trying to steal his fighter.

Milton Chwasky, a Butch Lewis–appointed lawyer who had filled in as Leon's attorney before the Ali fight, was supposedly representing Leon for his first defense.

Ed Bell and Lester Hudson, two Detroit attorneys, later replaced Chwasky.

Who actually had Leon's signature on paper? It's possible they all did. But it didn't matter.

Nova Spinks told *People* in May 1978, "From the moment Leon won the championship, it's been hell. Have you ever seen two or three dogs pulling on a rag? Well, Leon's the rag."

Arum took the lead in the Leon sweepstakes, producing the signed contract that proved Top Rank had control of Leon's first three title defenses and an option on the next three.

At that point Don King entered the picture and things got even stickier. King offered Leon two million dollars to defend his title against Ken Norton instead of Ali. Norton, a King fighter and the number-one challenger, had been passed over when Ali signed to fight Leon.

When Leon turned down King's offer, WBC president Jose Sulaiman (a personal friend of King) ordered Leon to fight Norton. If Leon failed to do so, Sulaiman told him he'd be stripped of the WBC title.

Arum knew Top Rank would make more money if Leon fought Ali, so he threw Norton a lowball offer of $200,000, assuming he would turn it down.

But Norton took it.

"They thought my ego would be so big I'd say no," Norton said at the time, "but every fighter is hungry for the title. I want that title."

Ali wasn't getting any younger and much preferred to fight Leon. He issued a statement at a news conference that aired as part of *CBS Sports Spectacular.*

"Mr. Ken Norton says he deserves the first shot," Ali announced, "but I'm truly the number-one contender in the eyes of the people of the world. My mail is ten-to-one in favor of Leon Spinks and myself getting together again. . . . The world is waiting for it. It's tradition. The first defense goes against the ex-champion. Leon Spinks should fight me."

It was then that Chwasky got involved. As Leon's lawyer, Chwasky announced that during the fight with Ali, Leon had aggravated a nagging rib injury that could delay the rematch. Skeptics pointed out that Leon had been seen a week after the Ali fight dancing at a New York discotheque until the wee hours, showing no signs of injury. They felt the whole thing reeked of Arum and that perhaps Leon's supposed injury was merely a stalling tactic to frustrate Norton into signing against a different fighter. Regardless, the Nevada State Athletic Commission slapped Leon with a ninety-day suspension for not disclosing the alleged injury before the first Ali fight.

Dave Anderson of the *New York Times* wrote in March 1978, "Ever since [Norton] called Arum's bluff and accepted the $200,000 offer in good faith, Arum has been acting in bad faith, first by staging Ali's nationally televised plea for a rematch and then announcing the Leon cartilage damage."

Arum now explains, "By that time Leon had gotten an advisor, some black lawyer from Detroit, I forget his name . . . yeah, Ed Bell . . . and he said he didn't give a shit what the rules were, he was gonna do a rematch with Ali because that was the most money to be made. Yeah, I did what I could to get Ken Norton out of the picture so the rematch could happen."

All of the jockeying, posturing, and angling was lost on Leon. The WBC edict meant nothing to him. Ali had given him a shot and he wanted to return the favor. And so he granted Ali the rematch.

Sulaiman held true to his word and stripped Leon of the title, handing it to Norton. The rematch would be for the WBA belt only, and of course, the lineal championship, which no sanctioning body could take away from Leon.

Arum offered Leon and Ali five million dollars each for the rematch, predicting the fight would be TV's highest-rated event. The agreement also produced a prizefight of sorts outside the ropes: Bob Arum vs. Don King. Their ring was the *Washington Post*.

King: "[Arum] is one of the most devious and evil individuals I have ever met, who builds a success road on deviousness."

More King after calling Leon a "totally illiterate black man": "[His illiteracy] is an indictment against the school system in the black ghettoes of the big cities of the United States. The teachers that passed Leon Spinks to the eleventh grade should be tied to a post and flogged."

Arum: "It was very unfair of King to say Spinks is illiterate. He is not illiterate. The kid can read very well. I have seen him read documents and newspapers. That is nonsense. He was in the Marine Corps. You can't get in the Marines if you are illiterate."

King: "[Arum] has a slave master's mentality of thinking he can treat people of color to do whatever is right for him. [He's treating Spinks] just like in the slave days when the house nigger could do anything against another nigger and get away with it. Here's a white man leading a black man into the paths of destruction."

Arum: "[King's comments] are beneath my dignity. Everybody knows what King is—a total charlatan. I'm a real 'slave master.' In his ninth pro fight, Spinks is going to earn five million dollars. I'm really treating him badly."

America didn't care who won the Arum-King slugfest. The real story was Leon, but there was nothing to write about because he was nowhere to be found. Throughout this entire mess—and even now that a rematch with Ali had been set for September 15, 1978, in New Orleans—Leon was still being Leon.

—◦—

Given a quarter of a million dollars for training expenses, Leon made sure not to hang on to a penny of it. He and his twelve employees—including Sam Solomon, Marine coach Art Redden, Gunnery Sgt. John Davis, Lester Hudson, Ed Bell, Roger Stafford, Mitt Barnes, full-time bodyguard Mr. T, part-time bodyguard Jerome Tunstall, and sparring partner Leroy Diggs—were put up at the Sea Pines Resort, an oceanfront getaway in Hilton Head, South Carolina, complete with the latest amenities and round-the-clock services.

When camp opened on June 1, everything was in place. The back room of the Hilton Head Community Playhouse had been outfitted into a training camp, and a personal chef was on hand. Staff members stood at the ready, each one decked out in a light-blue "Leon Spinks World Heavyweight Champion" jacket.

Leon's publicists fed the press the standard line: The champ was hard at work, running in combat boots, chopping down trees, eating up sparring partners. The truth was they had no idea where he was.

"We can't shackle him to the training camp," Sam Solomon told the assembled media. "When he's off, he's his own man. I go by his performance."

Leon's performance began when he showed up three weeks later. His day started with breakfast: three eggs, sausage, vitamins, and two bottles of beer. His day ended with a trip to the bar, where he'd drink, dance, and smoke cigarettes.

On July 1, only eight days after his arrival, Leon closed camp to have a birthday party. The festivities lasted through his actual birthday, ten days later.

Butch Lewis told *New York Magazine*'s Vic Ziegel at the time, "Leon's always looking for somebody to say he doesn't have to do something. And the people around him want to keep a smile on his face. He says, 'I think I'll go out tonight; it won't hurt me.' There they are, 'Yeah, Champ, anything you say, Champ.' He's surrounded by people who don't know anything about boxing. They're scufflers."

Leon went AWOL twice. Both times he was tracked down by a member of his entourage. The second time, when Lester Hudson found him in Detroit, Leon hadn't slept in three days.

Mr. T spent more time chasing the champ than guarding him. It was clear Leon was in the next phase of his lifelong bender—and this one came with an outsized budget and a never-ending supply of marijuana and cocaine. According to Mr. T, whatever hunger Leon had before winning the title was gone. The champ was buying—and blowing—cocaine by the pound.

"He'd wake up and snort it." Mr. T wrote in his autobiography, *Mr. T: The Man with the Gold.* "He had long fingernails and he would put it under his nails. The more cocaine he snorted, the less he trained, and the less he trained, the more out of shape he got.

"Leon was trying so hard to make friends with the ghetto dwellers. He would buy people drinks, share his smoke and blow with them, then ride them around with him. They would eat his food, drink his drinks, sleep in his hotel rooms, snort his cocaine and still try to rob and steal from him. Even Leon's ghetto friends said, 'He's a damn fool using all those drugs and not training.' They had lost respect for Leon and his name was mud."

Harold Petty, Leon's gym mate at the DeSoto, remembers Leon as a "wild man."

"He wanted to be accepted and that hurt him more than anything," Petty says. "He would come back [to St. Louis] after turning pro; he'd be driving this big old car and he'd be out there talking to everybody, talking to the kids, telling them to stay in school, saying all the right stuff. Then he'd leave and come back drunk."

Bruce Newman of *Sports Illustrated* wrote in late July 1978, "Usually Spinks heads for large urban centers like Philadelphia, Cleveland, or Detroit, diving into them as if they were foxholes that remind him of the Pruitt-Igoe housing project in which he grew up in St. Louis. . . . [Leon] is one of the few successful athletes whose money does not seem to be able to separate him from poverty."

Leon told Newman, "I'm a ghetto nigger, people shouldn't forget that about me. You can take the nigger out of the ghetto, but you can't take the ghetto out of the nigger. One of the great things about Ali was the things he did for the black man in the white society—but you don't never see no Ali down in the ghetto. . . . I go to the neighborhoods and give those people a chance to see the heavyweight champion of the world on their own ground."

Another ex-champion with a troubled past can relate. "When [Leon] had all his money and he was champion, he wants to go back and show everybody, wants to share it with these guys," Mike Tyson says. "'This is what I got! Look at me, ain't I bad? Didn't I make it? I'm the champ of the world!' I always liked Leon 'cause Leon was a street guy. He dressed like a street guy. 'Yo, look at his hat. His hat is fly.' He always had a sharp hat. Always getting in trouble like we were."

It was the getting-in-trouble part that helped Leon's camp keep tabs on their employer. In one instance Leon was spotted in his Coupe de Ville outside the main gate of the airport in Savannah, Georgia. This wouldn't have been newsworthy had he not been in the car with a young lady—necking for three solid hours—as his flight took off without him.

On another occasion a wire service released a photo in which Leon and a woman were shopping in a Las Vegas jewelry store. The article identified the woman as his wife, Nova. The article was wrong. And Nova saw the picture.

"I know who the woman is," she said. "If I ever see her face to face, I'll smash her."

Meanwhile, back at training camp, Leon's many advisors were still jockeying for power. Sam Solomon, Art Redden, and John Davis were all taking credit for Leon's success. But Davis got tired of waiting for Leon. After ten days he gave up and went back to Camp Lejeune.

Lester Hudson and Ed Bell were under the impression that they were calling the shots. Nova, now in Detroit, was under the impression that *she* was calling the shots. Michael and Kay thought they were advising Leon. Roger Stafford and Jerome Tunstall thought *they* were advising Leon.

Mitt Barnes, who had signed Leon before anybody else, accused Bell of choosing Hilton Head for Leon's camp site so that Bell could have an extended tennis vacation. The tension between the two didn't last long, because Barnes was ordered off the Hilton Head premises after calling Leon "ignorant" during an interview with the press. Barnes left but made it clear that Leon belonged to him for the next seven years.

Arum and Lewis both threatened to clean house and start from scratch.

Michael flew out to Hilton Head to confront Leon about his blown-out lifestyle. The two had it out, arguing as only brothers can. When Michael saw he was getting nowhere, he stormed out, leaving Leon alone at the heavy bag, swinging from his toes as tears streaked his face.

Eventually, the calendar ran out. It was time to leave for New Orleans, so Leon arranged to have sixty-one rooms reserved at the Hilton. Butch Lewis estimated that Leon knew only ten of the sixty-one freeloaders (for whom Leon was also footing plane fare). The hotel bill alone came to an estimated $7,000 per night.

Leon's entourage landed at New Orleans International Airport on September 1. A police motorcade escorted the champ's $45,000 limo to the Hilton. Leon was in the car with Mr. T, Solomon, Diggs, Hudson, and Bell. Before the motorcade even left the airport, one of the police motorcycle escorts bumped into the back of the limo. Leon jumped out and exchanged angry words with the officer until his aides calmed him down. According to Mr. T, when Leon got back in the limo, he said, "All right, give it here," which meant he wanted some reefer.

Mr. T wrote in his autobiography, "It was funny; Leon was getting high and all those police were around us. Leon was smoking reefers and waving to the crowds of people who had lined the street waiting to see him. He stood up in his sunroof limo, waving both hands now and smiling. The crowd loved him. People tried to run up to the moving car, but the police kept them back. The city of New Orleans belonged to Leon from that day up to the fifteenth. Whatever he wanted, wherever he went, anything, the city jumped to please."

On September 12, Bob Arum was on his way to breakfast at the Hilton. As he stepped off the elevator, Leon staggered past him and collapsed. Recognizing a drunk when he saw one, Arum said, "Leon, you're fighting Muhammad Ali in three days. Are you crazy?"

"Whatsa matter?" Leon mumbled. "I just got in from roadwork."

It was an obvious lie, but telling the truth wouldn't have changed anything. Drunk, out of shape, and slumped on the floor, Leon had seventy-two hours to sober up before stepping into the ring with an over-the-hill but determined Muhammad Ali.

7

For Leon, the three days leading up to "The Battle of New Orleans" were last-call at a once-in-a-lifetime bender. And like any garden-variety alcoholic, Leon got as high as he could before closing time.

By all accounts, Leon spent September 14, the day before the rematch, downing booze, smoking pot, snorting coke, and screwing women. It's remarkable that he made it to the Hilton that evening for the weigh-in, a prefight ritual that had been a nonevent until Ali turned it into a circus. This one deserved a big top. A chaotic crush of reporters, photographers, hangers-on, and boxing insiders crammed into the Grand Ballroom. One of the onlookers was Larry Holmes. The twenty-eight-year-old heavyweight got his start as a sparring partner for Ali but was now able to claim his own title: Leon's vacated WBC belt, which he'd taken from Ken Norton in a squeaker of a split decision a week earlier in Las Vegas.

"There ain't nobody in the world who can beat me," Holmes shouted, trying to convince the press that he hadn't backed his way into the championship. His histrionics didn't work. Few people, aside from members of his own family, saw Holmes as the legitimate titleholder. The boxing world recognized Leon as the king, and they were interested in only one fight: the Ali-Spinks rematch.

Ali, a genius at stealing ink, was uncharacteristically quiet, chewing on a toothpick. When he stepped up to the makeshift platform, camera crews rushed to the staged area as if a starting pistol had been fired. They converged on Ali and Leon so quickly that the platform began to collapse under their weight.

"Get back!" the announcer shouted, trying in vain to clear the area around a woman who had fainted. It took a team of gun-toting security guards to restore order. Once the crowd was under control, the ceremony of weighing the fighters took place.

Ali came in at 221; he had dropped three pounds in the seven months since losing the title to Leon.

Leon weighed 201. He'd gained four pounds since his first meeting with Ali, but some of that could be attributed to the fistful of gold medallions hanging around his neck and the new dentures between his lips.

After stepping off the scales, both fighters left the Hilton without exchanging as much as a nod.

Leon's activities on the day of the fight are sketchy, but the facts that can be gathered don't paint a picture of sobriety. In the early afternoon he brought an unnamed man and four women into his hotel room and locked the door. Mr. T said he knocked on the door at 5:15 and found him guzzling beer and snorting cocaine. Then Leon disappeared again, this time eluding even his bodyguard.

An hour before the opening bell was due to ring at the Louisiana Superdome, Nova found her husband in a hotel room across town sprawled out in bed, drunk. He wasn't alone.

Infuriated, she dragged him to his dressing room, where his cornermen—Solomon, Benton, and Michael—had been waiting for hours. Inexplicably, nobody was prepared.

Sports Illustrated's Pat Putnam recorded the chaotic scene in the dressing room when Leon asked for his protective cup:

"'Go get a cup,' Solomon said to Chet Cummings, a public-relations man for Top Rank. 'For God's sake, get Leon a cup.'

"'A cup?' said Cummings, who then turned to Vickie Blain, another Top Rank employee, and said, 'Go get Leon a cup for ice.'

"'Not *that* kind of a cup,' Solomon yelled, 'A *cup* cup, for God's sake. A *cup* cup!'"

Leon waited for the assistant to run to a neighboring dressing room. When the assistant returned, he handed the champ the only athletic cup in the house. It was the one Mike Rossman had just worn while taking the light-heavyweight title in a grueling thirteen-round TKO over Victor Galindez. Fresh it was not. Leon threw it on.

Then Kay Spinks led the room in prayer, asking the Lord to bring victory to the better man. Leon kissed a small cross and put it in his right sock. Then he walked with his entourage into the jammed arena as the crowd of 70,000 rhythmically chanted Ali's name.

It's no exaggeration to say that the Ali-Spinks rematch was one of the most anticipated fights in boxing history. It took in a record gate of $6 million, and drew what, at the time, was the second-largest television audience in history: ninety million viewers. Frank Sinatra, *Rocky* star Sylvester Stallone, and Lillian Carter were among those in the VIP row. Lillian's son, President Jimmy Carter, tuned in at Camp David with Egyptian President Anwar Sadat and Secretary of State Cyrus Vance.

"Leon had won the championship but he hadn't convinced people that he was a great fighter," says professor and fight scholar Gerald Early. "He hadn't even convinced those who knew the sport that he was a *good* fighter. What he had convinced people of was that he was a lucky fighter, and that on the night he'd fought Ali, he was really up for the fight. He was perfect proof of the adage 'I'd rather be lucky than good.'"

Muhammad Ali told *New York Magazine*'s Vic Ziegel during the lead-up to the fight, "If I beat him the first time I wouldn't of got no credit for it. He only had seven fights . . . the kid was nothing. . . . So I'm glad he won. It's a perfect scene. You couldn't write a better movie than this. Can the old champ regain his title for a third time? Think of it. A third time. And you know what makes me laugh? He's the same guy. Only difference is he got eight fights now.

"It will be no-o-o-o-o contest. I'll bring out the amateur in the boy. Bet your money on Muhammad Ali"

The oddsmakers believed him. Leon was the champ but entered the ring a two-to-one underdog. The odds probably would have been steeper had the handicappers known the extent of Leon's prefight binge—or that Solomon and Benton were still at loggerheads, both insisting they were in charge of the champion's corner.

Meanwhile, Ali had spent months in the gym trying his damnedest to grow young again—impossible for anyone, but also risky for an aging fighter. Reports had been circulating that Ali's speech was becoming slurred and that his reflexes were gone. He had come up with several excuses, the most questionable being that blows around his nose and mouth had closed his sinuses, causing his speech to thicken.

Ali had worked hard enough that when the bell rang he was able to put on a reasonable, if slower, impersonation of his vintage self. He set the pattern for the fight: He bobbed, backpedaled, jabbed, and clinched. He'd obviously studied the first bout and wasn't going to give away a single round this time. The famous rope-a-dope was shelved in favor of a dancing, picking, sniping offense. He peppered Leon with punches, never allowing the frustrated champion to get closer than a jab's length away.

As for Leon, his energy level was a far cry from that of the first fight. In Las Vegas he hadn't bothered sitting between rounds until

Michael convinced him, after the eighth, to take a breather. Now he was motioning for his stool when the bell rang to close the first round. When he reached his corner, he flopped down, exhausted. Then, searching for answers, he looked up to his cornermen—but had no idea which one he'd see. Solomon's solution to the internal power struggle had been to rotate the command: He would speak to Leon after the first round, Benton after the second, Michael after the third, and so on.

"I got up one round," George Benton told the *Washington Post*, "I think it was the third, when I saw [Leon] doing nothing. Then I went up the next round to try and tell him something, but everybody was talking from all angles. I couldn't get a word in edgewise. Fact is, one guy's telling the fighter to shake and boogie and wiggle-wiggle. Stuff like that. I still don't know what wiggle-wiggle meant. [At one point] one of the commissioners jumped up and said he was gonna fine us for [having] too many men in the corner."

Benton became so frustrated that after the fifth round he left the ring, showered, and returned to his hotel. "What can I do?" he said when departing. "There's ten amateurs in there."

Years later Benton would tell William Nack of *Sports Illustrated*, "It was like watching your baby drown. There was nothing you could do about it. I had no more control of the guy. I was useless. All I could do was get the hell out of it."

Mr. T wrote in *Mr. T: The Man with the Gold*, "As the fight wore on, Leon grew weary. His eyes were all glazed and he didn't even know where he was. He was just fighting out of instinct; his mind and reflexes were gone. Sam and Michael were hollering at Leon when he sat in the corner but he didn't hear them—he was in another world."

In the tenth round Ali delighted the crowd with a brief Ali shuffle, the fancy piece of footwork he'd made famous in his younger days. In the eleventh he fed Leon a steady diet of lefts. After the twelfth Solomon begged Leon to throw punches, to fight his fight, to avoid falling into Ali's traps. He might as well have asked him to run a one-minute mile.

ABC's Howard Cosell told viewers in round thirteen, "Spinks desperately trying to score, desperately trying to get to the former champion but unable to. Look at that! Now Ali is having fun! A touch of the shuffle . . . dancing from side to side . . . sensing he's in command . . . knowing that he's got this. Now tying up Spinks in the clinch. Just a quick combination there, only one blow landed, now tying up Spinks again. Getting perhaps a little rest but still setting the tone of the fight with that left. Notice the way he's clinching and tying Spinks up. He's fighting with a cautious wisdom now, trying to preserve his apparent wide lead. Look at that left! And again! And again! And Spinks unable to get at him! Of course, he's fighting, Spinks is, Ali's fight."

"The whole world watched as [Leon] stumbled around the ring trying to hit Ali," Mr. T wrote. "When the fight was nearing the end, Leon knew he had lost, so he just held on to keep from getting knocked down. When the fight was over, Leon was so glad that, if you didn't know any better, you would think he won instead of Ali."

Going by the judges' cards, which according to Louisiana rules were scored on the rounds system, the fight was nearly a shutout. Judge Herman Dutreix had Ali ahead 11–4. Referee Lucien Joubert and Judge Ernest Cojoe had it 10–4–1. The bout had been so one-sided that one of the few rounds Leon took—the fifth—came by way of default: Ali had been penalized for holding.

Leon showed no sour grapes. The instant he was no longer encumbered with the championship, he walked over to Ali, and in the center of the ring where he had just lost the title, lifted Ali's arm in victory. Leon says he did so out of respect. He must mean respect for Ali, because he never seemed to have had respect for the title when it was in his hands.

Some suggest that Leon, in his own way, felt as if he never deserved the title, that he'd borrowed it from Ali and was ready to give it back. If so, it might explain, at least partially, the seven-month joyride he had taken from Las Vegas to New Orleans.

"Behavior reflects intent," explains clinical psychologist Michael Conforti. "He may have partied the title away because on an unconscious level, he knew he was not able to live up to the myth: He was not going to transcend his circumstances. He recognized Ali as the champ because Ali had transcended his."

Robert Lipsyte suggests that Leon's gesture may have been "the fulfillment of his childhood hero worship. All was right with the world now: 'Muhammad Ali beat me. That's how it should be.'"

In Leon's dressing room after the fight, as Mr. T bawled his eyes out and Leon apologized for losing, Kay told her son, "We still love Ali because he gave us the title for a while so we gave it back to him. Today Ali was the better man. We want to thank Ali for allowing us to be here tonight."

At the postfight press conference, Leon shook off the notion that he'd thrown away the title on coke, booze, and whores.

"Intoxicated? Never," Leon said. "I was in great physical shape; it's just that my mind wasn't in it. During the fight there was so much stuff that went through my mind I thought all I can do now is survive and keep the fight going. If Ali did win, I wasn't going to let him win by knockout.

"There's a lot on your mind when you're heavyweight champion. Maybe it ruined me. Maybe I didn't know how to deal with it," Leon added.

To this day, nobody disagrees.

"After the first fight, all the pressure was on [Leon]," says 1980s heavyweight contender Gerry Cooney. "You start to think with fear. He was a tough guy for a while but he didn't live well. He started drinking and having a good time, and that catches up with you. He was reckless, didn't think about tomorrow."

Leon's friend Roger Stafford doesn't think victory was ever Leon's goal in the Ali rematch. "Leon didn't do nothing compared to the first fight," he says. "Everyone in Leon's corner was screaming to Leon, do this, do that, 'cause he had Ali in situations that he could take Ali out. But he wasn't doing nothing. Leon respected Ali so much that all he was thinking about was the money, the millions of dollars that he was getting. His mind was somewhere else. He didn't want to beat Ali."

Emanuel Steward said in 2011, "If [Leon] had been the same fighter in the second fight that he was in the first one, he could've beat [Ali]. But he didn't have that same intensity. Once he got the money, everybody was flocking around him everywhere. I didn't expect him to win."

The day after Leon's loss to Ali, Bob Arum told the press, "You have seen, in my opinion, one of the great tragedies of boxing, of America, and of a human being. Some of it I gotta take the blame for. Perhaps I was wrong to put the kid in a title shot when he wasn't ready. He obviously hadn't matured enough to accept the responsibility of being the heavyweight champion of the world. The message here is that a fighter has to have strong leadership, instead of a lot of sharks hovering around picking his bones."

Leon's magic carpet ride was over. Here's how quickly it ended: After the fight, when Leon returned to the Hilton, his entourage of seventy people had already disappeared. Boxing's father-son team Lou and Dan Duva were standing in front of the Hilton when Leon got out of his limo, alone, his head down, his hands in his pockets.

"It was the saddest thing I ever saw," Lou Duva told *Sports Illustrated.*

Instead of wallowing in self-pity, Leon did what any party-crazed night crawler would do: He kept on celebrating. He started in a downtown hotel, where he danced the night away, forgetting about his loss to Ali and any other problems that had supposedly been cluttering his mind.

One issue that clearly wasn't weighing on Leon was that the mother of his children, Zadie Mae Calvin, was chronically unemployed and financially strapped. Five days after Leon had defeated Ali, Zadie Mae gave birth to her and Leon's third son, Cory. By then, Little Leon was seven and Darrell was five. Any amount of money would have helped. All four were living with Zadie Mae's mother, Aline, and assorted other relatives in an overcrowded two-family brick house in north St. Louis—a neighborhood plagued by the same diseases that had afflicted Pruitt-Igoe—poverty, crime, and despair.

In an eerie replay of his own father's behavior, Leon had no presence in his children's lives. Three weeks after the Ali rematch, Zadie Mae filed a paternity suit in St. Louis Circuit Court. In it she asked the court to declare Leon the father of her three sons and order him to pay her a just sum periodically. She wound up dropping the suit when Leon agreed to fork over monthly child-support payments. But the money rarely came—either because Leon didn't have the wherewithal to send it or because he was already running out of cash.

"He partied and partied, he drank and drank, he smoked and smoked, he snorted cocaine and boy did he get high," Mr. T wrote in his autobiography. "I mean he would be so high that he would be foaming at the mouth and he was a sight to behold."

While Leon was busy burning through the last of his millions, Ed Bell and Lester Hudson were suing Bob Arum and Top Rank for "breaching their contract in almost every material aspect." They claimed that Top Rank failed to supply Leon's guests with agreed-upon transportation from the airport to the hotel; that Top Rank never gave Leon the fifty ringside seats he had been promised; and, the jewel of the suit, that Arum had publicly stated Leon was drunk every night leading up to the rematch.

In the midst of the paper storm, Bell and Hudson took their business to the only other game in town. They offered their client's upcoming fights to Don King, and King, having been shut out of the two Ali-Spinks bonanzas, was all too willing to oblige. But Ali was retiring, taking the lineal championship with him, and vacating the WBA title. A rubber match between Leon and Ali wasn't in the cards. The biggest money available to Leon would be in a title fight against Larry Holmes.

The only question was whether they could set up the fight before Leon shut the window on his own career.

8

OCTOBER 2, 1980. A CAPACITY CROWD OF 24,790 JAMMED THE
outdoor arena at Caesars Palace in Las Vegas. Frank Sinatra, Tom
Jones, and Paul Anka took their places in celebrity row. So did a
couple of thousand high rollers whose credit lines started at twenty
thousand dollars. The event was the stuff of legend. Muhammad Ali
was back. After a two-year layoff, the retired champ was returning to
the ring to take on WBC king Larry Holmes.

Holmes was undefeated in thirty-five fights, and since taking the
title from Ken Norton two years earlier, had successfully defended it
seven times. Yet, despite assuming the role of the people's champ and
boasting an impeccable record, he still felt upstaged by Ali. He had
good reason: Ali's shadow rivaled that of Paul Bunyan.

"Ali said he was the greatest and everyone said 'Yeah.' I said I was
the greatest and everyone said 'Yeah, right,'" Larry Holmes said in
the ESPN film *Muhammad and Larry*.

Before the fight Holmes bitterly reminded the press that, as
champ, he deserved top billing—the fight should be referred to as
Holmes-Ali, not Ali-Holmes as most papers had been calling it.
Tradition said he was right. The box office didn't agree.

The star here was Ali. The ex-champ had been coaxed out of
retirement by an eight-million-dollar payday plus the chance to win
the WBC crown for the fourth time. Holmes was to earn $2.3 mil-
lion, with the added bonus of having the opportunity to slay his
personal Goliath. Boxing purists viewed the fight as Holmes's shot

at the lineal title. And virtually everybody involved saw it as Ali's final hurrah.

In the two years since Ali had left the ring, speculation about his health had spread rapidly. Friends worried about his increasingly slurred and slowed speech and his deteriorating reflexes. Insiders spoke of pugilistic dementia and other ring-related conditions. His estranged physician, Ferdie Pacheco, had even gone public with a claim that he had seen a CAT scan showing small lesions on Ali's brain.

Three months before the Holmes fight, the Nevada Athletic Commission insisted that Ali undergo a physical. The two-day series of tests took place at the Mayo Clinic in Rochester, Minnesota.

Ali assured the boxing world, "They put their best machines on me and said I'm one hundred percent. My kidneys are perfect, my brain is perfect, my blood, my heart, everything. They gave me their stamp of approval."

The Nevada Commission released highlights of the report to the public. Dr. Donald Romeo accepted it on behalf of the commission and said the brain scan revealed "no trace of tumor or old clots" and dismissed the brain-damage rumors as "a bunch of bunk."

Thomas Hauser obtained a copy of the doctors' findings and disclosed them in his 1991 book, *Muhammad Ali: His Life and Times*. These are excerpts from the findings:

> *Other than occasional tingling of the hands in the morning when he awakens, which clears promptly with movement of the hands, he denied any other neurologic symptoms. . . . On neurological examination, he seems to have a mild ataxic dysarthria* [the inability to control speech resulting from damage to the cerebellum]. . . . *The remainder of his examination is normal except that he does not quite hop with the agility that one might anticipate and on finger-to-nose testing there is a slight degree of missing the*

*target. Both of these tests could be significantly influenced by fatigue.
. . . There is minimal evidence of some difficulty with his speech and
memory and perhaps to a very slight degree with his coordination. All
of these are more noticeable when he is fatigued.*

The commission gave Ali the go-ahead to lace up his gloves and
go toe-to-toe with Holmes. Perhaps those in power believed that an
icon such as Ali had limits beyond those of a mortal man. Or maybe
they didn't care if he got killed.

Fans who came early saw the prelims, throughout which chants
of "Ali!" rippled through the arena. The undercard featured Leon
against the six-foot-four Colombian power-puncher Bernardo
Mercado in a twelve-round title elimination bout. Mercado had
won twenty-six of twenty-eight fights and in March had stopped
Earnie Shavers with twenty-five unanswered blows in the seventh
round. But even though he was facing a legitimate opponent, Leon
was destined to spend the evening in the same manner as Holmes—
eclipsed by the outsize shadow of Ali.

Leon had spent the past two years bouncing around the heavyweight division with no apparent direction. He'd taken on Gerrie
Coetzee in Monte Carlo for a shot at Ali's vacated WBA belt, but he
hit the canvas more often than he hit Coetzee—three times within
the first two minutes of the fight. The bout was over before the bell
rang for the second round. Nobody was surprised. Bob Arum recalls
Leon partying away his training time before the fight and being so
irresponsible that he'd shown up five hours late for the press conference emceed by Prince Rainier.

Leon rebounded after the Coetzee fight and stopped Alfredo
Evangelista in five rounds, but then could only muster up a draw
against Eddie "The Animal" Lopez. (Had referee Mills Lane not
taken a point from Lopez for head butting in the fifth, Leon

would have lost a majority decision.) When Leon then TKOed the unknown Kevin Isaac in eight rounds, Don King matched him up with Mercado, the number-one challenger, and put the fight on the Holmes-Ali undercard. The winner of Leon-Mercado would get a shot at the winner of Holmes-Ali.

Leon tried his best to blow the opportunity, this time by nearly missing the previous day's weigh-in.

"Leon Spinks, please report to the weigh-in," ring announcer Chuck Hull said into the microphone. He read a similar announcement a few minutes later, and then a third after that. Still no Leon. Word began circulating that Leon's car had been parked illegally and was towed.

When Leon finally entered the Sports Pavilion at Caesars Palace and approached the scale, he was nearly a half hour late.

"We couldn't find a parking place," he casually explained.

Leon wriggled off the hook and was permitted to weigh in. Now training under Del Williams, he was at 204 pounds and in excellent shape. When the opening bell rang the following night, he looked fast and strong. But like most of Leon's fights, it didn't take long for the contest to spiral into a street brawl. Mercado blasted Leon's head with haymakers, but Leon absorbed them, got inside, and stayed there, hammering Mercado with an onslaught of body blows. Mercado never had a chance to breathe. Leon won nearly every one of the first eight rounds, and then, in the ninth, stunned his opponent with a left hook to the head. He followed with a flurry of blows, and when Mercado didn't respond, referee Ferd Hernandez did. He stopped the fight with eight seconds to go in the round.

Leon earned $125,000, minus expenses. One of those deductions included a $5,000 fine imposed by the Nevada Athletic Commission because Leon's cornermen had stood on the ring apron during the fight and cursed the officials.

It's unlikely that Leon cared. He had looked good, and in his next bout, only his fifteenth as a pro, he'd be fighting for the world title a third time. He just wasn't sure who would be in the other corner—Ali or Holmes.

The fans were hoping for Ali.

New York Times columnist Red Smith watched the fight on closed-circuit television with a standing-room-only crowd in Boston Garden. "Nothing could illustrate Ali's sentimental appeal, his popularity bordering on idolatry, better than that howling crowd in Boston," Smith wrote a few days later. "Even before Leon Spinks left the ring after the semifinal windup, they started a chant, 'Ali! Ali! Ali!' When the great man showed up, a big, grimy old hall 3,000 miles away trembled. When Larry Holmes appeared, booing rattled the tiles."

To say that Ali fans were disappointed with the outcome of the fight is an understatement. What they witnessed was a lopsided disaster—the type of mismatch that causes commissions to be formed, or replaced. Ali looked every hour of his thirty-eight years, 259 days. He appeared lethargic, and compared to the healthy, lightning-quick Holmes, he seemed to be throwing his punches underwater, a slow-motion replay of his glory days. Even ardent fans could see that the rumors of his failing health had some validity. Worse yet, the thirty-year-old Holmes, cast as the villain by the Ali faithful, was in his prime. He threw steady jabs and right crosses with pinpoint accuracy. After Ali absorbed ten rounds of inhumane punishment, Angelo Dundee got word from Herbert Muhammad to put an end to it.

Red Smith wrote, "If it had been any fighter except Muhammad Ali, he would have been thrown out of the ring and had his purse withheld. Only a deity or a myth could get away with the performance Ali gave against Larry Holmes. It should have been declared no contest.

"There was a heaviness of disappointment, maybe a reluctant acceptance of the fact that the past was past and would not be recovered. There were some small hoots but no widespread derision of the demigod who was letting them down. . . . On the subway, a man said the next day, about half the riders agreed that Ali had faked the whole thing to set up a rematch for another $8 million. Better that than to believe everything was over."

But for boxing fans, it *was* over. The new champion lacked Ali's charisma, political passion, and rapier tongue, but that couldn't stop the calendar from moving forward, the baton from changing hands. Despite the public's lingering idolatry of Ali, Larry Holmes held the heavyweight division in the palm of his gloved hand.

And Leon was next in line for a shot.

Three months later Leon was back in the papers. On January 15, 1981, he told Detroit police he'd been hit on the head while leaving a bar on the city's north side. He claimed he hadn't seen his assailants but woke up five miles away, naked, in the Crestwood Motel, minus $45,000 worth of clothes, jewelry, and gold front teeth.

As is the case with most stories that come out of late-night bars and short-stay motels, Leon's tale had some gaping holes.

Al Low, who promoted and managed Leon in the mid-1980s, heard the story this way: "He'd been drinking at Spears Bar on Woodward just north of Six Mile, and next thing he knew he was waking up in the motel without his stuff, including his gold teeth. But some eyewitnesses said he was drinking and playing pool at the Last Chance Bar on Woodward and Eight Mile, where he was known to hang out quite a bit, and left with one of the ladies who, ummm, quote unquote *worked* there."

Jackie Kallen, boxing manager and longtime friend of Leon, says, "I was under the impression that [Leon] went back to his hotel room with a girl, and while he was there he got rolled. I was never quite sure if it was her or if she had an accomplice."

Mr. T wrote in *Mr. T: The Man with the Gold*, "[Leon] kept on partying until one night some bitch set him up. He got high in a hotel room in January 1981 and she stole jewelry, his mink coat, money and drugs. He lied and told the police that he was robbed coming from a tavern. He said someone hit him on the back of the head and took his money and dragged him to a hotel, where they took all of his clothes. I tell you, Leon couldn't even lie straight."

If one is to believe Mr. T's story (and there's no evidence to the contrary), Leon may have been bending the truth to protect himself from Nova, who was running out of patience with his vagabond ways.

"One day I get a call from Leon," Emanuel Steward recalled in 2011. "It's the middle of the night and I answer the phone. 'Steward! Steward!' The voice is muffled but I knew it was Leon, so I say to my wife, 'Something's going on with Leon; I better go over there.' I go across the street and he opens up the door. There's some fighting going on, and an arm grabs him by the neck and pulls him back in. I look and there's Nova. Nova's about as big as Leon—six-one, six-two—and she's the one pulling him back. She had a girlfriend there named Ayesha who was about six-two or six-three, and they grab Leon and drag him to the kitchen and they throw him on the floor and say, 'Don't your ass move.' [Leon] looked at me and he said, 'Steward, you gotta help me.' And Nova said, 'Don't you dare. This motherfucker, we just caught him, he gave a car to some girlfriend. I was at the bank and I heard some shit and that bitch is driving around with my car. And we waited for him to come home and beat his ass.' Then [Nova] told me, 'Emanuel, get your ass on outta here. You got nothing to do with this. This ain't no boxing business.' And they were sitting at the table eating fried chicken, and I looked at them and said, 'Fuck it,' and went on back home."

On February 17, 1981, Leon filed for divorce. Nova's attorney requested that the circuit court judge of Wayne County, Michigan, order Leon to carry the mortgage on their house in Rosedale Park; pay tuition for Nova's son, Charles; and pick up five thousand dollars of Nova's legal bills. The lawyer also asked for Nova's $375 weekly alimony check to be bumped to $500 should Leon take the title from Holmes.

The divorce became final in 1982. The bills went unpaid.

❦

Nova's attorney may have had his eye on Leon's upcoming fight with Larry Holmes, but few fight fans did. In their view Leon had virtually no shot against the champion, and it didn't help when rumors surfaced that Leon had suffered a broken nose in training camp. Most agreed that Holmes took the fight simply to stay active. He had done much the same two months earlier when he defended the title against Trevor Berbick. These no-contests were keeping him sharp while he waited for a payday with rising star Gerry Cooney.

What many fans didn't realize was that Holmes had another reason for agreeing to the fight: He harbored a genuine dislike of Leon. In his 1998 autobiography, *Larry Holmes: Against the Odds*, written with Phil Berger, Holmes said Leon was the first opponent he "truly wanted to hurt." He also took issue with how Leon had disrespected the heavyweight title.

"He'd acted like a buffoon of a heavyweight champion," Holmes wrote. "He was a loose cannon, a guy who exposed himself as a dumb bastard the more you saw of him. I knew he'd end up a jive ex-champ, driving a Cadillac with about three bucks in his pocket and a brain like cornflakes."

According to Holmes, the friction had heated up in 1980 at a dinner held in Las Vegas for Joe Louis. Leon had gotten drunk and was going from table to table, plucking souvenir boxing gloves from the centerpieces and throwing them around the room. When he approached the table at which Holmes's wife, Diane, was seated, she and Leon had a bit of a tussle. It wasn't long before Holmes's posse was going at it with everybody in Leon's camp, including Mr. T.

Holmes's trainer Richie Giachetti attended the dinner and recalls, "Spinks was mouthing off, he wasn't conducting himself the right way, and he embarrassed himself. It was a shame to see it."

According to Holmes's autobiography, "He was loud and obnoxious, and bothering Diane. . . . I didn't want to muddy [the event] with violence, so when Spinks let go of the souvenir, and both he and Mr. T relaxed their threatening posture, I backed off. But I marked Spinks for a good butt-whupping, deciding right there I'd try to get him in the ring as soon as I could. Get him in the ring and beat him bad. Hurt him."

Boxing fans were far less enthusiastic than Holmes. A week before the "Motown Showdown," scheduled for June 12, 1981, ticket sales had produced a mere $500,000. Half the seats at Joe Louis Arena were unsold. To spur sales, the fight's promoter, Don King, dropped the price of the cheap seats from fifty to twenty-five dollars.

Holmes and Leon tried to build interest in the nonevent. But Holmes was no Ali when it came to hyping a fight. And Leon, despite growing up on the streets, had never learned to talk trash.

Holmes told the press that Leon had "the perfect style to make me look great" and that beating Leon would be considered his most meaningful victory. He also borrowed one of Leon's most popular phrases, repeatedly dismissing Leon as "Freaky Deaky" Spinks.

Leon asked the Associated Press to "tell Larry Holmes he's got my blessings and I wish him the best of luck, and tell him I'm comin' for it. I see him at the end of the rainbow with the pot of gold."

Holmes responded with, "Who's he ever beaten? He caught Ali on an off night and won a decision and then Ali got in shape and cleaned up on him in the rematch. He got himself knocked out and he's beaten nobody since then. If I hit him as many times as Mercado did in their fight, they'd have to carry him out of the ring. Besides, I can't allow myself to be beaten by Leon Spinks. I wouldn't be able to show my face back home. I just bought a new Rolls Royce, and I won't be able to drive it down the street."

Continuing the uninspired exchange, Leon told the press, "I'm going to fight him like I fought Muhammad Ali the first time. I'm going to cling to him like a T-shirt. He's a boxer and I'm a puncher. Holmes is going to try and dance and I'm going to try to keep him from dancing. I'll just be trying to win. Whether it's a knockout or not, I don't care. I just want to win the title back."

None of it was enough to bring out the fight fans. On the night of the bout, just three years after Leon had dethroned Ali, ten thousand people filed into the 21,000-seat arena to see him challenge the heavyweight champion of the world.

—✦—

This time around Leon had his own cup for the fight. He sat in his dressing room at Joe Louis Arena with his cornermen and his mother Kay, showing no signs of braggadocio. He had to be thinking what the rest of the boxing world already knew: The odds that he'd beat a peaking Larry Holmes were far slimmer than his tackling an over-the-hill Muhammad Ali.

When Kay Spinks reassured her son that he'd conquer Holmes, Leon said, mildly, "Aw, Mom, shut up. I'll just do the best I can."

He walked out to the ring to the cheers and jeers of the crowd, which included Kansas City Royals baseball players Larry Gura, Frank White, and Amos Otis. They were in town to play the Tigers, but the major league baseball players' strike suddenly freed up their schedule.

As champion, Holmes entered the arena after Leon, and to greater fanfare. Decked out in a white satin robe with red trim, he crossed the ropes and danced on his toes. Leon, draped in a burgundy robe, bounced in his corner, stretched his neck, and threw punches into the air. Michael stood next to him, wearing a black shirt, brown vest, white bow tie, black cowboy hat, and sunglasses.

Leon looked fit, much as he had when he won the title. When the bell rang, he did his best to replicate that miraculous showing. He rushed at Holmes in typical Leon Spinks fashion, trying to get inside, but the champion's five-inch reach advantage kept him away. Leon swung regardless.

In his autobiography, Holmes said, "Spinks was charging at me, bobbing and weaving like a disco dancer in a frenzy, trying to get inside my long reach. But he was also firing away like some damn kamikaze in boxing shorts."

At the outset, few of Leon's punches landed, but in the second round he began slipping Holmes's jab and working the champion's body. At two minutes and thirty-five seconds into the round, the timekeeper accidentally rang the bell and Holmes eased up, assuming the round was over. His corner even rushed into the ring with their stool. Leon didn't hear the bell and kept on wailing with wild rights and lefts, but the ring-savvy Holmes protected himself until the bell officially clanged.

By the third round, though, Holmes adjusted to Leon's awkward style. He picked at Leon with his world-class jab and then began following it with his right.

Gerry Cooney sat ringside. Going into the fight, he was convinced that Leon was too small for Holmes and that a fighter of Holmes's stature would overwhelm him.

"Holmes is an old pro," Cooney now says. "When Spinks tried to be the aggressor, Holmes knew how to cover up, take care of himself. He took the fight out of Spinks and then started catching him."

Holmes fired off combinations and each punch hit its target. He trapped Leon in the corner and rained blow after blow on his head. When a straight right from Holmes crunched Leon's jaw, Leon tumbled facedown onto the middle rope, rolled over, and landed hard on his back. Somehow, he got to his feet at the count of nine. Referee Richard Steele asked him if he was OK, and Leon said he was, despite having clearly lost his senses. He was so defeated, even Holmes may have felt compassion for him.

Holmes said in his autobiography, "I suddenly began to feel sorry for Spinks in spite of the way he had insulted Diane. I stepped back from [him] and yelled at Steele, 'Stop the goddamned fight. You want me to kill this man?'"

No one who was ringside that night claims to have heard Holmes cry out to Steele, and no such dialogue appears on the videotape of the fight. Regardless, Steele allowed one more exchange before coming to his own conclusion: Leon was finished. It didn't matter because Leon's trainer Del Williams was in the midst of throwing in the towel, and Michael, his face wet with tears, was rushing up the ringside stairs, desperately screaming to stop the fight. The end came at 2:34 of the third round.

A dazed Leon was led back to his dressing room as the crowd booed mercilessly. When the door shut, Leon sat for a postmortem with his inner circle. Nobody in the room would say it, but he'd probably just had his last shot at the big time.

The *New York Times*' Michael Katz reported the following exchange between Leon and Del Williams: "'I'm not giving up,' Leon said. 'We just got to go back to the drawing board, right Del?'

"'Yes,' Williams said.

"'We got to correct those mistakes.'"

Williams agreed again, though it was unclear if Leon was trying to convince himself or Williams.

After shooing away reporters and remaining behind closed doors for more than an hour, Leon emerged. He got into a waiting yellow limousine, swearing he'd get back to basics, train hard, and resurrect his career.

A few days later he was arrested for carrying an unregistered .357 Magnum in the glove compartment of his car.

9

In "The Road Not Taken," poet Robert Frost writes of facing a fork in the road and having to choose only one path. The same could be said for Michael, who had to decide between the direction Leon had followed and the one less traveled. By 1979 it had become clear he'd opted for the latter. He lived clean and trained hard—so hard that he had to undergo a knee operation after running on concrete in combat boots.

"Something had to give," his doctor told him, "and it wasn't going to be the concrete."

Following surgery Michael took a break from the ring, partly to recuperate but also to keep an eye on Leon, who was still celebrating the championship he'd lost to Ali in New Orleans.

For Michael, choosing the less popular path meant avoiding the headlines that were still ensnaring his brother. He settled into a quiet life in Philadelphia with his girlfriend, Sandy Massey, a dance instructor and part-time model he'd met after his operation.

Michael told *Sports Illustrated*'s Calvin Fussman later in March 1983 that "everybody needs somebody, and I didn't have nobody after Leon left Philadelphia. I had to stumble around with a big splint on my leg. So Sandy and I had time together. We wound up caring more and more for each other. Sandy showed me things that nobody had ever shown me. Her love. Her care. Her warmth. She was my first and only love. It was pure and golden."

With Sandy, Michael focused on building his own life instead of trying to safeguard Leon's. In 1980 Sandy gave birth to daughter Michelle at Philadelphia's Booth Maternity Center. A proud new father, Michael returned to the ring—more active, focused, and unbeatable than ever before. In thirteen months he reeled off seven victories, including a four-round TKO over former light-heavyweight champion Marvin Johnson. He built his record to 16–0 and was ranked as the number-one light-heavyweight contender behind WBC champion Matthew Saad Muhammad and WBA champion Eddie Mustafa Muhammad.

After the Johnson fight, in March 1981, the phone rang in Michael's Atlantic City hotel room. He picked up the receiver but didn't recognize the voice. It was opportunity knocking.

"Hello, you [expletive]," the caller said. "You ain't done nothin'. You know how gone Johnson was."

"Who's this?"

"It's Mustafa."

That was short for Eddie Mustafa Muhammad, who, it bears noting, had taken the title from the same Marvin Johnson a year earlier.

Mustafa had little respect for Michael. The former gun-toting street hustler felt that *his* ghetto, the Brownsville section of Brooklyn, was tougher than Michael's St. Louis slum—and he was tired of hearing about the unfortunate hand Michael had been dealt. He also resented the "easy road" paved for Olympic gold medalists.

Hoping to put an end to the buzz surrounding Michael's ascent in the rankings, Mustafa Muhammad gave him a shot at the title. The WBA champ signed for a guaranteed $350,000. Michael, despite his gold, signed for $125,000.

"I don't worry about Spinks," Mustafa Muhammad told UPI at the time. "He's an a-b-c fighter. He just uses the basics. There's nothing he can do to cause me difficulties. I think he'll get on his horse and run and that would be a very smart thing for him to do. He's never met anybody who can go inside like I can."

Michael responded to UPI, "I respect him. He's no pushover, but I know I'm going to win. I don't plan to stand there and trade with him. I'll be moving. I've got to get off first and then get the hell out of there. I don't know if I can take a good shot or not, but I don't want to find out. I'd be a fool to want to find out how hard he can hit. I think I'll dictate the fight. He's not going to give the title to me. It will take some convincing, but I'll manage to do it."

The showdown was set for July 18, 1981. Michael and Mustafa Muhammad would settle their differences at the Imperial Palace in Las Vegas.

In the five years since the 1976 Olympics, Michael was the only gold medalist from the U.S. boxing team who hadn't yet fought for a title—and the only one still undefeated.

Leo Randolph had turned pro in 1978 after earning his high school diploma the previous year. He took Ricardo Cardona's WBA super-bantamweight title in 1980 and then lost it in his first defense against Sergio Victor Palma. He collected his $72,000 purse, retired, and became a bus driver for the city of Tacoma.

Howard Davis continued training with his father on Long Island. He had been given a shot at Jim Watt's WBC lightweight title in 1980 but lost in a unanimous decision.

Sugar Ray Leonard had abandoned his plans to go to college in Maryland, choosing instead the path to the pros. It seemed he had little reason to look back. He'd won the WBC welterweight belt in a TKO over Wilfred Benitez, defended it once, and then lost it to Roberto Duran before regaining it in a rematch. He'd then won the

WBA junior-middleweight title and, as Michael was training for Mustafa Muhammad, was prepping for a super-fight against WBA welterweight champ Thomas Hearns.

Leon, of course, had snatched the title from Ali before drinking, snorting, and womanizing it away.

Michael was holed up at the Concord Hotel in the Catskills in upstate New York; he kept his training camp lean and spent the days, in his words, "doin' time."

But the differences between the two brothers didn't end in camp. Unlike Leon, who avoided training and loved to fight, Michael was reluctant to get in the ring.

In a *New York Times* profile published five days before the Mustafa Muhammad fight, Michael Katz wrote, "[Michael] does not like boxing, but he is very good at it. He has a powerful and accurate left jab, a fine hook and the famous Spinks jinx, or overhand right. He hasn't lost a fight in five years, since Keith Broom ... outpointed him at Olympic training camp in Vermont."

Katz continued, "It was as if [Michael] were wrestling with the loneliness of this sport he does not like, this sport he appreciates only for taking him and his brother Leon out of the ghetto. Training camp is bad enough, but even that does not compare to, [in Michael's words], 'the terrifying five loneliest minutes, the time when they knock on your door and say, Mike, you're on next.'"

Michael told Katz, "Your mind be doing some funny things in that ring. You be hurting and tired and you're in there all alone. Your corner be telling you they're with you and every punch you throw, they're throwing, too. 'And every punch I feel, you feel, too?' you ask them, and they say, 'Somewhat.'

"And running, you get so tired you about want to pass out, like that hill [near the Concord Hotel] I call Death. Every day, you're lookin' at Death. Then you lie in bed at night and you try not to move, and all of a sudden you're punching. I wake up in the morning and the sheets and covers are all over the place."

Meanwhile, Mustafa Muhammad was facing his own challenges. The twenty-nine-year-old defensive master was fresh off a ten-round loss to heavyweight Renaldo Snipes. It was nothing new for a light-heavyweight to try his hand in the heavyweight division, but the Snipes fight was a particularly bad move for Mustafa Muhammad. He'd barely won a round. Worse yet, he had gained nearly 27 pounds to fight Snipes and now had just two months to lose it.

The weigh-in was scheduled for 12:30 a.m. so both fighters could sleep late the day of the fight. Michael came in at 173¾ pounds. But when Mustafa Muhammad stepped on the scale, he topped the 175-pound limit by 1¾ pounds. He was given two hours to make weight. The ramifications were huge: If he didn't lose the weight by 2:30 a.m., he'd be stripped of his title. (He would still be allowed to fight Michael, but only Michael could leave the ring with a title. If Mustafa were to win, the title would be considered vacant.) On the other hand, if Mustafa Muhammad lost the extra poundage in such a short amount of time, he'd also lose a lot of energy, not to mention sleep. He chose the lesser of two evils: Drop the weight.

There were two hours and 1¾ pounds to go. Preferring not to drain more energy than necessary, Mustafa Muhammad ducked the steam room and brought his entourage to a nearby twenty-four-hour health club. Fellow champ Matthew Saad Muhammad, whose past included its own spate of gang-related blemishes, came along for moral support.

While Michael was in his hotel room sound asleep, Mustafa Muhammad skipped rope and sweated off the weight. He worked, perspired, and grunted for twelve straight minutes. Then he stepped on the scale. 175¾ . He changed into a fresh sweat suit and repeated the drill. 175¼. He changed again, worked some more, but this time didn't bother wasting time getting weighed. He rushed out of the gym and got back to the hotel at 2:19 a.m. Two minutes later he stood buck naked on the scale, still sweating from the face, neck and ears. His entourage leaned in as the ring official slid the weights along the top and bottom bars. When the balance beam came to rest, the scale read 175 on the nose. His friends jumped, screamed, and hugged as if their man had just beaten the scale by a first-round knockout.

But Mustafa Muhammad was too smart to celebrate. He'd surely heard that Las Vegas had Michael as the favorite in the fight; he also realized he'd left a lot of strength back at the gym. Silently, he slipped on his white terrycloth robe, draped a towel over his head, and went up to his room to collapse.

"I'm in my bed sleeping in the morning—and Leon comes in my room and wakes me up," Mustafa Muhammad remembers. "'Get up! Get up! Let's go hang out. Whatever you and my brother got goin' on, that's between y'all.' He didn't care about none of that. I'm like, 'Leon, get outta my room.' The guy didn't have a care in the world. He was a party guy, the most fun-loving guy that ever lived."

It's unconfirmed how long Leon's escapades lasted that morning, but when the opening bell rang later that afternoon, he was seated at ringside, rooting on his brother.

The fight itself was not on anybody's top-ten list; the first three rounds played as if they were in slow motion, with Michael awkward, off-balance, and uneasy. It was shaping up to be a tactical battle, interesting from a purist's point of view but lacking in the fireworks department. The excitement was found only in the stakes: The belt was on the line and neither boxer was taking control of the fight.

After seven rounds the title was still up for grabs. Mustafa Muhammad was ahead by one point on two judges' cards; Michael had the extra point on the third.

But in the eighth the fighters' fortunes veered in different directions. Michael nailed the champ with a jab that shut his right eye, and when the eye stay closed, he pounded it with lefts for the remainder of the fight.

"After that I was aiming for the eye but I don't know how often I got it," Michael told Jack McCallum of *Sports Illustrated*. "By the end of the fight I was just aiming for anything above the neck."

In the twelfth Michael decked the champion with a piston-pumping combo: two lefts followed by an earth-rattling right to the jaw that sent the champ down for an eight count. Once Mustafa Muhammad was back on his feet, Michael blasted him to the ropes with a fusillade of rights and lefts. By the time the attack was over, Michael had thrown two dozen punches to Mustafa Muhammad's one lone counter.

"My eye swelled," Mustafa Muhammad says, looking back. "Michael stuck his thumb in my eye and my eye blew up. I had to hold my head up to see out of the other eye. With my head up like that, he just came right over and got me. He hit me hard, but I just got up and looked at him. But I made a plan. He was not gonna knock me out. We were gonna go fifteen hard rounds."

Mustafa Muhammad had followed his plan—the fight had gone fifteen rounds, and for him they *were* hard. Judge Duane Ford had Michael winning nine of the last ten rounds. Judge Chuck Minker had Michael taking eight of the last ten; Lou Tabat gave him seven of the ten. The final tallies were 145–139 (Ford), 146–138 (Minker), and 144–140 (Tabat).

When the decision was announced and Michael officially became the WBA light-heavyweight champion, he and Leon wrapped their arms around each other in the ring. "We shed tears," Michael told the AP. "We both wanted this."

It wasn't what Mustafa Muhammad wanted. He bitterly complained that Michael had fouled him. To this day he says Michael's combination was "one-two-three-elbow."

After the fight Mustafa Muhammad vented to the press. "The referee saw him repeatedly sticking his thumbs and elbows into my eye. He just didn't do anything at all. Today was his day. You can't beat an Olympic hero in America. He didn't do anything but run."

Carlo Rotella, author of *Cut Time: An Education at the Fights*, sees Michael through a different lens. "Michael had a distinctive style and a distinctive rhythm as a fighter; the combination of angles and rhythms he gave an opponent was very different. The usual term is awkward. Awkward means you can't hit him flush. That style made it very hard to engage him for a lot of fighters, especially accomplished fighters. So when fighters say 'he ran, he was awkward' what they're saying is, 'I couldn't find a way to deal with this style. I couldn't figure that guy out.'"

Matthew Saad Muhammad crashed the press conference to stand up for his pal. While Michael was speaking to a group of reporters, Saad Muhammad interrupted to say the wrong fighter had gotten the decision. On that, he was in a minority of one.

"I didn't mean to cut you off," Michael said to the WBC champ, "But I was talking. Will someone please remove this man from the premises?"

Saad Muhammad left without incident and took the WBC title with him. If the paths of those two belts were going to converge, it wasn't going to be soon.

10

By 1983 Michael had established himself as an elite light-heavyweight. He'd won all twenty-two of his fights, and in the two years since beating Eddie Mustafa Muhammad, he had defended the WBA belt five times. He was now the only member of his Olympic team to hold a title. But in the minds of boxing fans, he was still one hurdle away from greatness. That hurdle stood five-five and change, possessed a forty-one-inch chest, was as cuddly as a fire hydrant, and went by the name Dwight Muhammad Qawi. A year earlier Qawi had upset the fearsome Matthew Saad Muhammad to win the WBC light-heavyweight championship.

With twelve knockouts to his credit, Qawi owned a record of 19–1–1. He'd successfully defended his title three times in two years, knocking out Jerry Martin, Saad Muhammad a second time, and Eddie Davis. None of those fights went the distance.

By meeting in the ring, Qawi and Michael would be unifying their division—making it only the second such division in the sport. (The other was the middleweight division, which was ruled by Marvin Hagler.) Better still, they'd be bringing fight fans a dream match: a lean, gawky, unorthodox boxer with a seventy-six-inch reach versus a steam engine in shorts that would sooner take a bullet than give up an inch of canvas.

The fight hadn't come cheaply. Butch Lewis had booked the pricey 14,000-seat Convention Hall in Atlantic City. He'd also guaranteed each fighter $1.2 million, with add-ons bringing their purses to $2.1 million. It was more than either man had ever earned in a single bout, and the fattest purse the division had ever seen.

But signing fighters was one thing. Capturing the public's imagination was another. Insiders had high hopes that this bout would vault the light-heavyweight division out of irrelevancy. Could Michael Spinks and Dwight Muhammad Qawi finally carry the division into the big time?

Born Dwight Braxton, Qawi had joined the Nation of Islam in 1975 and changed his name five years later (although, for publicity purposes, he kept Braxton for this fight). Unlike Michael, Qawi hadn't thrown a single punch as an amateur. He hadn't even begun his pro career until the age of twenty-five. He'd spent his youth on the unforgiving streets of Camden, New Jersey, and after being convicted of armed robbery, spent his early twenties inside a concrete cell at Rahway State Prison. He walked out of Rahway in 1978 with nothing to offer except a crunching jab, a jaw-splitting right hand, and the aura of an ex-con who'd seen far tougher battles than those regulated by a referee.

Qawi and Michael weren't strangers. They had sparred back in 1980 when Michael was training to fight Dave Conteh, whom he went on to stop in nine rounds.

"We did eight five-minute rounds a day," Qawi remembers. "You could hear a pin drop when we were in the ring. Michael was very safe, methodical, sneaky, but I was eating him up every day."

Michael agreed that their sessions were tough, but he told Phil Pepe of the New York *Daily News,* "There were a couple of times when I jabbed him to death for eight or nine rounds, but neither of us really got the better of the other."

When hyping the fight, trumpeted by Butch Lewis as "The Brawl for It All," the media preyed on those sparring sessions, particularly the enmity that had supposedly developed between the two fighters. Michael told *Sports Illustrated* that he had lent Qawi $45 for a radio, and after two years the debt was still unpaid.

"I'll send you the money in a first-aid kit," Qawi wisecracked. It was one of countless one-liners from the Camden Buzzsaw. Here's another: "I'll roll out the red carpet for Michael to come down the stretch. Only the carpet will be made of his blood."

When Qawi is reminded of those taunts, he waves his hand, dismissing them as nothing more than gate-building trash talk. But Michael didn't take them lightly. He brought in the legendary Eddie Futch to help his regular trainer, Nelson Brison (Butch Lewis's brother), prepare him for the fight. Futch came up with a strategy designed to unravel Qawi.

He saw Qawi as a crouching puma with an arsenal of devastating combinations—kind of like Joe Frazier with a pinch of Archie Moore. Qawi cornered his opponents, worked inside, and countered right hands with a lethal right of his own.

At the prefight press conference, Qawi emphasized his in-your-face style. "I'll be so close to him that people will think we're Siamese twins, with my head connected to his chest. He'll be looking for a breather, but he won't get one."

Futch's solution was to jab, jab, jab, jab, jab. Lead with the left. Remain in the center of the ring. Stay an arm's length away at all times. Jab, jab, jab, jab, jab.

In layman's terms, Futch wanted to turn Michael into a different fighter for the next fifteen rounds of his career. He couldn't have had a more disciplined pupil to work with. But Michael's training was about to be interrupted by a chain of events that neither he nor Futch could have seen coming.

By 1983 Michael had been with Butch Lewis for six years. He saw him not only as a promoter and ad hoc manager but also as a friend and brother, and even a father. Leon had dropped the responsibility of being Michael's role model on the streets of Pruitt-Igoe years ago. It was now in the hands of Lewis.

"That's the closest I've ever known of any fighter and manager in history," Emanuel Steward said in 2011. "Michael was a very insecure person and Butch represented strength, just the opposite of what Michael was. He depended on Butch for everything. Michael found somebody that was successful and he attached to him like an older brother or a daddy, and that's where he stayed. Leon never had that and I don't think he could have had that. His mental makeup is different. Michael is what you call a scary fighter [fearful in the ring]. That's why he gravitated to a guy like Butch, a strong-personality-type person."

Sportswriter Wallace Matthews remembers working on a story in Lewis's Manhattan apartment. "[Michael] called him for some advice, and I could hear [the conversation] from Butch's side. It was like he was talking to a fifteen-year-old. Michael was going to fly somewhere. If I remember, Butch was saying, 'Now, listen, Michael, don't you park that Benz at the airport.' It was something my father would have told me. It struck me as, like, this guy takes an unusual interest in his fighter. Most managers and trainers, they don't give a fuck. It's like whatever. It's your problem. And it just seemed to me that they were very close. And he spoke about him, you know, very affectionately."

Never did Michael need his friend's support more than during the months leading up to the Qawi fight.

On Wednesday, January 5, 1983, two months before the bout, Michael took his twenty-year-old brother, Leland, for a ride through Philadelphia in his new Mercedes. At about 1:45 a.m., he passed a red light as he turned a corner. Flashing police lights suddenly lit up behind him.

"We didn't think the lights were meant for us," Leland later explained to Calvin Fussman in *Sports Illustrated*. "Before we knew it, they were following us and there was another [police] car coming toward us."

There are differing reports as to exactly what happened next. According to two police officers, they chased Michael—who had been weaving in and out of traffic on City Avenue near Fifty-Second Street—for twenty-five blocks with their sirens wailing and flashers cranking. Michael disagreed, claiming there was no high-speed chase. Both sides agree that Michael was pulled over on Wynnefield and Parkside Avenues.

"I saw the flashing lights," Michael told various reporters at the time, "but they were so far behind me, I didn't know if they were police or an ambulance or a fire truck. When I realized they wanted me to pull over, I did."

"They jumped on us," Leland told Fussman. "They said, 'Get out or we'll blow your heads off.'"

Michael and Leland obeyed. As they were getting out of the car, one of the officers spotted a .45 caliber revolver resting on the floor of the front seat. The gun contained six spent shells.

"It was a gift," Michael told police.

The excuse was so unimaginative it almost had to be true. Michael explained that the gun was a keepsake given to him by a fan in Montreal after the Olympics. The shells were spent, he said, because he'd taken the pistol out of his house and fired a celebratory round into an open field six nights earlier on New Year's Eve.

It turned out the gun had been reported stolen in Toronto in 1975. Michael was charged with possession of an unlicensed weapon and released after signing a $1,000 bail bond. Butch Lewis was there to support him upon his release. Lewis was also by his side three months later when Michael appeared in court to plead guilty and pay a $1,770 fine.

On Friday, January 7, two days after the gun incident, Michael's fiancée, Sandy Massey, was heading home in her new 1982 Ford Mustang, a gift from Michael. While on the Schuylkill Expressway just outside of downtown Philadelphia, she crashed into an oncoming Buick Regal that had crossed into her lane. The head-on collision sent the driver of the Buick, sixty-year-old Joseph McCormick, to the hospital with chest injuries, a broken hip, rib fractures, and facial lacerations. Sandy wasn't as lucky. She was pronounced dead at 4:52 a.m.

Funeral services took place at the Sanctuary Church of the Open Door on the city's west side. Dwight Qawi sent flowers and his manager, Rock Newman, attended.

Butch Lewis managed the press, as did Eddie Futch, but neither one could hide their fighter's grief. Michael wept openly during interviews. He wept openly during workouts. And he wept privately in his dressing room.

"You're alone and you want it to end," he told the *Boston Globe*. "You want this whole thing to be over with so you can join the rest of the world and the rest of your family.

"I don't know what an average person goes through in a lifetime, but I've been through a lot up to now—and I have lived life as cautiously as I possibly can. My life hasn't been a bowl of cherries."

Michael had always found solace inside the ropes. And so he tried desperately to concentrate on the battle in front of him, training with Futch on the skills he needed to beat Qawi.

"Michael went to pieces," Futch told *Sports Illustrated*. "It was hard for him to get his mind on the fight."

Michael may have had trouble focusing on the match, but that was not true for the rest of the boxing community. Boxing writers across the country were heralding the fight, which was to air on HBO, as the bout that would finally put the light-heavyweight division on equal footing with the heavyweights.

The only person who wasn't ready for the attention was the WBA champion.

The twinkling lights of the Atlantic City Boardwalk belied the squalor around it. While tourists were plunking down more than a billion dollars at the casinos in 1983, much of the rest of the city was in decay. Those who ventured off the boardwalk saw boarded-up storefronts lining the streets, hookers working the corners, and vagrants camping out in doorways. Comedian Alan King famously said of the place, "It looked like Fantasy Island on the inside and Beirut on the outside."

On the night of the Spinks-Qawi fight, twenty-three-mile-per-hour winds ripped through Atlantic City as a rainstorm drenched the East Coast. Still, more than nine thousand ticket-holders braved the elements to make it past Dock's Oyster House and James's Saltwater Taffy to Convention Hall.

Walk-up sales were a different story. Butch Lewis had to chew on five thousand unpunched tickets, but his spirits were surely buoyed when he collected the $956,375 gate. HBO reported a healthy viewership even though foreign TV sales were underwhelming. The jury was still out as to whether the division was ready to carry the burden of the public spotlight.

Columnist Jerry Izenberg of the Newark *Star-Ledger* wrote, "Light heavyweights are sort of the parsley of the boxing world. Everybody acknowledges that parsley has a use but no one quite knows what it is."

Of course, neither Michael nor Qawi had signed on to resurrect the division, nor did they have much interest in the size of the gate. Each fighter aimed to leave the ring as the sole champion of his weight class.

Both faced obstacles. Michael was in a raw emotional state. Qawi had been fighting a cold for nearly two weeks.

"I remember at one point during training camp [Dwight] said he was feeling flat," manager Rock Newman remembers. "So [co-trainer] Quenzell McCall told him to take a glass of beer and put a raw egg in it. Dwight is obsessive, so he started to obsess on that, and it wasn't good. He put on quite a bit of weight drinking a beer or two a day. It was not an ideal situation. So there was a struggle with his weight."

Quenzell McCall told *Sports Illustrated,* "We kept him off his feet as long as we could. We loaded him up with grapefruit and orange juice and gave him aspirin and plenty of rest. And a doctor gave him penicillin. We were concerned that he might develop a fever, but fortunately he didn't."

Qawi insisted he was ready to go. As for Michael, his resolve was tested shortly before the opening bell when his daughter Michelle came into the dressing room.

"Where's Mommy?" the two-year-old asked her father.

"I was just so stunned to see my baby," Michael later told *Sports Illustrated.* "I couldn't hang on. I couldn't say nothing. I couldn't take it. What can you say to her when she asks that?"

Ten minutes after Michelle's visit, Michael was climbing into the ring, wearing a white robe and white trunks with black trim. A pair of white socks with three fat horizontal black stripes wrapped his calves. He threw a few punches into the air as Qawi made his way through the ropes. The thirty-year-old Qawi, looking rock-solid and fit in a red robe and red trunks, shifted from side to side and repeatedly glanced over at Michael.

When the opening bell sounded, two questions surely ran through Eddie Futch's mind. Would his grieving fighter stay focused? Could Michael pull off the fight plan they had devised?

In the first round, Michael abandoned the plan and stung Qawi with an overhand right—the "Spinks Jinx."

"I think what that shot did was get Michael some respect," Rock Newman says. "I won't say [Dwight] was cautious, but it may have taken away a smidgeon of his aggressiveness."

After the right landed, Michael immediately went back to Futch's plan, and used his reach advantage to win six of the first seven rounds with his left. Jab, jab, jab. Few of those punches landed, and most had so little mustard that Qawi simply swatted them away. But Michael was on the move and neutralizing Qawi's punching power. His floating clearly irked his opponent. Qawi tried everything—including making faces and sticking out his tongue—to get Michael to stand in one place and duke it out.

Qawi explains, "I wanted to get him to slow down, to come at me, to mix it up more. The referee wasn't letting me fight my fight. Every time I got close inside, he would say, 'Break.' He favored Spinks."

Leon, watching from ringside, couldn't sit still. He continually ran around the press section, shouting, and according to Richard Hoffer of the *Los Angeles Times,* looked like a madman. Few fight fans followed the cruiserweights, a nascent division shoehorned in between the heavies and light heavies, but those that did knew that Leon had taken its meaningless *North American Boxing Federation* title by scoring a decision over Jesse Burnett five months earlier. They also knew that Burnett had won only eight of his previous twenty fights, and that Leon had gone on to suffer a beating at the hands of the younger, faster, and more skilled Carlos de Leon twelve days before Michael met up with Qawi.

When Michael took to his stool after the sixth, Leon rushed over to him, an oversize black cowboy hat sitting awkwardly on his head. It didn't take a shrink to see that the dynamic between the brothers had changed.

"Double jab, then the right!" Leon yelled up at him.

Michael shouted back, "Straighten your hat, Lee!"

A flash of recognition crossed Leon's face.

"Oh, yeah," he said and adjusted it before returning to his seat.

Michael didn't need Leon's help. He had taken six of the first seven rounds on all three judges' cards. But in the eighth Qawi woke up and changed the tone of the fight.

Sensing he'd lost too much ground, he charged out of his corner a different fighter. He flicked away Michael's jabs and fired missiles with every ounce of leverage his 174-pound frame could muster. Michael hit the deck not once, not twice, but three times. The first and third times, he'd slipped. But the second was ruled a knockdown, even though Qawi appeared to step on his foot.

Referee Larry Hazzard admits he got it wrong. "I blew that call," he says now. "Qawi got credited for a knockdown when I saw on the replay clearly that Michael tripped. Certainly when he got up, you could see that there was absolutely no sign physically that he had been hit with a solid punch."

More significant to Qawi, however, was that each time Michael went down, he'd been retreating.

"All three should've been knockdowns. If somebody goes down because they're running, that's a knockdown," Qawi says.

"Make that jab sharper," Futch told Michael after the eighth. "You're laying it out there. You can't do that with this guy."

Qawi stayed on the attack in the ninth but had trouble maintaining his momentum. From then on the fight was a seesaw, a back-and-forth drama that had the crowd on its feet.

"Not once during this fight, which rubbed the nerve-endings raw," wrote the Newark *Star-Ledger*'s Jerry Izenberg, "was there a single instant when anyone—the fighters, their corners, or the highly divided partisan crowd—would say for sure how it would end."

When the two fighters touched gloves to start the fifteenth, they were both venturing into relatively uncharted territory: Michael had gone the distance only once—when taking the crown from Mustafa Muhammad—and Qawi had never gone past eleven.

"Final three minutes," announcer Barry Tompkins told the HBO audience. "The crowd on its feet chanting 'Michael, Michael, Michael.' They feel their man has won the fight. Dwight Braxton [Qawi] literally has three minutes to knock his man out."

Tompkins's announcement was news to nobody. Yet Qawi got no closer to his man than he had throughout the evening. The round was Qawi's, but it didn't seem to be enough to close the gap that Michael had built in the early rounds.

Izenberg wrote, "Even as they were still rechecking the official cards, [Michael] raised a right hand, still encased in its sweat-soaked boxing glove, toward the ceiling of the room that made Miss America famous and shouted at the top of his lungs, 'I did it! I did it!'"

A beaming Butch Lewis decked out in full Lewis regalia—white shirt, white necktie, and white suit—made his way through the ropes and put his arm around Michael. Kay, her face hidden by oversize sunglasses, entered the ring and stood beside her son as they listened to the scores of the judges, all three of whom awarded Michael the victory: Tony Perez and Frank Cappuccino had scored it 144–141; Tony Castellano had it 144–140. Michael shouldered his way to the man he had just dethroned. He put his arms around his neck and said, "We'll do it again."

Charles Leerhsen wrote in *Newsweek*, "Spinks raised his hands in the air and called for his daughter. 'Michelle,' he said as the child was pressed against his sweaty cheek, 'we did it!' On the way back to the dressing room, [Qawi] grabbed angrily at Spinks, but the undisputed champ calmly turned his hand away. 'What you've got to realize, Dwight,' he said, 'is that fighting is just the game that we play.'"

Through the years, Qawi has offered a number of reasons for his loss. At ringside he claimed his cold hadn't cleared up and that he'd been drained of energy throughout the fight. Later he mentioned pneumonia. He even accused Butch Lewis of paying off Larry Hazzard.

Now he says that he'd suffered a broken nose and a deviated septum during a sparring session with his younger brother a year before the fight. "I never had it checked out. I thought it would go away. But it really inhibited me. I couldn't breathe through my left nostril. I should've postponed the fight."

But Qawi does have one beef that he has repeated time and again since the bell rang to end the bout. "Spinks really ran like a chicken. I wanted him to mix it up with me, but he just didn't. It was like he had a lot of dog in him."

His manager agrees. "Dwight is right," Rock Newman says. "Michael ran and, as we said during the fight, he ran like a little bitch. I hated the tactic. I told Eddie Futch, '[Michael] didn't beat Qawi. Your black ass did.'"

Michael told William Nack of *Sports Illustrated,* "I wanted to be like that guy on the TV program, Elliott Ness. Untouchable. When he tried to swarm me, I was catching him with jabs and hooks. My left hand is awfully sore now, but I was going to work it until it fell off. I beat him with one hand."

Sports Illustrated ran a photo of the fight on its cover. In it Michael is about to wallop Qawi with a left. The caption read, His Left Was All Riight!

Qawi says the photo is a misrepresentation of the fight and it haunts him to this day.

"The cover should have told the story of the fight: how Spinks ran like a thief, how I knocked him down. The fact is my nose was broken," he told the magazine in 2006. "He got a decision, but lots of people thought I'd won, including me. That cover shot hurts more than my nose did."

When all was said and done, "The Brawl for It All" was not quite the battle the boxing world had envisioned, nor was it the fight that would catapult the light-heavyweight division to the grand stage. That didn't matter to Michael. He and Leon partied all night on Butch Lewis's dime at Resorts International.

Later that day, when William Nack of *Sports Illustrated* knocked on Michael's door at the Claridge, the champ said, "I was still dancin' going out the door. My waistline is sore from the dancin' and my neck is tired and sore from the fight. I was hiding my head and [Qawi] was hitting me in the neck with those roundhouse punches. I'm achin'. I laughed all night. . . . Leon fell asleep at the table, so I drank his Crown Royal.

"I was laying in bed, and I was thinking, I won more than $1 million last night. And I won the prize. I kept saying it to myself, over and over again. I got him. I got him! I beat that bum. I beat him! I looked at the headlines in the papers and I kept saying, I won, I won!"

It was true. Michael had gone from drowning in a black hole of despair to holding his daughter in victory after the biggest fight of his career.

But what he had not realized was how much brighter his spotlight would shine.

And how much farther his brother would fall.

11

DETROIT. WEST SIDE. 1985. AN ASSORTMENT OF FIGHTERS WHACKED heavy bags, speed bags, and trainers' mitts as sweat dripped off the hems of their signature red-and-gold T-shirts. The heat was cranked to one hundred degrees so the fighters could get loose and stay that way. The dank, low-ceilinged room had the signature smell of ointment and leather; the background score was a percussive patter of gloves hitting canvas, jump ropes smacking linoleum. This was the Kronk Gym, and the brittle, yellowed newspaper clippings tacked to wall-mounted bulletin boards validated its pedigree. Hector Camacho. Julio César Chávez. Thomas Hearns.

The gym occupied the basement of the Kronk Recreation Center, a well-worn graffiti-marred, two-story brick building at Fourteenth and McGraw. Across the street the McGraw Hotel, a fleabag with grime-covered walls and semen-stained mattresses, took in guests by the hour. The surrounding streets were dotted with broken bottles, used condoms, and discarded needles. Had you walked a block in any direction, odds were you would have found a liquor store with security gates or a check-cashing stand with barred windows. Had you walked the same route at night, odds were you would have run into a bullet. Even the boxers left the area before dusk, with the exception of Hearns, who'd built enough local cred that he could park his gold Mercedes on the street and know it wouldn't be violated.

On the second floor of the rec center, young men ran up and down the muggy basketball court while seniors played Ping-Pong or gin rummy. But it was in the basement, underneath the swimming pool, where the Kronk legend had been built. Its architect, Emanuel Steward, was a savvy boxing trainer who took over the gym in 1971, giving up a five-hundred-dollar-a-week paycheck as a master electrician to earn thirty dollars a week as director of the boxing program. Until his untimely death in 2012, Steward had groomed dozens of champions within the gym's chipped red and gold walls. By his own count, the onetime Golden Gloves bantamweight champion had managed and trained more than forty world champions and six Olympic gold-medal winners.

On a late winter day in 1985, Steward was overseeing a roomful of boxers, most of them Kronk regulars—young fighters dreaming of taking the title the way Leon Spinks had. One of those hopefuls was Leon himself, now a thirty-one-year-old has-been.

A year earlier Leon had approached local Detroit car dealer Sam Lafata and asked for financial backing to help restart his career; Lafata brought him to meet his friend Steward.

"[Leon] was in a desperate mode," Lafata recalls. "He needed money and he was very, very serious at the time. He said he wanted to get his life back. I took him over to the Kronk."

Emanuel Steward said in 2011, "I got involved as a co-manager. Leon was the roughest guy in the ring; the biggest 178-pounder I ever saw. He was an animal. I remember he was fighting a guy at the Olympic trials, All-Army champ, and Leon was so strong that he made the guy almost run. He was so fuckin' tough that nobody would deal with it. I never saw anybody who could overpower everybody. That was the Leon that I knew."

But by the time Lafata and Steward joined forces to back Leon, their fighter's Olympic triumphs had become a distant memory.

"[Leon] was a real long shot for me," Lafata says. "I was doing him a favor really. We might have signed a little contract at that time, but that was nothing. I never took anything from him. To be honest with you, I didn't see a future in him."

Leon promised his new managers he would take boxing more seriously this time around.

"Being around the Kronk Gym is just like when I first started fighting," Leon told a reporter from London's *Daily Telegraph*. "A dedicated atmosphere. Young guys coming up, getting in condition. All the kinds of things I need to be around. It got to be play, play, play. I was drinking so heavy and worrying that I got bleeding ulcers. I had to go to the hospital. I could drink like a madhouse. Me and a friend would drink three or four fifths a day. A day! I mean, get drunk, go to sleep, and get drunk again."

A seemingly rehabilitated Leon was sparring with Vernon Bridges, a wannabe who'd compiled a record of 4–11–1 and was known as "Burning Bridges" to the Kronk regulars. Leon, who had retired after his humiliating loss to Carlos de Leon, was 12–4–2. And rusty. Those closest to him thought he should have stayed away from the ring. After the de Leon slaughter, a teary-eyed Michael told *Ring* magazine that he had tried desperately to talk Leon out of the fight but that Leon's mind had been made up. He also said that if it weren't for Leon's famous name, Don King would never have shown any interest in making the matchup. Michael's biggest concern wasn't so much Leon's body, it was his brain. Even the godlike Ali had succumbed to Parkinson's syndrome, a condition similar to, but milder than, Parkinson's disease. By early 1985 Ali's hands shook uncontrollably, and his speech was nearly inaudible.

Back at the Kronk Leon lunged at the taller Bridges, but his punches were zipless, his footwork ill-timed, his offense awkward. Like the Leon of old, he kept charging, but that ferocity—once his biggest asset—had turned into a liability. Bridges toyed with Leon, turning him every which way but upside down. After four rounds Leon's eyes were puffy, and his shirt—which advertised "Look Out, Leon Is Back"—was smeared with blood.

A trainer watching the exchange turned away. "He's shot," he said to no one in particular.

"It's dog eat dog out there," Leon told the *Telegraph* in the dressing room after the session. "Nobody cuts you any slack."

Leon sat on a bench and stared down at his shoes. If he was thinking about quitting, the notion didn't stick. He continued down the comeback trail but brought little to the ring other than a calling card that read "Former World Heavyweight Champion."

His first two opponents, Lupe Guerra and Rick Kellar, were hardly household names, even in the Guerra and Kellar households. Leon sent Guerra to the canvas in the first and second rounds before flooring him for good in the fourth. For the first time in Leon's career, Michael wasn't ringside.

"I'd rather see him be an exotic dancer than get abused in the ring," Michael told the *New York Times'* Michael Katz. "I couldn't take it."

Six weeks later, on April 9, Leon stopped Kellar in two rounds when "King Kong" hit the deck six times, each time from a jab to the midsection.

"This guy was a nobody, but he could've become a somebody if he beat me," Leon said about Kellar, an assessment that could have just as easily applied to Guerra. "I want to be back on top again," he told UPI. "I want it bad—real bad—and I'm going to do anything I can to win."

On June 29, 1985, three weeks after Michael defeated Jim MacDonald to retain his undisputed light-heavyweight title, Leon stepped into a temporary ring at the Sonoma County Fairground in Santa Rosa, California. His opponent was Tommy Franco Thomas, a policeman from Shinnston, West Virginia. Thomas's record of 34–6 may have been slightly misleading, given that he'd compiled it against fighters even more obscure than himself. The promoter of the bout, Randy Haupt, was hoping that Leon's name would bring in a big crowd. But when the bell rang and the 4,000-seat arena was only half-filled, it was apparent that the former heavyweight champ was no longer much of a draw.

The gate brought in $41,000, a quarter of which went to Leon. The fight went the full ten rounds and Leon won a unanimous decision. But make no mistake: Going the distance with a man who chased criminals in Shinnston wasn't much of an achievement for Leon Spinks.

A few extra watts of electricity charged the Las Vegas air as Michael Spinks approached the scale at the Riviera Hotel and Casino.

Larry Holmes tipped the scales at a hair over 221, which came as little surprise to the three hundred fans, reporters, and photographers who had jammed past the glass doors to witness the weigh-in. All eyes were on Michael, who in twenty-four hours would be challenging Holmes for the International Boxing Federation (IBF) heavyweight championship. Michael had to hit 190 to qualify. He had weighed only 175 three months earlier when defending his light-heavyweight title against Jim MacDonald. The crowd was eager to see if he'd managed to gain fifteen pounds. And if he had, they wondered, how the hell would he be strong enough to beat Holmes? The matchup was as competitive as a hammer versus a nail.

Michael had more to worry about than his waistline: He was also fighting history. No reigning light-heavyweight champion had ever come to the bigs and taken the title. It wasn't from lack of trying. Nine champions had stepped up; they'd failed thirteen times. Bob Foster missed twice, in part because he'd given up twenty-one pounds against Frazier and forty-two against Ali. Billy Conn tried twice and failed both times; he'd given up thirty pounds in each of his two losses to Joe Louis. Even Archie Moore, who'd matched Rocky Marciano's weight in 1955 and outweighed Floyd Patterson in 1956, lacked the punching power of a natural heavyweight.

Most ring insiders agreed that Michael was out of his league.

Billy Conn told the *Chicago Tribune:* "It's like betting on a tooth-pick against a lumberyard."

Los Angeles Times writer Jim Murray, anticipating last rites, wrote, "On September 21st at the Riviera Hotel in Las Vegas, Larry Holmes, a 225-pound fighter with a 45½-inch chest and an 18-inch neck, will get in a 16-foot square ring with a 175-pound 'opponent,' one with a 38-inch chest and a 15½-inch neck, and will be turned loose on him. Bring a priest."

The burning question was why Michael would put his considerable legacy on the line by stepping into the ring with a heavyweight champion he couldn't beat.

"I don't care about getting more recognition," Michael told the *Miami Herald.* "Fame brings more than money and respect—it gets everybody into your life. I've never been into that. But it's a heavy challenge, and that makes it exciting."

And so the über-challenged Michael stepped into the glare of the klieg lights at the Riviera. But now his face seemed fuller, his neck thicker. He had the back of a lumberjack and the face of a barroom poker player.

When the weights on the scale found their proper grooves, Duane Ford of the Nevada State Athletic Commission announced the reading. "Michael Spinks," he said through the PA system. "Two hundred even."

Michael gave the crowd a wink and made a circle with his thumb and forefinger. Things were A-OK.

Silence gave way to a flurry of questions. *Ten pounds over the minimum? No way. Check the scale. Twenty-five pounds in three months?* Even Larry Holmes looked confused.

"He must have drank a couple of cases of water and didn't go to the bathroom," the champ told the gathering.

Rumors had been flying for weeks about Michael's workout regimen, which had been cooked up by a strength-and-conditioning coach named Mackie Shilstone.

A walk-on wide receiver for Tulane in the early 1970s, Shilstone had been conditioning Michael's light-heavyweight body for three years—but turning him into a heavyweight was a new challenge. According to Shilstone, his biggest accomplishment had not been bringing Michael to two hundred—that was Michael's "walking around weight." His triumph lay in converting that weight into lean, energetic, heavyweight-worthy muscle. He'd cut the fighter down to 185 pounds and then rebuilt him from scratch, putting him on a 4,500-calorie-a-day diet made up of 65 percent carbohydrates, 20 percent protein, and 15 percent fat.

Michael had told the press, "I'm eating nuts, bolts, screws, razor blades, and sledgehammers." In truth, he was loading up on vegetables and grains and depriving himself of his favorite snacks.

According to Shilstone, "He'd get this candy and hide it under his bed. The funny thing was I'd go into his room, and one day I found it. I asked him, 'Are you gonna go eat the candy under the bed?' He said, 'No, I don't really want it. I just want to know I can have it.' So one time I took it away. I came back later and he'd [replaced] it."

The process hadn't stopped in the kitchen. To make Michael a more "explosive" fighter, Shilstone had him run sprints instead of doing traditional long-distance roadwork, and he put him on a weightlifting regimen. Talk to Shilstone and you'll walk away thinking he's a genius. Talk to others and you'll think his approach was nonsense.

Holmes's trainer, Richie Giachetti, believes the media took the story and ran with it.

"That was a hype job," Giachetti says. "Anyone who's an athlete knows you don't do sprints. There's no substitute for doing long distance to get in shape. Sprints help you to fight in bursts, but they don't help you when you have to go fifteen rounds."

At the weigh-in Giachetti told Holmes that a 200-pound Michael would not be the same fighter he had been as a light-heavyweight. The extra body mass, according to Giachetti, would make Michael slower and stiffer. Throw Michael's bad knee into the equation and you've got a seriously compromised fighter.

Holmes agreed with Giachetti and brushed off the weight issue, just as he discounted anything he didn't find agreeable.

"The heavier he is, the easier it'll be for me," Holmes told reporters. "This will probably be one of my easiest fights. . . . The only way Michael Spinks could beat me is if I was out drinking all night long. I haven't been. So I said to myself, is there any way he can beat me? The answer is no. No way."

Michael dismissed Holmes's trash talk. But Holmes was accurate about one thing: Michael was about to get into the ring with one of the most successful heavyweight champions the sport had ever seen.

❧

Las Vegas, 1985. Michael was not the only fighter chasing history. Holmes, who had fought ten times since beating Leon in 1981 (including a racially charged mega-bout against Gerry Cooney), was one win away from tying Rocky Marciano's unbeaten record of 49–0.

Now thirty-five years old, Holmes had been talking of retirement since the previous year when the WBC ordered him to fight its number-one challenger Greg Page or be stripped of the championship. Holmes said no to the fight, reportedly because Don King's offer of $2.5 million was insulting. Behind the scenes, though, many thought Holmes was afraid of blemishing his sterling record.

Before the WBC could take away his title, Holmes defected. He accepted the belt of the newly formed IBF, providing instant credibility to the nascent organization, and gaining the freedom to pick his own opponent in the process. He chose a $3.1 million payday against Marvis Frazier, who aside from a legendary surname had little offer. It took Holmes two minutes and fifty-seven seconds to dispatch Frazier and improve his record to 45–0.

Through it all, Holmes claimed he wasn't interested in Marciano. Nobody was buying it. Why would they? Despite his talk, he seemed to be on a mission to break the record. In the eighteen months following the Frazier fight, he got by Bonecrusher Smith, battered the underqualified David Bey, and unwrapped a gift decision over Carl Williams. That left one victory. And one undefeated light-heavyweight champion.

Seth Abraham, then president of HBO Sports, recalls how the idea of Holmes-Spinks first came about. "[In 1985] I was at Pietro's seafood restaurant in Las Vegas with my father-in-law and one of my wife's uncles and a bunch of HBO people," he says. "And who shows up but Don [King] and Butch [Lewis], so I moved everybody down and sat with them. And we start talking about Holmes and Michael. Larry was chasing Marciano's record at the time, and he had fought a barely breathing guy. I had had conversations with Larry, and I was concerned that he wanted to fight *me* next to tie Marciano, and then fight *you* to break Marciano. So the dinner was not a negotiation as much as it was a probing, diplomatically, to see if Larry wanted to take the fight. Don was interested in history and in helping Larry break Marciano's record. Butch's determining factor was, frankly, money. It wasn't a question of breaking Larry's undefeated record; it was a question of winning the heavyweight championship of the world."

In June Michael had been at the Riviera entertaining the press corps after stopping Jim MacDonald in the eighth round. The Mac-Donald fight was his tenth defense of the WBA belt and his fourth defense of the WBC title he had taken from Qawi. Holmes's publicity agent Dick Lovell placed an emergency call to the hotel and reached the Riviera's public relations representative Laura Herlovich. Moments later she interrupted the press conference.

"Michael is not aware of what I'm about to say," Herlovich announced. "Dick Lovell, who represents Larry Holmes, just called to offer Michael Spinks $550,000, plus $150,000 in training expenses, to fight him in August."

Michael's postwin euphoria puddled at his feet. He'd already turned down $1 million to fight Holmes. This new offer was even more insulting.

"That was the emergency call?" Butch Lewis said to Herlovich. "Hang up on him."

Herlovich hung up, but the negotiations, which had been going on for the better part of a year, were coming to a head. Within a month Lewis and King finalized a deal with Abraham and HBO. Holmes would take in roughly $3.5 million. Michael would earn close to $1.5 million, more than ten times his purse against MacDonald.

The public cared less about the money than about the fight's historical significance. Rocky Marciano had been a revered champion, and the matchup had the statisticians and historians working overtime to come up with noteworthy insights:

- The date. After all the shenanigans, the fight was set for September 21, 1985, exactly thirty years from the night Marciano wrapped up his flawless career by knocking out another ambitious light-heavyweight champion, Archie Moore, in Yankee Stadium.
- Holmes's legacy. The fight marked Holmes's twenty-second title defense; he'd been champ for seven years. He was chasing only Joe Louis, who'd defended his title twenty-five times in a twelve-year span.
- Michael's legacy. In stepping up to heavyweight, Michael had become the first light-heavyweight to leave his division as an undefeated champion.
- The record books. If Michael took the fight from Holmes, he and Leon would become the first pair of brothers to capture the heavyweight title.

The alphabet-soup organizations tried to cloud the picture. The WBA recognized Tony Tubbs as the heavyweight champ; the WBC recognized Pinklon Thomas. But no one else on the planet—perhaps not even Tubbs or Thomas—agreed. Holmes was champ, period. And the winner of Holmes-Spinks would walk away with the IBF heavyweight title, *Ring* magazine's heavyweight title, the lineal title, and a sizable chunk of boxing history.

On September 21, 1985, a chilled air was blowing through the outdoor arena that had been set up in the parking lot behind the Riviera.

A stiffly moving Muhammad Ali sat ringside—Parkinson's syndrome was taking its toll on the once-invincible champion. The right hand that had battered Joe Frazier in Manila now trembled as he went to sign autographs.

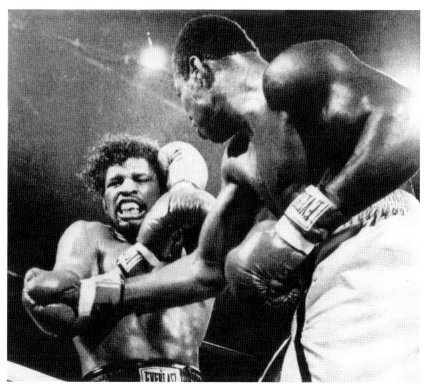

Leon got another title shot, this one against WBC champ Larry Holmes, on June 12, 1981, at Detroit's Joe Louis Arena. Holmes entered the fight with a grudge stemming from an earlier incident. AP IMAGES

Holmes punished Leon and dropped him in the third round. Referee Richard Steele stopped the fight shortly after the knockdown. AP IMAGES

Michael leaves the Philadelphia courthouse where he was arraigned on the charge of possessing an unregistered handgun. AP IMAGES

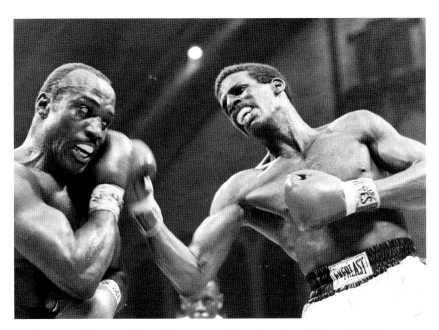

March 18, 1983: Now WBA light heavyweight champion, Michael defeats WBC champ, Dwight Muhammad Qawi, by unanimous decision. Qawi accused Michael's promoter, Butch Lewis, of paying off referee Larry Hazzard. AP IMAGES

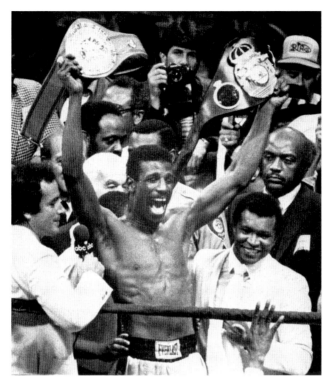

Michael raises the WBA and WBC belts after unifying the title. Butch Lewis (right, in white) looks as happy as his fighter. AP IMAGES

In 1985, Michael beefed up to take on IBF heavyweight champion, Larry Holmes. Holmes (lower right) looks on as Michael tips the scale at an even 200 pounds. AP IMAGES

September 21, 1985: Michael becomes the first light heavyweight champ in history to take the heavyweight title. Never before had two brothers been world heavyweight champions. AP IMAGES

A pith-helmeted Leon (left), sporting new front teeth, gives the latest heavy-weight champion a congratulatory hug. AP IMAGES

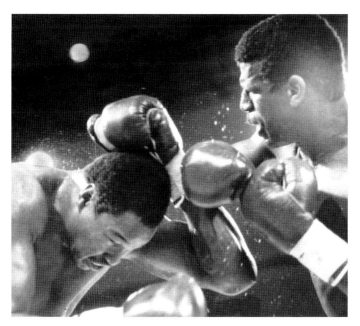

Michael beats Holmes a second time—in a razor-thin, hotly disputed decision. AP IMAGES

Stripped of his belt for leaving the HBO heavyweight series, Michael took a $4 million payday to fight six-foot-six Gerry Cooney. The only title on the line was *Ring* magazine's, which recognized the lineal champ. Michael downed Cooney in the fifth; the fight was stopped later that round. AP IMAGES

Michael shows off his *Ring* magazine belt after the Cooney fight. He's flanked by referee Frank Cappuccino (left) and promoter Butch Lewis (right). Lewis is gunning for Tyson. AP IMAGES

Michael trains in Pleasantville, NJ, for his fight against undisputed champ Mike Tyson. The fight, billed "Once and for All," would gross over $100 million. Michael would earn $13.5 million. AP IMAGES

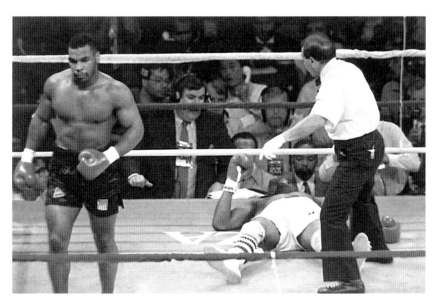

June 27, 1988: The opening bell for Tyson-Spinks was delayed. Rumor was that Michael was too intimidated to leave his dressing room. The holdup lasted longer than the fight: Michael was knocked out in 91 seconds. AP IMAGES

July 27, 1988: Michael wipes a tear from his eye during his retirement luncheon at New York's famed Tavern on the Green. AP IMAGES

Leon was rarely present during his sons' early years, but has been more involved with them as adults. He was often seen rooting on Cory, a former undisputed welterweight champion. AP IMAGES

Marciano's relatives, including his brother, Peter, were also on hand, courtesy of Caesars Palace. Jersey Joe Walcott could be spotted in the crowd, along with Mr. T, Robert Duvall, Grace Jones, Redd Foxx, Hector Camacho, and Leon Spinks. Leon sported a white sweatshirt—the hood was pulled over his head and topped by a pith helmet. Camacho was in silver lamé, but most eyes were on that helmet. Pia Zadora sang the national anthem. It just so happened that her billionaire husband, Meshulam Riklis, owned the hotel.

Standing in their corners, the two fighters loosened up: Michael in white trunks with black trim, Holmes in white trunks with red trim. Ring announcer Chuck Hull introduced the referee, Carlos Padilla, and the judges, Dave Moretti, Harold Lederman and Larry Wallace, to the crowd of 11,000. He then announced the fighters: "From St. Louis, Missouri, the undefeated light-heavyweight champion of the world, Michael Spinks. From Easton, Pennsylvania, the undefeated heavyweight champion of the world, Larry Holmes."

The bell clanged.

The fighters met in the center of the ring, but, surprisingly, Holmes did not take it to Spinks. Instead of throwing his hallmark right, he stayed outside. His once-feared jab was slow and off the mark, like a jackhammer with a weak battery. Michael was on the move, ducking the left jab while training his eye on Holmes's right fist. He kept his upper body in motion, twitching and jerking his head in case Holmes pulled his right out of its holster. Michael's awkward movements clearly frustrated the big man, who continued to fire only lefts. Most missed.

You didn't need a stopwatch to see that Michael was quicker than Holmes. Instead of slowing down from the extra poundage, Michael seemed spunky, energetic, and strong. Butch Lewis, obviously enjoying what he was seeing, taunted Holmes from ringside.

"You're an old man!" Lewis repeatedly shouted at Holmes, his words being picked up by the HBO microphones.

Judge Harold Lederman says, "[Butch Lewis] was yelling and screaming. He wasn't in the corner, either, he was on the apron or in the first row. He kept pounding on the canvas. The Nevada commission was so stupid, they didn't know enough to chase him away. You could feel the banging; it was unbelievable."

By the third round Michael seemed to sense that Holmes didn't have enough to hurt him. He ducked the jab, moved inside, threw combinations, and then ran like a bandit from a holdup. His punches failed to wobble Holmes, but they were piling up points by the dozen.

Holmes landed a few big punches, mostly to Michael's midsection. But he had lost control of the ring. His eyes were swelling and a small cut opened on his forehead. Despite pleas from his corner to throw the right, he kept it cocked but inexplicably didn't pull the trigger. He chose instead to stalk Michael, presumably waiting for the chance to connect with a knee-buckling bomb. When completely flummoxed, he bullied his smaller opponent. Michael complained to Padilla of holding, thumbing, and elbowing; Padilla warned Holmes twice, but the big man continued to roughhouse and strong-arm. His moves were straight out of a bar fight and didn't endear Holmes to the crowd. Those watching the bout live booed heartily, and when Holmes thuggishly tried to shove Michael to the floor, a water bottle sailed into the ring.

Holmes had never been a saint between the ropes but neither had he bullied his way to the top. A seasoned champion, he knew what he had to do: lure Michael into a slugfest. Had Michael taken the bait, he probably would have met the same fate that Leon had in 1981. But Michael didn't have Leon's impetuousness, and he wasn't about to do anything rash now. He continued to slip the jab, deliver five- and six-punch combinations, and leave town without waiting for a receipt.

HBO commentator Larry Merchant midbout, "If [Spinks keeps] fighting Holmes in this fashion, if his stamina doesn't betray him, we may have one of the great upsets in prizefight history."

Trainer Nelson Brison to Michael, "You're doing good. Don't get careless, now."

Richie Giachetti to Holmes after the eighth round: "You're the champion. You can't let this guy take it to you. Keep the jab, work off of it. Throw the right hand. If you miss, come back with the left hook. Then you bring the right uppercut. . . . Throw the goddamned right uppercut."

Going into the ninth, just as Michael was enjoying a razor-thin lead on the judges' cards and the name Mackie Shilstone was being bandied about in living rooms around the country, the needle on Michael's gas tank dipped into the red zone. His gloves dropped to his beltline and he took a solid right hook to the body. He appeared hurt as he sucked in huge gulps of air, but he quickly marshaled a defensive strategy, refusing to give Holmes a stationary target. He circled the ring, moved sideways, avoided the ropes, and jerked his body in the manner of a guy squirming inside an itchy wool suit.

Holmes, as everyone knew, was fighting more than just a twenty-nine-year-old light-heavyweight champion; he was battling age. Like Ali at the end of his career, Holmes knew what he had to do but couldn't find the wherewithal to do it. He was no longer the indomitable fighter who had beaten Ken Norton, Earnie Shavers, and Gerry Cooney. He did, however, have twelve years of professional ring experience, and that fact wasn't lost on Michael, who continued to stay away, thereby sacrificing the late middle rounds.

In the eleventh Michael seemed to gather strength, but his biggest spurt of energy came when he yelled at Leon, who was leaning on the ring apron in his pith helmet and shouting advice to his brother. HBO commentators Sugar Ray Leonard and Barry Tompkins, unaware of what prompted Michael's outburst, remarked that he'd better save his energy for the last few rounds of battle.

It was good advice, because it was becoming increasingly apparent that the fight was going the distance. And while Merchant, Leonard, and Tompkins had Michael well ahead on their cards, the official judges didn't. After fourteen rounds Dave Moretti and Harold Lederman had the fight even; Larry Wallace had Michael ahead, 135–133. There were three minutes left, and the heavyweight title was still up for grabs.

"The Volkswagen is beating the eighteen-wheeler . . .," Larry Merchant told the HBO audience. "We may be going into the last round of a great champion's career."

"Three minutes left and you have the feeling Holmes is going to need all of them," Barry Tompkins added.

Richie Giachetti told Holmes, "It's the last goddamn round. You gotta go after him. There's no tomorrow, you hear me? You got to take it to him. Let it all hang out."

Nelson Brison told Michael, "You got three minutes and you're champion."

Holmes answered the bell for the fifteenth with renewed gusto. He planted his feet to the canvas and swung for the fences. Michael answered the challenge, trading punches with Holmes in the middle of the ring, landing several. But going toe-to-toe with the big man came with risks. Holmes unloaded a powerful right across Michael's temple, and as Michael struggled to clear his head, Holmes came in for the kill. Just then, a dazed Michael got to his toes and retreated in a fashion known to boxing fans as "getting on his bicycle" but referred to by Dwight Qawi as "running." Michael continued to lurch in every direction, staying clear of the big man. By the time

Holmes landed another right, Michael was clearheaded enough to retaliate with a six-punch assault.

When the bell rang Michael shot his fists into the air. He didn't need to wait for the judges' scores. Nor did his cornermen, who rushed to his side, jubilant. Nor did Holmes, who skulked back to his corner, head down, mouthpiece dangling between his teeth. Nor did the announcers who gave the fight to Michael. Nor did the crowd, which rhythmically chanted "Mi-chael! Mi-chael!" Still, uncertainty crackled in the air. Boxing fans knew the sport had become notorious for dealing out questionable decisions, a few of which had kept Holmes champion in recent years.

After a few minutes ring announcer Chuck Hull took hold of the microphone. "Ladies and gentlemen, here is the decision of the judges: Judge Dave Moretti scores 143–142, Judge Harold Lederman scores 143–142, and Judge Larry Wallace scores 145–142, for the winner by unanimous decision, and *new* heavyweight champion of the world, Michael Spinks."

On the word *new,* a whoop erupted from Michael's circle as his handlers, friends, and family broke into delirium. Michael could be seen in the center of the mob. He was hugging a heavyset guy wearing a hooded sweatshirt under a pith helmet.

The shocking victory registered a ten on boxing's Richter scale. Once again Michael commanded the covers of *Sports Illustrated* and *The Ring*. His story was a natural. He'd taken the heavyweight title from Larry Holmes in the biggest upset since Leon had wrested the belt from Ali.

Bernie Lincicome wrote in the *Chicago Tribune,* "Holmes was too old and Spinks was too weird. Spinks fought like a man with a bad rash, dipping and flopping around the ring while Holmes posed like a statue, waiting for the chance to pound an opponent who was never there. He pawed at Holmes more than punished him. He slapped and slipped and used his youth to outlast Holmes. On two of the judges' cards, had Holmes been able to win the 15th round, he would have kept his title by split decision. It would have been a greater larceny than roulette. Spinks landed more punches than Holmes, though none will leave scars. He dashed in and out of Holmes' arms like a shameless flirt."

Muhammad Ali was full of praise for Michael's historic feat and told *Jet* magazine, "All light heavyweights can lift their heads up now, no more second-class citizenship."

Michael said to reporters afterward, "Muhammad Ali told me during Jersey Joe Walcott's retirement party to stay with Holmes for six rounds, and then he'd have no legs after that. I took Ali's advice, and I kept giving Holmes head movements to mess with his mind. I had him hypnotized and mesmerized."

When Michael appeared on CBS's *NFL Today* with Brent Musburger the morning after the fight, he was a far cry from hypnotizer or mesmerizer. He showed up for the interview in a large white hat, red warm-up suit, and bare feet, and delicately lowered himself into his chair. After the interview he slid out of his seat and crawled to a nearby couch.

"My feet hurt, my arms hurt, my head hurts," he told Terence Moore of the *Atlanta Constitution*. "I'm just so tired that I don't even have time to think about what happened last night. But I'll be all right before I get to my first title defense. Oh, no. My first title defense. I don't even want to think about that."

Then he groaned.

But the ache in Michael's bones didn't match the distress in Holmes's head. The now ex-champion, who had often accused the media of shortchanging him during his reign, didn't disappoint at the postfight press conference. He stepped to the podium wearing dark-brown prescription sunglasses that masked the swelling under his eyes. Then he tried his best to undo any shred of goodwill he still had left.

"I'm thirty-five fighting young men, and [Marciano] was twenty-five fighting old men," he said. "To be technical, Rocky Marciano couldn't carry my jockstrap."

Peter Marciano had tried to interject, but Holmes shut him down with a pointed finger. "This is my press conference and you can just shut up."

He then called Marciano a "freeloader" for attending the fight on Caesars's dime and said, "If it wasn't for me, Peter, you wouldn't never have been invited to Caesars Palace, where all your expenses are paid. If I hurt your feelings, so fuckin' what."

Butch Lewis and Don King, lifelong enemies, found common ground as they cringed in the back of the room. But Holmes was just getting started. He accused the media of being racist and hindering his reign as champion. He called Boston a racist city and dug into *Boston Globe* reporter Steve Marantz, presumably for an unflattering article he had written years earlier.

After his tirade he choked out a rambling apology. "If I hurt anybody's feelings, I'm very sorry. But I was giving my people something to look forward to in our lifetime."

Dave Anderson recognized that Holmes had irrevocably damaged his reputation. "Seldom, if ever, has a champion been such a bad loser," he wrote in the *New York Times*. "It is one thing to grouse about styles, it's quite another to attack verbally not only a departed champion, but also the surviving members of that departed champion's family. Larry Holmes assured himself of being disliked by many boxing buffs, if not dismissed as worthy of being ranked with the great champions."

Perhaps the only saving grace to Holmes's outburst was that at some point during the histrionics, he mentioned that he was retiring, that he had business to attend to in Easton.

It appeared as though boxing fans had seen the last of a dominant, underappreciated, overconfident, admirable, and cantankerous champion.

12

MICHAEL STRETCHED OUT ON THE COUCH, RESTING HIS ACHING body in the oversized living room of his country estate. Having moved to one of Delaware's priciest enclaves, he was now a resident of "Chateau Country," the home of the Vicmead Hunt Club and the exclusive Wilmington and Greenville Country Clubs. The best way to get there by car was to leave north St. Louis, gun it, and never look back.

It took two months for Michael's bruises to heal, but his new-found fame showed no signs of subsiding. As boxing's new king, he was being bombarded by sports fanatics and groupies; he was deluged with interview requests and sponsorship opportunities. As he told *Ebony* magazine, people saw him through a different lens now that he had become heavyweight champion. "The crowds around me are bigger," he said. "And there seems to be a certain kind of affection for me. I guess that's what happens when you're involved in a historic event."

The problem for Michael was that he didn't crave the lime-light, and in fact, had always tried to avoid it. He'd bought the 6,700-square-foot home earlier in the year with the guaranteed purse from the Holmes fight. He was drawn as much to its setting as he was to its colonial charm. The two-story stucco, built in 1850, was set on three acres and tucked out of sight by lush landscaping. It was the ideal place in which to hide from autograph seekers. Better still, it was a mere five miles from Butch Lewis's home, a sprawling eleven-room ranch that Lewis had built on an equally exclusive plot two years earlier.

Michael rarely left his house, choosing instead to let his metallic gray Mercedes-Benz 380SEL sit idly in the driveway. He shared the five bedrooms with his sister Karen and her three young children; his daughter Michelle could also be found there when she wasn't with her maternal grandmother in Philadelphia. His other siblings—Leland, Evan, Eddie, and Leon—came and went. Those who visited saw little evidence of Michael's profession. No boxing trophies. No medals. No awards. And no sign of his freshly minted red-and-gold IBF belt.

As for braggadocio, the new champ left all the trash talk to Butch Lewis. Many insiders admired his trust in Lewis. Others questioned whether Lewis was worthy of it.

Michael's longtime friend James Caldwell says, "It was quite a partnership. Butch was really a good guy to Michael. I don't think he looked at Michael as a money ticket. Butch seemed a lot more genuine than some of the other people that had been around Michael. Other commercial people were pulling at him, people that wanted him to sponsor certain things. He was uncomfortable with that. So when Butch came along, he had somebody that he felt had his genuine interest in mind and would represent him properly."

Kenny Loehr has never trusted the relationship. "I don't think Butch Lewis [was] good for Michael," he says. "He kept a close watch on Michael's money. Whenever I seen Michael, he had to ask Butch for money."

Amelia Patterson worked at Butch Lewis Productions on and off for more than seven years; she organized boxing matches, coordinated TV shows, and managed public relations. She knew all aspects of the complex, multifaceted Lewis: the funny man, the holy terror, the down-in-the-trenches workaholic. She also knew Lewis, money manager for Michael Spinks.

"Michael's mom didn't like that Butch was handling [Michael's] money," Patterson remembers. "She was complaining, 'You need to have someone else handling your money.' But Michael trusted Butch. He had that kind of devotion to him. He could've had his own separate accountant, business manager. I mean, don't mix apples and oranges. So he had one person controlling his whole life."

Ross Greenburg, former executive producer of HBO Sports, recalls, "You could tell there was a bond there and that [Michael] totally and wholeheartedly trusted Butch Lewis and everything he did for him. [But] Butch took a nice paycheck every time Michael fought. There was a lot of money to be had, so you could say he was doing a nice job of promoting [Michael]. But I had heard on many occasions that he was taking 50 percent of his purses for his fee."

Top Rank's Bob Arum says, "It seemed to me that they had a very trusting relationship. It's a relationship that everybody looked to as being a credit to the sport."

Leon, meanwhile, had no such support. By 1986 he'd run through half a dozen promoters and even more managers. He was staying with his girlfriend Betty Green at her apartment in Detroit and scraping by on the $400 weekly allowance fronted him by his Kronk management team: Emanuel Steward, Sam Lafata, and Marv Haupt. His Rosedale Park home now belonged to the National Bank of Detroit. (Thomas Hearns would later buy it for a cut-rate $55,000.) His last five fights had brought in $26,400—the fifth contest producing an eight-round TKO over the unknown Kip Kane for the equally unknown WBC Continental Americas heavyweight championship. The victory was so meaningless that Leon had vacated the title and agreed to slim back down to cruiserweight and fight Dwight Qawi for the WBA championship. (After losing to Michael, Qawi had stepped up to cruiserweight and won six fights in the talent-starved division.) He and Leon were due to meet in Reno, Nevada, on March 22.

But Leon had more immediate concerns, one of which was the losing battle he'd been waging against his bankbook. Less than a week before the bout, he'd filed for bankruptcy with no hope of paying the $301,303 due his various creditors. He owed $85,000 to Don King Productions, $18,000 to D's Fur Works, $500 to Detroit Edison, and $500 to Michigan Consolidated. The case was closed four months later and Leon was absolved of his debts.

In the meantime new creditors were lining up. Two days before the Qawi fight, Nevada District Judge Jerry Carr Whitehead signed an order earmarking $32,000 of Leon's $70,000 purse for Jerry Sawyer, Leon's former manager.

Marv Haupt dismissed his client's financial worries and assured the media that big money was in the offing for Leon. The winner of the Qawi fight would defend the title in a bigger-money match against Olympic bronze medalist and rising cruiserweight Evander Holyfield.

As for Qawi, he'd been aching for another shot at Michael. He'd been negotiating a rematch, but when told by Lewis it had been canceled, Qawi erupted in a temper tantrum during which he kicked a spit bucket at Lewis. Neither one had forgotten.

Qawi's manager Rock Newman says, "Butch tried to get him suspended from the sport. So by this time there was a lot of bad blood between Dwight and the Spinkses. Dwight didn't just want to beat Leon, he wanted to humiliate him."

Leon was oblivious to Qawi's intentions. His toughest opponent didn't come in the form of an ex-con with padded gloves. It came on the rocks, straight up, or with a twist.

"We're in Reno and both fighters were staying in the Peppermill Casino," Newman remembers. "The fight was being shown on Saturday on *Wide World of Sports*. On Wednesday morning I go down at five because Dwight's gonna have his last run of the training camp and I'm gonna warm up the car. I see Leon and a couple of his friends walk in the hotel. I think, 'Damn, he's already been out for a run, he's training hard.' He didn't have jogging clothes on. He looked like he had spent the night in the casino or something. Then he walked past me and he was reeking of alcohol. Absolutely reeking of alcohol. So then he sat down at the blackjack table and he was flirting with the dealer. He told her that he was Leon Spinks. She said, 'No, you're not. Leon Spinks doesn't have any teeth.' He turned around from the table, pulled his teeth out, and grinned back at her with that big [Leon] grin and said, 'How do you like me now?'

"I was nervous about that fight because Dwight had so many things going on in his personal life and Leon still packed a heavy punch. But [when I saw Leon drinking at the casino], I told Dwight there's no way in the world Leon can go a whole bunch of rounds. I said, 'He'll come out and shoot his load.' Seventy-five percent of my nervousness went away."

Drinking does compromise stamina. It also beefs up the waistline. And unlike the heavyweight division, which had no weight limit, the WBA cruiserweight division dictated a ceiling of 190 pounds. As one might expect, Leon had trouble making weight. He spent the day before the fight at the Grand Central Sauna & Hot Tub Company trying to sweat off six pounds.

That evening Steward and Lafata went to Leon's hotel room to check in on him. When they got there, Leon was lying on the bed naked, cocked like a broomstick. He had a lady friend with him, and the place was littered with bottles of beer and containers of fried chicken.

For Steward, it was a first. "He says, 'Coach, it ain't like it look.' I said, 'It looks like you're having sex, it looks like you've been drinking, it looks like you're living like a gigolo.' I had never in my life experienced a fighter that did this stuff. Even today nobody tops Leon."

Lafata remembers, "I walked out when I seen the scene. It just bothered the heck out of me. You do so much to help him, and it just breaks your heart. I said, 'What the hell am I doing here? What am I wasting my time for?'"

Needless to say, one day in the sauna wasn't enough for Leon to make weight. He wound up having to run for an hour in order to tip the scale at exactly 190. Qawi, on the other hand, was a fit and determined 189 despite battling personal demons, including a family tragedy that had culminated with his father's murder.

So when boxing fans tuned into ABC's *Wide World of Sports* on March 22, 1986, they thought they were watching the man who'd beaten Muhammad Ali make an earnest effort to revive his career in a lighter weight division. What they actually saw was an out-of-shape, hungover ex-fighter go up against an angry and bitter cruiserweight champion who was out to disgrace him.

—~—

Reno was not the kind of town photographers flocked to for beauty shots. In the eyes of Bernie Lincicome, sports columnist for the *Chicago Tribune*, the town "looks as if someone took a giant push broom and shoved all the debris of the high desert up against the Sierra Nevada mountains, which are the only redeeming feature of the place and are, to their credit, a safe distance from the mobile home, pickup truck, brown-grass capital of the Western world."

Promoting itself as "The Biggest Little City in the World," Reno had built its reputation on gambling, divorce, and boxing. Jess Willard, Max Baer, and Sonny Liston all fought there; the town had played host to the notorious 1910 "Fight of the Century" between Jack Johnson and Jim Jeffries.

When Leon Spinks and Dwight Qawi squared off at the University of Nevada's Lawlor Events Center, boxing in Reno was in its heyday, grabbing big-name fights that weren't quite big enough for Las Vegas. Leon hadn't fought in a noteworthy venue since losing to Carlos de Leon in Atlantic City three years earlier. This was yet another shot for him to regain the national spotlight.

In the dressing room before the fight, Leon gathered with his handlers. Predictably, Kay Spinks used the opportunity to hold an impromptu prayer meeting.

Emanuel Steward never forgot the scene. "Before the fight Mama's having a prayer about this young man who's been working so hard and put so much into it, and my assistant vice president Prentiss Byrd couldn't take it anymore. He just walked out. 'I gotta leave,' he said. 'I can't hear this part.'"

Leon, sporting a neatly trimmed beard and mustache, entered the ring in gold Kronk gym shorts. He had seven-and-a-half-inches on Qawi in height and five in reach. He also had the punching power of a true heavyweight.

"Before I fought [Leon], I saw him fight against some guy," Qawi says. "He looked pretty good. I was concerned. He could still fight. He had two or three losses before he fought me, but he was always dangerous. My strategy was to take it right to him and whip him like he stole something."

As soon as the bell rang, the two fighters came out slugging, giving the crowd its money's worth. But then Leon went to the ropes and stayed there, counterpunching. His lack of training was already evident.

ABC announcer Alex Wallau in the first round, "Leon has been less aggressive than is his normal style here. . . . Right now, you'd have to say that Leon is just dead at this weight. He has no legs to move away, he has very little zip in his punches at this point."

Leon absorbed many more blows than he dished out, and the ratio became more lopsided as the fight progressed. His friends and family shouted from ringside to box, move, get off the ropes, but it was clear that Leon didn't have a game plan, nor did he have the wellspring of energy he had dipped into eight years earlier against Ali.

In the fourth round Qawi taunted Leon, mugging at him, sticking out his tongue, hitting him at will, daring him to hit back. But Leon's battery was dying. His punches were slow, late, and off the mark. Worse yet, every time he swung and missed, Qawi responded with a sharp, targeted combination.

"I was just having fun," Qawi says now. "That was about getting his brother to come out. I wanted to get a rematch with Michael. I put a whipping on Leon. I heard his people yelling, 'Move, move, get off the ropes, Leon.' I turned around and told 'em to shut up."

Steward worked Leon's corner that night. "Qawi would get him over to the ropes and beat on him. Then he says to me [while hitting Leon], 'Got any more of these guys over at the Kronk? I like beating on a big man with little gold Kronk britches on him.' He's really rubbing it into me."

By the sixth, Steward had seen enough. Leon was standing straight up—an easy target—and Qawi went at him like a plumber banging on a rusty pipe. Steward threw in the towel, and referee Mills Lane put an official end to the fight at 2:56 of the sixth round.

As he walked away from the ring, Lane told ringside reporters, "[Leon's] knees were beginning to buckle with each blow. He was not throwing any punches in return and he was getting hit with a lot of solid blows. There was no point in getting the kid killed."

After the onslaught had abated, Leon stood with his right hand resting on the rope, blood streaming from his lower lip, his eyes glued to Qawi. Perhaps he was upset at being mocked, because he had no problem with the premature stoppage of the fight.

"What took you so long?" he said to Steward. "I could get killed with someone like you in my corner."

Years later Steward would recall, "I hate losing a fight, but I stopped it. Leon came over to me and said, 'Don't be so damn serious. Let's go have a drink.' I just had to laugh. That was typical of Leon."

Marv Haupt put on his game face and told the press that Leon had lost because he was too weak at 190 pounds. You'll see Leon again, he said, but it will be as a heavyweight.

That was pure spin.

"If Leon would have been serious, he would have beat Qawi," says Lafata now. "But it's hard to explain Leon. He just never took anything serious. He just thought that he's good enough to handle himself. But of course once he got in there, after being out all night, that was very, very discouraging, especially with the work that we put into him. And you couldn't follow him around. He had his own way. Trying to keep up with him was physically impossible. People told me we should have [locked him up]. If we would've let him sit in jail, he would've kicked the hell out of Qawi. We should've locked him up and slept with him."

In his dressing room, Leon did his best to keep his career alive.

"You still love me, dontcha?" he asked the few people still with him.

"We still love you, Leon."

The truth was that his handlers agreed with Lafata. They figured that Leon had blown his chance—that he would have had an easy time beating Qawi had he stayed sober for even one week leading up to the fight. They weren't going to watch it happen again.

"After he showered, [Leon] came out in the casinos with a big smile on his face," Lafata says. "Of course, we were ready to go home. I had had it. I said, 'Leon, you're on your own now. I really can't handle this anymore. Not in this business.' And he understood.

"I have no idea how he ended up getting back from Reno. He got paid and I didn't see him after that. I wanted no part of him. I was ashamed of myself for what I put Emanuel through. I honestly feel that he handled [Leon] just to help me out. He probably knew from day one that Leon didn't have a chance."

Three months later Leon was back in the news when the Nevada State Athletic Commission suspended him for testing positive for the depressant phenobarbital following the loss to Qawi. According to Leon, he had taken the medication before the fight to alleviate stomach problems he'd developed after dropping twenty-three pounds to make weight.

The suspension was of no concern to Leon's handlers. They'd already moved on.

13

THE SPLINTERING OF THE HEAVYWEIGHT TITLE BEGAN WHEN THE WBC stripped Leon of his belt in 1978, and it hadn't let up since. Cynics suspected payoffs. Fans blamed the promoters, particularly Don King, the cunning matchmaker with the gravity-defying hairdo, who seemed to double his fortune—legitimately or not—every time a title bout was signed. When Michael beat Holmes in September 1985, boxing had three champions: one each for the WBC, WBA, and IBF. Writing in the *New York Times,* Dave Anderson lamented, "The heavyweight division crumbled like crackers into alphabet soup."

Anderson now says, "That's the beauty and the disgrace of boxing—you had three champions. The public may favor one of them, but the other two guys can say, 'Well, but I'm the champion.' Of course, they're not. There should be only one champion. That's what boxing was for years, going back to Jack Johnson and John L. Sullivan. But all of these alphabet organizations emerged because of television. There were three or four networks and each one could claim they had a championship fight."

In the eyes of the public, Michael was the legitimate titleholder— he'd beaten the lineal and most established champion, Larry Holmes. Plus, it was nearly impossible to follow the paths of the other belts.

Here's a recap.

The WBC belt: After the WBC stripped Leon for fighting Ali, the championship went to Norton. In his first defense Norton lost it in a barnburner to Holmes. Holmes then defended the belt sixteen times before dumping it and accepting recognition by the newly formed IBF. (He became the IBF's first heavyweight champion and defended that belt three times before losing it to Michael.) Tim Witherspoon beat Greg Page for Holmes's vacated WBC championship, but promptly lost it to Pinklon Thomas.

The WBA belt: Ali had retired and vacated the title after taking it from Leon in New Orleans. John Tate won the vacated belt by beating Gerrie Coetzee but lost it in his first defense to Mike Weaver, who lost it in his third defense to Michael Dokes, who lost it in his second defense to Gerrie Coetzee, who lost it in his first defense to Greg Page, who lost it in his first defense to Tony Tubbs. Few people realized it—how could they?—but in October 1985, Tony Tubbs was the WBA heavyweight champion.

So it stands to reason that when Don King showed up at Seth Abraham's Greenwich Village apartment that October to peddle a Pinklon Thomas–Trevor Berbick WBC title fight, the HBO Sports president had zero interest.

But King and Abraham had aired many fights together, and King wasn't about to give up. He returned to Abraham's apartment the following night to pitch the same fight. This time instead of dismissing the bout, Abraham used it as a springboard to a bigger idea.

"[Don and I] were watching the World Series between the St. Louis Cardinals and the Kansas City Royals," Abraham recalls. "I said to Don, 'So, let me ask you a question. Seven games, World Series, undisputed baseball champion. Could we use this Thomas-Berbick fight as the first bout in a heavyweight world series?'

"Don stayed until about 2:30 in the morning; the game was long over. We sketched out the seven fights we'd need to unify the three different titles. I said to Don, 'Come back and tell me the matchups and the license fees.' If Don came back and said seven fights at $250 million, obviously it's a nonstarter. But Don came back about a month later and the number wasn't on Mars. It was on Earth. It was high, but it wasn't out of the galaxy."

The number was $20 million. And the schedule was relatively straightforward. The tournament would start with three title fights, one each for the WBC, the IBF, and the WBA. After that the WBC and the IBF champions would fight mandatory title defenses. Then the WBA champ would fight the WBC champ, and the winner of that bout would fight the IBF champ.

Negotiations between the fighters and their promoters began on December 24, 1985, at HBO's offices in New York and wrapped up in mid-January in Atlanta. The talks may have gone more quickly if Butch Lewis had been sold on the idea that the tournament was in Michael's best interest. But since Lewis represented the fighter generally considered the "true" champion, he'd had the luxury of waiting until he was all but certain Michael would be the last man standing.

The series kicked off on March 22, 1986, at the Riviera in Las Vegas. In the opener Trevor Berbick took the WBC title from Pinklon Thomas in a twelve-round unanimous decision.

Michael was up next. He'd be defending the IBF title on April 19. The bout? A rematch with the ex-champion who'd retired from the sport seven months earlier with his head held high and his foot planted defiantly in his mouth.

⌐⌐

Larry Holmes had held the title from 1978 to 1985, but he'd never captured the public's imagination in the same way that Muhammad Ali or Joe Louis had.

According to Carlo Rotella, author of *Cut Time: An Education at the Fights*, "Holmes fought his way up through the deepest, most dangerous heavyweight division of all time. He stood for pretty much every virtue that mattered to the working class in the first half of the twentieth century: craft, will, resilience, ability to perform at a high technical level for a long time, to endure suffering, to beat the best. The money was good; the adulation was good. But there was always, 'You're not Muhammad Ali.' He was always second fiddle."

Perhaps that's why Holmes had lashed out at the fighter whose win streak he had chased and missed. Whatever the reason, his diatribe against Marciano and Marciano's family didn't help his cause. He'd sounded petty, angry, and bitter, and although he had tried his best to undo the damage, his apology didn't sway the court of public opinion.

New York Times sportswriter Dave Anderson says, "I always found Larry Holmes to be a terrific guy in a quiet setting. But when you gave him a microphone in a press conference, you never knew what he was going to say. He realized he said the wrong thing about Marciano the next day, but it was too late. And it's a shame because it tarnished him at the time."

Holmes issued an apology in his 1998 autobiography, *Larry Holmes: Against the Odds.* "[I said things] to Peter Marciano and Rocky's kids that were uncalled for and simply wrong. Somewhere in there I must have realized I'd gone too far because in my fashion I tried to apologize. I said, 'Rocky was one of the greatest fighters of all time. For anybody to accomplish forty-nine victories, even if they were all bums, is some kind of record. If I didn't think he was a great fighter, his pictures wouldn't be on the walls of my motel near Easton.' But, of course, it was too little, too late. As they say, 'The insult is halfway around the world before the apology gets its boots on.'"

The Spinks-Holmes rematch was scheduled to take place in Las Vegas, and Holmes had few allies left. He sent a letter to Bob Lee, president of the IBF, appealing to Lee's sense of fair play. In the note he listed the judges that he felt were off-limits. According to

Holmes, Lee sent back a reply that said Holmes had been treated fairly the first time around and would be treated the same way again.

That wasn't enough for the fuming ex-champion. A week before the fight, Holmes lifted his moratorium on interviews and targeted the very officials who held his future in their scorecard-wielding hands. He told the press he didn't trust the Nevada judges, that they were "incompetent" and "must have been drunk" when they scored the first Spinks fight.

Just when Holmes had been trying to endear himself to the press and the public, he dug himself a bigger hole than the one he'd put himself in earlier.

—◆—

April 19, 1986. When ring announcer Chuck Hull introduced Larry Holmes to the full house at the Hilton, the ex-champion was hit with boos and catcalls. Judging by the steely look in his eye, Holmes was focusing on settling his scores with Michael, the Vegas judges, and a legion of sportswriters he felt had never warmed up to him.

Following tradition, the champion, Michael Spinks, was introduced last.

"And in the blue corner," Hull proclaimed, "now fighting out of Wilmington, Delaware, weighing 205 pounds, he is undefeated in his professional career, twenty-eight wins, no defeats, nineteen knockouts. He is a former undisputed light-heavyweight champion of the world, the current IBF champion of the world: Michael Spinks."

The crowd of 8,300 cheered as Michael raised his gloves in response. It was no accident that Michael's sculpted body seemed as solid as the ring posts; Mackie Shilstone had put him on a training regimen even more intense than the one he'd designed for the first Holmes fight. This time around Michael had trained in bursts. He'd broken up 440-, 880-, and 1,320-meter runs with one-minute breaks to simulate the pattern of a fifteen-round fight. He worked out with weighted gloves to replicate late-round fatigue. And he leapt sideways on and off plyometric boxes to strengthen his legs (while simulating his signature lateral boxing style).

Despite Michael's conditioning and his championship status, he was still the underdog against Holmes—just as Leon had been when defending his title against Ali in New Orleans.

Before the fight HBO commentators Barry Tompkins, Larry Merchant, and Sugar Ray Leonard put the onus of the match on the big man, wondering whether he'd finally pull the trigger on his powerful right hand.

Tompkins said, "So, we'll watch the right hand of Larry Holmes. He didn't throw it in the first round of the last fight."

"What we have to see here is if Larry Holmes is going to be the aggressive fighter he says he's going to be and sustain the pace that that requires," Merchant added.

Leonard predicted, "I would be surprised if Larry doesn't jump on Michael right in the first round."

As Leonard forecast, Holmes went right at Michael as soon as the bell clanged. He punched, bullied, and manhandled the smaller man. Then, shortly into the round, he threw Michael to the canvas.

"Get up," Holmes snarled.

Michael got to his feet. To Mills Lane he said, "It's OK, ref. It's OK."

Holmes's thuggish behavior set the tone for the first four rounds, and Michael spent those twelve minutes ducking, dodging, and dancing out of harm's way. He turned and twisted his body back and forth, holding up his hands to protect his head, and rarely threw a punch. His awkward defensive antics seemed to anger Holmes all the more. The big man swung hard and often—clearly looking for a knockout. He landed a number of solid shots but missed with just as many. Michael withstood the tidal wave of anger and adrenaline gushing out of the ex-champ, but there was no doubt that Holmes won those rounds big.

The pattern began to shift in the fifth. Holmes had said before the fight that he was going to take punches and wear Michael down. But Michael's strategy of staying away started to pay off, and Holmes was the one wearing down. Michael began unleashing stinging punches. Jab, jab, right hand. The crowd broke out into chants of "Mi-chael! Mi-chael!" as their fighter came alive. Jab, jab, right hand. Holmes took the punches without retreating, but he lacked the adrenaline of youth.

Tompkins told the HBO audience in the sixth, "Very, very slowly, you have the feeling that the momentum of this fight is switching to the champion. Almost imperceptibly."

As Holmes's energy continued to wane, Michael began showing the confidence of a fighter who knows his opponent can't hurt him. Jab, jab, right-left-right-left. It wasn't pretty, it was tactical, but Michael was putting points in his column.

Judges Frank Brunette and Jerry Roth gave Michael the fifth and sixth rounds. They also awarded him every round from the eighth through the thirteenth. Joe Cortez agreed on all rounds except the fifth and the ninth, both of which he gave to Holmes. After the thirteenth Michael had a slight edge on two of the three official scorecards, but the bout was still up for grabs and neither fighter had much juice left. The early rounds had worn Holmes down, and thirteen rounds of running, dodging, and counterpunching had sucked the energy out of Michael. The remainder of the fight would be fought between two depleted and desperate champions.

Richie Giachetti told Holmes after the thirteenth, "Ya gotta keep throwing punches. Look at him. Look at him over there. Look at the ice and everything on him. Let's go, dammit. Ya gotta want it. You gotta go get it, baby."

Michael kicked off the fourteenth with a flurry of pinpoint blows and took control of the ring for the first two minutes of the round. But just as his fans were figuring he could cruise to the bell, Holmes pounded him with a right that sent his knees to within an inch of the canvas. Remarkably, he sprung back up (he would later give credit to the plyometric boxes), but he spent the final sixty seconds of the round on Queer Street. One more punch from Holmes would surely finish him, but, inexplicably, that shot never came.

HBO's Barry Tompkins: "Larry Holmes himself said, 'I don't want to leave this to the judges,' and now he's got a chance and he's not pouncing on Michael Spinks."

Michael stumbled away from Holmes, threw a couple of lackluster punches, and walked sideways with a facial expression that said he was no more certain he was battling for a championship than walking home from a grocery store. When the big man finally advanced, Michael let loose with a hail of blows that kept Holmes from landing another one of his right-fisted hammers.

Tompkins: "Spinks just trying to brawl Holmes to keep him off of him."

Leonard: "[Holmes] had [Michael] out on his feet. And now Spinks showing the heart he has as a champion and he's trying to come back."

When the bell rang to close the round, Michael thrust his gloves above his head. That he was still on his feet no doubt gave him a sense of victory. He might have felt differently had he known that HBO's unofficial judge, Harold Lederman, and the network commentators had Holmes winning the fight by four points. (Michael was still narrowly ahead on two of the three official judges' cards.)

The fourteenth round had been the most aggressive of the twenty-nine fought between the two men, and the fifteenth topped it. Both swung heavy punches. A small contingency of Holmes fans chanted "Lar-ry! Lar-ry!" but the rest of the house overpowered them with shouts of "Mi-chael! Mi-chael!" Both sides felt their man was getting the better of the other, and both could make a case for their position. As the clock ran out, Holmes and Michael emptied their war chests, and as the bell rang, Michael landed a solid right cross. The fight was over and destiny was exactly where Holmes didn't want it: in the hands of three Nevada judges.

Tompkins on-air to Sugar Ray Leonard: "So this one has come to an end. . . . You have to think Larry Holmes is the winner of this fight. That's what Larry Merchant had on his card, that's what Harold Lederman had on his card. You and I saw the fight that way. But again, I harken back to many fights that you and I have done here in Las Vegas, Ray, and I've seen some awfully strange decisions."

Sugar Ray Leonard: "That's true, Barry, but judging by the way Larry approached this fight, Larry was the aggressor from round one. I think you have to look at that as your criteria, the fact that Larry was very effective, he was able to land some sharp right hands that stunned Michael Spinks."

Holmes went to his corner and huddled with his handlers. Michael stood in the center of the ring; Leon, wearing a do-rag that hung out from under his black-and-gold cap, hugged him and yelled into his ear, "I love you." Michael patted him with his gloved hand and walked back to his corner, where Butch Lewis was waiting.

Chuck Hull grabbed the overhead microphone. "Ladies and gentlemen, here is the decision of the judges. Judge Frank Brunette scores 144 Spinks, 141 Holmes."

The crowd cheered for Michael but quickly became silent. This was going to be a split decision.

"Judge Joe Cortez scores 144 Holmes, 141 Spinks."

Now the crowd booed, fearing that their new whipping boy, Holmes, might have won back his title.

"Judge Jerry Roth scores 144–142 for the winner by a split decision, and *still* the IBF heavyweight champion, Michael Spinks."

The crowd erupted into a single, joyous roar. Michael shot both arms into the air and his handlers danced wildly around him. Holmes said nothing; he shook his head. His facial expression was one of disgust. He'd just earned $1.125 million (Michael's take was two million dollars), but for him, this was about much more than money. Michael went over to Holmes in a conciliatory manner, but Holmes rebuffed him. The big man turned away and slipped into his robe.

Michael went back to his cornermen and yelled for his daughter. "Where's my baby?" he shouted. "Where's my baby?"

Someone brought Michelle over to Michael. The toddler, oblivious to what her father had just been through, reached over and wiped the sweat from his arms and his face while watching him give an interview to Larry Merchant.

"I knew from twelve on it had to be my fight," Michael said.

Then, when asked about the fourteenth round, he added, "I think the big right hand he caught me with, I didn't know what happened, but I knew I was hit. All I knew was that I was stationary and sort of in limbo. . . . Right away my mind thought, 'You're here too long. I must be dazed, let me get the hell on outta here.' So I dashed. And I recovered just like that."

Standing next to Michael, Lewis steered the interview in the direction he wanted it to go, which was away from Holmes's punishing right hand and toward the big punches that Michael had landed in the later rounds.

"You hurt him, too," Lewis prompted Michael.

"Oh sure, I hurt him a few times. I know I rattled him," Michael told Merchant.

Shortly thereafter Holmes was in a somber mood, icing his right hand in his dressing room. (It would later be revealed that he had fractured his thumb in the third round.) He told Merchant he was leaving the game, that there was no sense in chasing ghosts, that he'd be "walking around punched out and punch drunk" if he didn't hang up his gloves. Then, he added, "I can still be proud of what I accomplished, and I can say to the judges, the referees, and the promoters to kiss me where the sun don't shine—and because we're on HBO, that's my big black behind."

He'd done it again. The crotchety ex-champ was sticking to his guns. But was he right? Did the judges have it in for him? Had his fate been determined before the opening bell?

Dave Anderson wrote in the *New York Times*, "On my scorecard, Spinks was ahead, 144–142, earning eight of the last ten rounds after Holmes burned out. Holmes's hesitation in throwing another right hand in the fourteenth round Saturday night was typical of an old fighter whose reflexes weren't there anymore. It happened to Muhammad Ali and to Joe Louis. And Saturday night it happened to Holmes, but he has preferred to think there was a plot to make sure he didn't regain the title."

At the time, Jim Lampley was a commentator for ABC Sports. "My perception had been that Spinks's two wins over Holmes had more to do with Holmes's shot reflexes than with what Michael had done," Lampley says, looking back. "But I didn't give Michael enough credit for his calculated aggression and the way he measured distance—and how brilliantly he confused Holmes."

Harold Lederman, HBO's unofficial ringside scorer, has little doubt as to the winner. "There's no question Larry won the second fight," he maintains. "But [Larry] didn't endear himself to anybody.

Whoever was working the fight couldn't have been too pleased with him. If that made any difference, I don't know. But Michael was the benefactor of some very questionable judging."

According to Richie Giachetti, "The judges, they said Holmes's comments didn't bother them, but in the back of your mind, you think about something and you react to it. He called the judges blind and crooked and it more or less turned people off."

Tell that to Jerry Roth. "I was one of the judges and it didn't affect me one way or the other," he says now. "From a judging standpoint, it's a three-minute round. I watch the round, I judge that round on the three minutes, and that's it. I don't care about [a fighter's] comments—that doesn't enter my mind at all. As a professional judge, you've got to eliminate those kinds of things from your mind."

Author and boxing scholar Carlo Rotella says, "[Michael] won two unscorable, complicated, unsuccessful matchups with Holmes. I say 'unsuccessful' because those two guys never found a way to settle who was the better fighter. You couldn't score those fights and say Holmes won, and you couldn't score them and say Spinks won. These are exactly the kinds of fights you can't score on TV because you don't know how hard they're hitting."

Jerry Izenberg wrote in the Newark *Star-Ledger*, "You could have wound up scoring the fight with twenty different arithmetical combinations and who is to say you'd be wrong? You could have given it to either fighter or called it a draw and thrown your scorecard up in the air and suggested everybody start all over tomorrow."

A month after the fight, Holmes began a short-lived crusade to clean up boxing, testifying for ninety minutes before the Assembly Independent and Regional Authorities Committee in Newark, New Jersey. According to UPI, he "painted a picture of corrupt boxing judges, lackadaisical physicians, exploitative promoters, and unsafe equipment."

One of Holmes's accusations targeted the competency, although not the integrity, of Frank Brunette and Jerry Roth, the two judges who'd been responsible for his second loss.

It should come as no surprise that in Holmes's efforts to clean up the sport, he made no mention of Joe Cortez, the ref who scored in his favor. Nor did he take issue with any of the controversial decisions that had tipped his way throughout his seven-year reign as champion. Apparently, every corrupt official in boxing was targeting Holmes.

In the end the ex-champ's crusade had virtually no effect on the sport, and even less on Michael.

The quiet, gangly boxer from Pruitt-Igoe was still unbeaten, still the lineal champion, and still wearing the IBF belt.

And the heavyweight division was waiting to be unified.

14

To be the last man standing in the HBO tournament, Michael would have to win his next three fights. The first would be a tune-up against a handpicked opponent. The second a mandatory defense against the IBF's number-one contender Tony Tucker. Then Michael could sit back and watch the fireworks between the WBC and the WBA champs and take on the winner in a final unification match.

The first of those three fights took place on September 6, 1986, at the Las Vegas Hilton. Michael's opponent was Norway's Steffen Tangstad, the unknown European champ who had compiled a 24–1–2 record against a grab bag of mediocrity. He had little power in his left hand, less in his right, and no speed in his hands or feet. A substitute teacher by trade, Tangstad had mortgaged his cottage and gone to the United States when Norway banned boxing in 1981. Michael Katz quipped in the New York *Daily News* that if the Norwegian were to win, "boxing might be banned in this country, too."

Tangstad entered the ring looking the part of a champion—he stood six-two and weighed a solid 210—but the threat ended there. Michael, an 8–1 favorite, had an easy night, hammering at Tangstad with hard left jabs in the second, knocking him down with a right cross in the third, and flooring him twice—each time with a left hook—in the fourth. After the last knockdown, referee Richard Steele asked Tangstad if he'd had enough. Tangstad said he had.

"There was a buzzing sound in my head," Tangstad recalls. "I knew that I could maybe catch Spinks with another good punch, but if he caught me with another good one, I would have been out, and I had never been out in my life. I didn't like that feeling. And I wanted to go back to another life. So that was my last fight. I retired."

Ticket sales for the Spinks-Tangstad fight had been weak, in part because American boxing fans had no awareness of Tangstad, but also because they still hadn't accepted Michael as a true heavyweight. It didn't help that Michael continued to shy away from the spotlight. To a public accustomed to headline-hungry champions, he defied the myth. He was a wallflower in a roomful of tough guys.

"Michael didn't have the attitude to be a heavyweight," says Holmes's trainer Richie Giachetti, "the attitude that you're the baddest guy in the world. Michael never run off his mouth. He never talked the trash talk."

The executives at HBO noticed the same thing, at least as far as the trash talk was concerned. Ratings were low, and the network craved the kind of electricity generated by more flamboyant champions. Only a few weeks before the Tangstad fight, lightning struck.

"I started paying attention to [Mike] Tyson when he was fighting on the USA Network," recalls former HBO Sports president Seth Abraham. "He was fighting in upstate New York, in the Catskills area, at the time. He wasn't a champion, he wasn't even in the top ten, but here he is with a string of one-round knockouts. So Michael Fuchs [then chairman of the board and chief executive officer of HBO] and I got the idea of signing him to a series of fights at HBO's expense and then giving him to the promoters, free, if you will, with HBO paying his license fee to [Tyson's managers] Bill Cayton and Jim Jacobs. We put him on a couple of undercards and he exploded in terms of talent. Then we realized that it would look very phony to do this heavyweight series with Tyson out of it. [So we negotiated] a very complicated deal that put him into the series."

HBO added Tyson's fight against Alfonso Ratliff to the under-card of the Spinks-Tangstad match. Even Tyson couldn't fill the 9,000-seat arena, but he did boost the tally to a respectable 6,000. The public knew that the Tyson-Ratliff matchup was more ludicrous than Michael-Tangstad. The casinos wouldn't even take bets on who would win the fight; they'd only give odds on *when* Tyson would win it. The over-under was five rounds.

The smart money was on "under."

"Tyson fought my old sparring partner from Chicago, Alfonso Ratliff," Tangstad says. "He was way over the hill. He had no chance against Tyson. After he sparred with me, he was kayoed by Tim Witherspoon. He was a pushover for Tyson and he had nothing left."

Tyson put Ratliff out of his misery midway through the second round. The victory brought Tyson's record to 27–0 with twenty-five knockouts and earned him a shot against Trevor Berbick for the WBC belt.

Michael was on a collision course with the media magnet from Brooklyn. Spinks-Tyson was the type of matchup that made for a big-money fight: the lineal champ versus a seemingly indomitable rising star. But since the bout would be part of the HBO tournament, Michael would get only a fraction of what Butch Lewis felt he deserved for such an event. The promoter's wheels started turning. In order for Michael to cash in on the title before taking the marquee fight against Tyson, he'd have to consider matchups outside of the series.

That's when all hell broke loose.

In November 1986 Tyson fought Berbick in the HBO series, taking the WBC belt from the Jamaican-born champion in a second-round

KO that turned Berbick's legs to noodles. At twenty years and four months, Tyson thus became the youngest heavyweight champion in boxing history.

HBO now had a compelling storyline and its twenty-million-dollar outlay was looking more and more like a shrewd investment. But Butch Lewis was trying to fill the pockets of his fighter, not of the network executives. He'd already begun talking with Dennis Rappaport and Mike Jones about setting up a fight between Michael and their fighter, Gerry Cooney, outside the series.

Rock Newman, who'd left Qawi's camp and taken a public relations position with Butch Lewis Productions, witnessed the negotiations. "With Butch and Dennis you had two of the most mercurial, egotistical maniacs going at each other," Newman says. "Dennis always had a limo to greet him and a guy to wait for him all the time. I remember a negotiation going on until three in the morning, or so, which is not uncommon for Butch's style. He's a night owl. Up all night long. In Butch's office, three o'clock or so in the morning, enough cigarette smoke to kill an elephant, and Scotch, you know, alcohol, and 'motherfucker' and 'fuck you' and 'kiss my ass' and 'suck my dick.' And Dennis finally broke it up and said, 'That's it, we'll never talk again.' And I'm like, 'Hold it, Dennis! Dennis, wait!' And Butch is like, 'Let that motherfucker go. Fuck him.' Dennis went to the elevator. I went to the elevator after him. We rode downstairs and probably talked a half hour, forty-five minutes. And he comes back up and the stuff starts again. At one point we looked out the window and it was getting light outside."

As it turned out, money wasn't the only stumbling block to making the fight. Michael's contract with HBO allowed him to defend his title against a nontournament fighter, such as Cooney, provided that Cooney join the HBO series if he were to win. This ensured that

HBO would wind up with an undisputed champion. But Cooney wanted no part of the tournament under any conditions. That left Lewis scrambling for a way to make the payday without jeopardizing Michael's agreement with HBO. It's called having your cake and eating it too.

"Word started filtering around the boxing grapevine that Butch was in negotiations with Gerry Cooney," Seth Abraham recalls. "At first he denied it. He was hoping to pull out of the series and keep the IBF belt. But he clearly got legal advice that he had a much better chance of [pulling out] if he gave up the belt."

The advice Lewis received addressed the specificity of the contract's language. The agreement had been worded in a way that bound "Michael Spinks, IBF champion" to the series but made no such demands on "Michael Spinks, heavyweight." So, if Michael were to give up his title, he could leave the series and fight whenever, wherever, and whomever he wanted.

Once shown the loophole, Lewis, with Michael in tow, ran through it. Lewis announced that Michael would not defend his title against the number-one challenger, Tony Tucker, and, as expected, Michael was stripped of his IBF belt. It made little difference to Michael. He had Lewis's negotiating skills as well as basic mathematics on his side. The Tucker fight would have earned him $500,000; the Cooney bout would land him seven million dollars.

"To me, the fact that Butch would say, 'Hey, I can get more money fighting Cooney,' is irrelevant," Seth Abraham says. "He signed a contract. If you buy an apartment and the seller comes back and says somebody just offered me $250,000 more, I'm gonna sell it to them, what are you going to do? [You're going to sue.] Well, somebody offered Butch more money for the apartment, except he had signed a contract, as did Michael, to sell the apartment to HBO. It's no different."

Lewis was indeed blinded by the large payday with Cooney. But it's also likely that he remembered how his old friend Joe Frazier had taken Ali's vacated title in 1968. Frazier's manager, Yank Durham, had pulled his fighter out of the eight-man WBA heavyweight tournament, choosing instead to have Frazier step in at the end and take on one man—Jimmy Ellis—for the championship.

In this case the maneuver led to HBO's suing Lewis and Michael. The court sided with Michael, allowing him to leave the HBO tournament with impunity.

Ross Greenburg, then executive producer of HBO Sports, recalls a meeting held around that time in the HBO offices. "I can vividly remember sitting there in a semi state of panic as Butch Lewis and Don King went after each other from across the table calling each other MFs, and the bombs falling verbally, and the fingers pointing. It was like watching two people on the verge of a confrontation on a street corner. It was ugly. Butch was a fiery guy who lost his temper and you could see in his eyes a kind of sinister anger, very similar to King. They often went toe-to-toe, but this went to another level."

"They were actually going to go at each other using the conference room tabletop as the ring," Abraham says. "I won't repeat the epithets that were being thrown around. It was end-of-the-world stuff. As I stood there, I couldn't decide if they wanted HBO to stop them or if they didn't. We took about an hour break to let everybody cool down."

When Michael pulled out, the IBF title was vacant and HBO had a hole in its schedule. Abraham says they did the best they could under the circumstances. "We took the number-one and -two ranked heavyweights—Tony Tucker and Buster Douglas—and had them fight. Was it ideal? No."

Ross Greenburg remembers, "[Michael's departure] didn't feel like as much of a loss because Tyson was on such a roll; the Tyson train had left the station. Tyson had actually overwhelmed Spinks publicly. If *Tyson* had left the series, it would've been devastating."

As it happened, the HBO series did go on, costing the network more money as a result of having to add more fights. But the HBO execs knew they'd get it back, because the Tyson locomotive was definitely gaining momentum.

Steve Lott, Tyson's cornerman, recalls the whistle-stops. "Don King got champion after champion after champion in the ring, and the objective was to make Mike [Tyson] look good in each fight, and that's what happened when he fought those former champions. All of those fights came with a lot of pressure because [Tyson] was not only expected to win, he was expected to win spectacularly."

On March 7, 1987, Tyson won the WBA belt in a lopsided twelve-round decision over Bonecrusher Smith. On May 30 he defended his WBC and WBA titles by knocking out Pinklon Thomas in the sixth round. That same night Tony Tucker took Michael's vacated IBF belt by stopping Buster Douglas in the tenth, thus setting up a Tyson-Tucker match for the undisputed championship.

Michael, beltless for the first time in six years, was still the lineal champ—and about to become a millionaire seven times over by passing through the ropes at the Atlantic City Convention Center and taking on Gerry Cooney.

✦

Beginning in the 1940s the Catskills attracted Jewish families from New York City who yearned for the fresh air and cool breezes of upstate New York. The area, two hours north of the city, offered a paradise of grand resorts, bungalow colonies, summer camps, stand-up comedy, and big bands. It was also where heavyweight champions set up camp. Rocky Marciano trained at Grossinger's, Sonny Liston at the Pines.

By 1987 the lure of the Catskills had given way to the sunny climes of California and Florida. But the Concord was still going strong as upstate New York's largest resort, stretching out over two thousand acres, offering fifteen hundred rooms, and featuring a dining hall that sat three thousand guests.

One of those guests was Michael Spinks. There, he hunkered down with Butch Lewis, Eddie Futch, and Mackie Shilstone to prepare for "The War at the Shore" on June 15. Most of the guests didn't recognize him. Despite his historic victories over Holmes and his current status as lineal champion, Michael had been eclipsed in the public imagination by Tyson. To those who did approach him—mostly gaga teenagers and their mothers who mistakenly called him Leon—he was genuine, playful, and accommodating.

In terms of size, Cooney was Michael's biggest challenge to date. Standing six-six and weighing 238, the hulking Long Islander had four inches and thirty pounds on Michael. His left hook was the stuff of legend. On his way to a 28–1 record, he had knocked out twenty-four opponents, nine of them in the first round. On the flip side he had fought only three times since losing his 1982 mega-fight with Larry Holmes.

Reporters flocked to the Concord in search of training-camp dirt they could bring back to their editors. But Michael was no Leon—there were no late-night through-the-window escapes to the local watering hole, no disappearing acts for weeks at a time, and no drugged-out debauchery. The best they could dig up was another unorthodox training regimen devised by Mackie Shilstone. What came out of Michael's camp was the picture of a single-minded fighter, free of a champion's bravado. Michael, the writers reported, offered frank answers and spoke openly of being scared of supersize heavyweights like Cooney. As the *Los Angeles Times* put it, Michael's "ego lagged woefully behind his achievements." The paper even quoted Michael as saying, "I'm in no hurry to get in the ring with that man. I could start crying. Training is fun, but thinking about the actual fight is scary. Man, those three steps up to the ring . . ."

Before the fight Michael told reporters that he wasn't thrilled about getting in the ring with Cooney. "I don't even watch films of him. He hasn't fought enough rounds for me to get much out of it, and besides, all they show me are guys going down, going down, going down. I find that very terrifying.

"Even though I'm a heavyweight, I'm probably the smallest heavyweight out there, and I have to admit, boxing all these big guys all the time, it isn't like lying on the beach or a walk in the park. It's work. It's serious work. It leaves me with an attitude of, I mean, really, really wishing, hoping that overnight I just wake up and I'm all that I would ever want to be as a heavyweight, weighing maybe around two-fifty and punching like a Mack truck."

Mackie Shilstone remembers sitting with Michael at training camp. "We're watching TV and the [commentators] are all saying Michael's not gonna stand up against this guy. And [Michael] said, 'They don't think I'm going to make it.' Cooney was this giant man. I think of all the athletes that Michael faced, Michael had the greatest apprehension about him."

Cooney was a slight favorite going into the fight—the odds more the result of his size than his skills. He'd fought only seven rounds in the previous five years, and word on the street was that he was battling depression with an arsenal of alcohol and drugs.

Kevin P. Porter, Cooney's sparring partner, recalls, "I was with him up in Great Gorge [while he was training to fight Michael]. I could see guys bringing cases of beer to Cooney's condo. . . . I think he had a drug problem too. He always gave these little speeches about his brother—he had a brother who was strung out on something—but I don't think he was talking about his brother, he was talking about himself. It eventually came out about his partying.

"I tried to tell Dennis [Rappaport] that Cooney would not be able to get to Michael Spinks. [Michael] would be able to elude him, and when he hit Cooney, he would hurt him. If you could avoid the left hand, Cooney was easy to get to. I thought Michael would eventually knock him out."

It turned out the public didn't care. Nobody was salivating over a match between a hungover Cooney and a gentle lineal champion. Hundreds of venues showing the fight via closed-circuit hookup were starved for business. The managers of one such venue, Joe Louis Arena in Detroit, pulled out of their contract when they sold only sixteen tickets. Even theaters that pulled the race card (against the wishes of Butch Lewis) weren't able to build a gate.

In the *Los Angeles Times,* Richard Hoffer gave his view as to why the Cooney fight wasn't the draw that the promoters thought it would be. "[They] misjudged badly," Hoffer wrote. "Cooney's mysterious appeal, that of a white puncher, inspired a gate of more than $30 million for his challenge of Holmes in 1982. As he remains white and a puncher—as an 86-second destruction of Eddie Gregg last year reminded us—it was thought that his appeal was intact. Promoter Butch Lewis reports that a closed-circuit distributor in the South has a promotional tape that advises fans to 'be there for the pride of their race.' But nothing sells Cooney any more. Seven rounds in five years do not qualify even a white heavyweight with a left hook for contention."

Despite lagging closed-circuit sales, all 16,000 seats in Convention Hall were filled on fight night. Mike Tyson sat ringside. So did Sugar Ray Leonard, Evander Holyfield, and Jersey Joe Walcott. First-round NFL draft pick Vinny Testaverde was on hand, as was *Miami Vice* star Don Johnson and celebrated jockey Angel Cordero Jr.

Ring announcer Ed Darien introduced the challenger as "'Gentleman' Gerry Cooney" and Michael as "the heavyweight champion of the world."

Michael came out swinging. Rather than run from the towering Cooney, he lunged at him with left jabs, overhand rights, and short left hooks—twice backing up the 238-pound behemoth. Cooney landed his own shots, though, and the momentum swung back and forth throughout the first two rounds.

Frank Lotierzo, Michael's former sparring partner, sat ringside. What he saw didn't surprise him. "I went to watch Cooney work out at Caesars," he recalls. "I see how he's training and I tell [Cooney's trainer] Victor Valle that Gerry is reaching with his jab. 'Tell Gerry after he jabs to hook off his jab, that will get him closer. Michael will bring his hands down and Gerry can step in and come through with his finishing punches.' Victor Valle looked at me, like, 'Who is this guy?' Well, in the first round, by accident, Cooney throws a jab and a left hook and he misses Michael by an inch. If he were to hit Michael with that left hook, he would've put him in the ocean. But the left hook went right by Michael's face and [Cooney] never did it again."

Cooney didn't connect with that hook, but in the second round he accidentally butted Michael's head, cutting the brow over his right eye. By the third round the cut was obviously a factor. Cooney took control of the fight in the latter half of the third and kept it throughout the fourth. After the round the fight was even on the judges' cards. Harold Lederman had Cooney up 39–37, John Stewart had Michael up 39–37, and Tom Kaczmarek had the fight even. But things were trending in Cooney's direction.

Newsday's Wallace Matthews recalls, "Michael was cut early in the fight, and I remember Leon was in the corner. He was down on his knees and he was crying as he was watching the fight because he thought his brother was going to get beat. And I remember seeing him pounding the ring steps with his fists because Michael was a bloody mess."

Rock Newman was in the Spinks camp and remembers how the blood woke Michael up. "Our cut man, Percy Richardson, instead of being the cool, calm, collected cut man that keeps the fighter calm, looked at [Michael's] eye and screamed, 'Cut! Oh my god!'" says Newman. "Michael, sitting on the stool, got so goddamn amped up that he went out and fought like a wild man the next round."

In that next round—the fifth—Michael threw combinations that were more easily measured by the knockdown than by the punch. Cooney barely threw a punch in return.

Rat-a-tat-a-tat-a-tat, down.

Referee Frank Cappuccino gave Cooney a standing eight count; then Cooney, still dazed, walked back into the hailstorm.

Rat-a-tat-a-tat-a-tat, down.

Cooney took a second standing eight and again came back for more. Michael unleashed yet another assault, showing no sign of tiring. This time Cappuccino didn't wait for the knockdown. The fight was over.

"When Cooney was down, his eyes are right in my eyes," Cappuccino recalls. "I'm thinking he's saying to himself, 'Goddamn, when the hell's he gonna stop this fight?' He kept staring at me. Eyeball to eyeball."

Mackie Shilstone gives himself some credit for the machine-gun outbursts of Michael's fists. "We had trained for Cooney using surgical tubing," he says, "and we did it on a bike because Michael's knees were bothering him. We would only run three days a week and I had him punching [while] on a bike, hundreds of punches against surgical tubing. I said, 'This is gonna come back and be the victory.' Michael hit Gerry Cooney, I'll never forget it, eighty-three punches in two minutes and thirty-seven seconds. Had the referee not stopped that onslaught, Michael would have kept punching him, because we'd trained to 175 punches in three minutes. He just killed him. Punched him into submission."

Michael explained at the postfight press conference, "I had been training to fight aggressively. That's the way we wanted to fight. We wanted to back him up. They say he punched so hard, but he had to hit me. He was confusing for a while, but I saw how to fight Gerry. I saw exactly where he was coming from. I saw everything. I went in with the strategy to be there and not be there. I planned to never be on the ropes. That's where he wanted me to be."

Cooney has a list of excuses as long as his reach. "I was worn out," he says. "The fight was on, the fight was off. I never believed the fight was gonna happen. I had no motivation. I wasn't taking care of myself. I shouldn't have been in the ring that night. I was drinking every day. He got me at a bad time in my life. It was the most regretful fight I ever had.

"[Michael] didn't belong in the ring with me. He didn't belong in the ring with a heavyweight. Michael was a very good light-heavyweight, not a heavyweight. If he fought me on any healthy day of my career, I'd knock him out easily. That's the truth. If I'm in shape when I go into that fight, he ain't gonna last. I'm gonna catch him."

Wallace Matthews recalls, "Cooney's first reaction [after signing to fight Michael] was to call a friend and say, 'I'm fighting for the light-heavyweight title.' He thought it was a joke. He thought he couldn't possibly lose to this little guy. And [after the fight] he was making all kinds of excuses. He couldn't get his wind. It was all kinds of bullshit: 'I never got loose.' The typical things that losers say after a fight."

Kevin P. Porter, Cooney's sparring partner, writes off the excuses as meaningless. "Even if Cooney was in great, great shape, nope, he [wouldn't have won]," Porter says. "Michael had a lot of arsenal—that overhand right and a couple of hooks. Michael can punch. He's in tremendous shape and he can punch."

Harold Lederman, one of the official judges that night, disagrees. "Gerry wasn't Gerry in that fight. Something was wrong. There were rumors about alcohol. If Cooney was in his prime, there's no doubt he would have knocked out Michael. I will back that 'til the day I die. He had a huge left hook and if he was sharp, if he was really on his game, he would have flattened Michael. There's no doubt about it."

Jim Lampley called the fight and now sees it as a defining event in Michael's career. "I drank all of the Kool-Aid regarding Cooney's size," he says. "It was not my perspective going into the fight that Michael could jump inside, beat Gerry to the punch as quickly and aggressively as he did, round after round, and pummel him the way that he did. I was stunned by his performance. Michael was a much better fighter than I thought he was, and he was a much better fighter than Gerry Cooney. At that point Gerry didn't have the sheer physical and emotional presence to compete with Michael Spinks. I way underestimated what Michael Spinks was.

"There isn't any one distinctive thing about him as a fighter. They used to print 'Spinks Jinx' because it was attention getting, and yeah, he had a sneaky right hand, but it wasn't an eye-catching dominating weapon like Joe Frazier's left hook. And so at the end of the day, if you're gonna win forty or fifty some-odd fights in a modern boxing career, there are going to be a few nights that stick out where you were sensational, you were dominant, and you were as good as you could be, and that's Spinks in the Cooney fight."

As far as Michael was concerned, the timing couldn't have been better. He'd just shown the skeptics that he could take a big man with a huge punch and topple him—and he could do it with pizzazz. So six weeks later, on August 1, 1986, when Tyson took a twelve-round decision from Tony Tucker to become the undisputed heavyweight champion, boxing fans wanted to know: Was Mike Tyson really the undisputed champ if he hadn't beaten Michael Spinks, the lineal champion?

The WBA, WBC, and IBF all said yes.

Butch Lewis and Michael Spinks disagreed.

15

By the late 1980s no legitimate promoters would touch Leon. The few small-timers that were hanging around plastered his name wherever they could, hoping to turn a quick buck. They had Leon hopping the globe, squaring off with no-name opponents in far-flung venues for two-bit pay. Boxing insiders shook their heads, wondering how much lower the ex-champ could fall. They found out when he landed in the New Japan Pro Wrestling ring, sleepwalking through mixed matches with the likes of Tarzan Goto and Antonio Inoki (the same Inoki that nearly destroyed Ali's legs in 1976). Leon's boredom was so contagious—and the matches so obviously staged—that even the rabid fans who had paid top dollar to see the bouts left the arenas with the same vacant look in their eyes.

In the two years following Leon's loss to Dwight Qawi and his unceremonious dismissal from the Kronk gym, Leon fought nine boxing matches. He lost seven.

Rocky Sekorski knocked him out in Minnesota. Jose Ribalta knocked him out in the first round in Florida. Leon managed to squeak by Jeff Jordan with a split decision in Japan, but he got knocked out by Angelo Musone in Italy and then could only muster up a draw against Jim Ashard in Oregon. Terry Mims outpointed him in Ohio, as did Ladislao Mijangos in Texas and Randall "Tex" Cobb in Tennessee. Tony Morrison flattened him in thirty-three seconds in Connecticut.

The Morrison debacle, which took place on May 30, 1988, was all the Connecticut Athletic Commission needed to clamp an immediate thirty-day suspension on Leon. The head of the commission, John Burns, said Leon would be required to undergo a physical if he ever wanted to fight in Connecticut again. Burns also said he'd be notifying other state commissions of the suspension, implying that those states should consider a similar ban.

Two weeks later an obscure and highly suspect matchmaker named Dickie Hohn set up a kickboxing-karate match between Leon and "Bad" Brad Hefton at Le Moyne College in Syracuse, New York. The fight would be legit and Leon would make $15,000. Reporters got wind of the mismatch and exposed it to the public. It didn't take a martial arts expert to realize that Leon's cornermen would be doubling as pallbearers.

Jeff Gordon of the *St. Louis Post-Dispatch* wrote, "Full-contact karate is cable TV's answer to dogfighting. It's not for the squeamish. Along with conventional jabs and hooks, jaw-crushing roundhouse and side kicks are staples of this blood sport. . . . Pitting Leon against Hefton would be like matching a Frito-fed schnauzer against a meanly bred pit bull. Defeat would be swift and final."

Ferdie Pacheco was quoted as saying, "It's almost to the point where they should be arrested for contributing to manslaughter. What do they want to do? Put Leon on a slab?"

In the end the Hefton fight never materialized, and neither did Leon's paycheck. Unfortunately, the promoters kept knocking. And Leon kept answering.

Butch Lewis knew money when he smelled it. Two undefeated heavyweight champions squaring off in the ring. It hadn't happened on this scale since 1971, when Ali met Frazier in "The Fight of the

Century" at Madison Square Garden. Michael Spinks vs. Mike Tyson would be a box-office extravaganza.

Michael had chopped down the great white oak, Gerry Cooney, and the stage was set for him to take on the toughest man on the planet.

Meanwhile, the toughest man on the planet was knocking down wannabe after wannabe. After beating Tony Tucker for the IBF belt, Tyson kayoed Tyrell Biggs in seven and then temporarily re-retired the twice-unretired Larry Holmes in four. America had wanted a mythic champion, and Tyson was a perfect fit for the role.

Yet Tyson insists he always had respect for the lineal titleholder. "I don't care what anybody says. Spinks was the champ. I was [just] the alphabet champion. You gotta beat the man that beat the man that beat the man. That's just the history of boxing. I don't care how many organizations they make. That's the rule. You can't lose the title unless you lose it in the ring."

Boxing purists agreed, but the public would need some convincing. Tyson's face was splashed across newspapers and magazines; it filled America's television screens and radio airwaves. Boxing fans weren't only tracking Tyson's ring career—they were also following his much-publicized rocky marriage to TV actress Robin Givens, which was becoming more tumultuous by the minute. The name Spinks hadn't been this irrelevant since Leon and Michael were boxing out of the DeSoto.

To make the fight happen, Lewis would have to cross a number of bridges he'd burned when pulling Michael out of the HBO tournament. He figured he could patch things up with HBO—its executives would surely be interested in a spectacle of this size—so he started talking with Tyson's co-managers, Jim Jacobs and Bill Cayton. Jacobs handled the boxing decisions, Cayton the financial ones.

The pedigrees and deal-making styles of the negotiators, Rock Newman remembers, were worlds apart. "You had Butch, who was an absolute maniac madman, and he's negotiating against Jacobs and Cayton, who fancied themselves these sophisticated, cerebral businesspeople," Newman says. "They truly looked down their noses at Butch. Cayton was just utterly condescending. Both Cayton and Jacobs were very deliberate in their speech, in their enunciation and articulation. They'd use a [fancy] word every now and then and Butch would say [in a high-pitched voice], 'Motherfucker, what the fuck does that mean? What the fuck is he talkin' about?' I remember Cayton saying, 'If nothing comes out of this, I will have learned how to say *motherfucker.*'"

Ill feelings were not limited to one side of the table. Wallace Matthews of *Newsday* quoted Lewis as saying that Cayton and Jacobs should be "generous with us instead of trying to play the great white fathers and dictating to us."

Matthews now says, "That was Butch's nice quote about them. Behind the scenes he said, 'They're a couple of cold-blooded, reptilian motherfuckers.' He especially hated Cayton. God, did he hate him."

Discussions began in earnest in January 1988. Lewis sat across from the two negotiators he so despised, working to get their offer into a range he found acceptable.

At one point Cayton looked at his watch. "It's 11:42," he said. "Our final offer is five million dollars. You have three minutes to accept this offer or the fight won't take place within the next twelve months. More importantly, we won't talk for the next twelve months."

Lewis looked at his own watch. "So let me understand. If I don't take this offer by 11:45, which I'm not going to do, we can't talk again until 11:45 on this day one year from now?"

Cayton looked back at his watch. "That is correct."

Rock Newman and the rest of Lewis's staff were praying Lewis would put aside his pride and make the deal.

"Internally, we all were urging Butch, 'Make this fuckin' deal, man,'" Newman says. "But he put his balls up on the goddamn table and steadfastly refused."

Once again the fight was as good as dead, but Lewis continued pounding on its chest. He figured that if he could land Ali back in 1976, he could revive this fight now—he just had to figure out how. He found his answer when he took the negotiations out of the boardroom and onto his own turf: the street.

"Butch called us together and said, 'We gotta go guerilla,'" recalls Newman. "Going guerilla involved paying somebody in the Tyson camp to give us Tyson's schedule—whether he was going to a basketball game, whether he was going to a bordello. Wherever [Tyson] was, we always knew. He couldn't step out of a car, he couldn't turn around, he couldn't go to a game, he couldn't go to a club, he couldn't go to a party where we didn't have somebody saying, 'You know, you a bitch, man, you scared of Michael Spinks.' [Sometimes] we would send females. More than once Tyson was at a club and a female would ease up to him and say, 'You're acting like a bitch not fighting Michael.' He was like, 'No, *you* the bitch.' It was down and dirty, man. I'd be getting calls [from the mole] at two, three o'clock in the morning. I'm telling you, it was clandestine shit. [We paid that guy] somewhere around $75,000."

In *Bad Intentions: The Mike Tyson Story*, author Peter Heller wrote, "During one encounter in Los Angeles, Tyson almost fought it out with a guy who wouldn't let him off the hook about not fighting Spinks. Coincidentally, Butch Lewis was in the same restaurant at the time. As more and more people asked [Tyson] why he was avoiding Spinks, Tyson grew madder and madder. Was all this orchestrated by Butch Lewis? When asked, Lewis just laughed and said, 'No comment.'"

Michael had also campaigned for the fight. Lewis had told him that a matchup with Tyson would be a great way to cap off his career in terms of both glory and money, so Michael had gone on *Late Night with David Letterman* in June 1987, a week after the Cooney fight. A white bandage above his right eye marked the site of Cooney's headbutt.

Letterman asked Michael which boxing organization he represented.

"I represent T.H.E."

"T.H.E.?"

"Yeah. *The* heavyweight champion. That's my title."

After a hearty laugh from the studio audience, Michael went on to say that he wanted to fight Tyson because the public wanted it.

"It makes good business sense to take on Tyson," he said. "And it brings me one step closer to having my career come to an end."

Letterman treated the comment as a straight line, getting a laugh by suggesting that Tyson's punching power might terminate Michael's career on the spot. Nonetheless, it was clear that Michael was looking to wrap up his life in the ring. He'd been a reluctant warrior since signing on with Lewis back in the projects. After thirty-one professional fights, he didn't want to push his luck. He'd seen what had happened to Joe Louis's mental health, Muhammad Ali's motor skills, and Leon's wallet. He wasn't about to follow in their footsteps.

Boyhood friend James Caldwell says, "We had talked years before and [Michael] was mentioning that he didn't want to stay in the game so long that he ended up in a bad position down the road mentally or physically."

Steffen Tangstad remembers, "After [our] fight Michael came to Norway and told me that he'd been in the game for so long he was looking for a way to get out of the business and 'ride out into the sunset like a lonely cowboy.'"

Michael's eagerness to leave the sport was tempered only by an intense fear of going broke. He had seen plenty of poverty at Pruitt-Igoe. According to Rock Newman, Michael had vowed to Lewis he'd never blow his money and had developed a nearly pathological fear of spending it.

"Butch had a nickname for Michael," says Newman. "He called him 'Slim' and 'Skimmer.' That had something to do with Michael being so tight [with money]. Butch controlled everything. I don't know if Michael ever wrote a check in his life.

"We were on a long promo tour for the Cooney fight. We went from Boston to New York to D.C. to Miami [all in the same day] and I didn't eat the entire day. I think I grabbed a couple of grapes in D.C. Michael and I got in the limo in Miami. And Michael had a long black coat on and he's sitting in the limo eating a cookie. I saw inside the pocket on that big-ass coat he had a big bag of Oreo cookies. So I said, 'Mike, I'm starving, gimme some of those cookies.' He went in that bag and he pulled out *one cookie*."

Childhood friend Jesse Davison shares similar stories. "I remember a time Michael came home and his mama asked him for some money and he started fussin'. I said, 'Michael, that's your mama, you're supposed to help her pay the gas bill, the electric bill. Let her have some money.' He used to hide his money in a pouch [points to the inside of his pant leg]. It had a key on it. He'd say, 'Turn your head, Jesse,' and then he'd open his wallet. He'd get out three or four hundred dollars and hand it to me. 'Here, Jesse, take my mama to the store.'"

There's no doubt the Tyson fight would fill Michael's pouch and then some, but Tyson's co-manager Jim Jacobs still wasn't onboard. He'd been dragging out the negotiations purposely, figuring that the delay would help lessen Lewis's financial demands. But the fifty-eight-year-old Jacobs, who'd suffered from leukemia for many years, suddenly developed pneumonia and passed away at Mount Sinai Hospital in New York.

Tyson's cornerman Steve Lott remembers how Jacobs's death broke the stalemate. "The unforeseen happened. Jim [Jacobs] died," Lott says. "Shelly Finkel got involved and was kind of putting the fight together behind Bill Cayton's back. And because Shelly was handling closed circuit around the country, he wanted the fight made, so he offered Butch a lot of money. Then he went to [Tyson] and said the fight can be made and [Tyson] said, 'Bill, I want the fight.' So Bill had to make the fight."

With the bout on, Butch Lewis looked as prescient as Nostradamus. Michael, who was originally slated to fight Tyson in the HBO tournament for somewhere in the neighborhood of two million dollars, would now make $13.5 million. After taxes and expenses, he'd pocket a little less than half that amount. Add that to the cash he'd taken home against Cooney, and he'd be able to take his ride into the sunset. And he had Butch Lewis to thank.

The hype for the Spinks-Tyson fight, which was promoted under the banner "Once and for All," spilled out of America's newspapers and cable boxes. Real estate mogul Donald Trump, host of the Atlantic City spectacular, predicted the live gate alone would bring in $12.3 million, which would make it the largest in boxing history. Sixteen hundred U.S. venues signed on for the closed-circuit feed. Thirteen hundred passes went out to the press. If Trump was to be believed—and no one seemed to be disputing him—the fight was on its way to grossing more than one hundred million dollars.

With the bout growing closer, both training camps moved their headquarters from the Catskills to Atlantic City. As reporters searched for compelling prefight stories, the two Mikes could not have displayed more opposite personalities.

Mike Tyson: "I'll break Spinks. I'll break them all. When I fight someone I want to break his will. I want to take his manhood. I want to rip out his heart and show it to him. People say that's primitive, that I'm an animal. But then they pay five hundred dollars to see it. . . . I'm a warrior. . . . If I wasn't in boxing, I'd be breaking the law. That's my nature."

Jim Lampley: "A great deal of Tyson's persona in those days was constructed, was theatrical. The perception was larger than life. The way he bounced Tubbs off the canvas in Tokyo, the fact that a single punch caused Berbick to fall to the canvas three separate times. This was the highlight reel of [Tyson's] early knockouts. Obviously those people had extremely questionable credentials, but he was flying them through the air, knocking them for loops. There was a comic book quality about [Tyson]."

Michael was afraid of Tyson and had no qualms about saying so. "The fear is always there, especially at night," he told Earl Gustkey of the *Los Angeles Times*. "It's in the background. When I'm in bed at night, and the fight suddenly comes into my mind, my heart rate goes up and I can't sleep. I'll put the fight out of my mind, for a minute or two. Then it comes back. . . . Hey, I'm not talking just about Tyson . . . I go through this before every fight."

Author and boxing writer Thomas Hauser had gone to the kickoff press conference for Tyson-Spinks. "[The two fighters] walked out together," Hauser recalls. "Michael was sort of mock-crying, saying [in a high-pitched crying voice], 'I don't wanna go. I don't wanna go.' He was trying to make a joke out of it, but you could see that he had already come face to face with [Tyson], and

[Tyson] had given him that ugly look, and Mike was horrifically scary in those days."

On June 26, 1988, the night before the Spinks-Tyson showdown, ABC cleared airtime to carry the weigh-in live, marking the first time a weigh-in had been covered in such a fashion since Ali took on George Foreman in 1974. The event, held at Trump Plaza, was a dud. As Brian Schmitz reported in the *Orlando Sentinel*, the air inside Trump Plaza had so little electricity that "Don King's hair fell."

The lack of buzz had less to do with the public's expectations than it did with Michael's demeanor. He simply had no bravado. The best he could do was show up in an oversize white straw hat and raise his arms in victory in front of the standing-room-only crowd. But when he stepped on the scale wearing nothing but a pair of white slacks, he looked like a true heavyweight, and the scale agreed. It read 212¼ pounds.

Tyson, in shiny black trunks, was next. Between the glowering expression on his face and the bulging muscles rippling through his upper body, he had the look of a guy who wrestled steer in his spare time. The scale registered 218¼ pounds and his height was marked at five-eleven, although the naked eye said he'd had the benefit of a generous measuring tape.

The two fighters did not exchange so much as a glance. The tensest moment came when Robin Givens, who had gone public with a purported miscarriage two weeks earlier, showed up in a black leather dress and her own entourage.

Tyson made no statements regarding his private life, but before leaving he spoke briefly with reporters about the upcoming fight. His words reflected the old-school teachings of his trainer and mentor Cus D'Amato, who had taught him to unleash his inner rage in the ring.

"This is a hurt business," Tyson said. "When you see guys like Trump, Kennedy, and Rockefeller—bluebloods—when they come to a fight, regardless of what they may represent, they come to see someone get hurt, and my objective is to inflict as much punishment as possible."

Add to Tyson's "crazy killer" persona the fiasco that was his personal life. He spoke openly of how he'd become unglued since D'Amato died in 1985. Now his marriage was imploding. Multiple news stories hinted that Givens had taken control of Tyson's life. Word leaked out that she had tried to fire cornerman Steve Lott, and that she was in the process of replacing Bill Cayton with Don King.

"I had written a story, 'The Troubled Times of Mike Tyson,' or something, maybe a week before the Spinks fight," says *Newsday's* Wallace Matthews. "And this was a story where Robin Givens told me that Mike was beating her up. And I had several meetings with her and her mother, and spoke with her sister. And they all painted the same picture of Mike as violent and abusive and out of control. So I had all of his stuff on tape and I was trying to get in touch with Tyson to get a response, and at the time Mike wasn't talking to me. So I reached out to Jose Torres, who was close to Mike. And I said, 'Look, Jose, I gotta talk to Mike. It's really important. I've got something very damaging from his wife.' And I remember Jose saying, 'Ohh shit. Ohh shit.' So about ten minutes later, Tyson called me and denied [the accusations]. He just sounded horrible. And at the end of the conversation, he was in tears and he said to me, 'Listen, man, thanks, and I'm really sorry that we had to talk.' And as soon as I put down the phone, I said this guy is not in his right mind."

On the day of the fight, Monday, June 27, Tyson shut down. He refused all but one interview request, that of Newark *Star-Ledger* columnist Jerry Izenberg. *Washington Post* writer William Gildea and the *Star-Ledger's* boxing beat writer Chris Thorne went with

Izenberg to Tyson's hotel room. There, the champ was holed up with his trainer, Kevin Rooney.

Izenberg loosened up the tight-lipped Tyson as Gildea, Thorne, and Rooney looked on. "So, Mike, where do you run in the morning?"

"On the boardwalk," Tyson said. "It's flat."

"What do you think about when you're running?" Izenberg asked, steering the conversation toward boxing. "Do you think about how you want to fight Michael Spinks? About how you expect him to fight?"

"Oh, no," Tyson said. "Mostly I think about Cus. I think about Cus talking. His voice."

Izenberg knew virtually everybody in the boxing game, and D'Amato was no exception. He started imitating the trainer's high, whiney voice.

Tyson laughed. "Yeah, yeah," he said, his eyes twinkling. "We used to have fun. Now it's all about the money, the money, the money. Why did Cus have to die? Why did Jimmy [Jacobs] die on me?"

When telling the story now, Izenberg says, "This is a guy who's just been married, and his trainer, who's supposed to be the closest guy in the world to him, is standing next to him. And then he says to me, 'There's nobody in the world I can talk to. Nobody.'

"And he leans forward and he puts his head on my chest and he starts to cry. And he cried so hard that I had to go upstairs to my room and change my shirt. It made a helluva story 'cause the column I wrote [the next day] started, 'The heavyweight champion of the world cried yesterday.'"

Hours before the extravaganza, sports reporter and broadcaster Dick Schaap told the nearly ten million viewers of *ABC World News Tonight*, "It is a classic showdown. The most intriguing matchup of undefeated heavyweight kings since the first Ali-Frazier fight, and possibly the richest fight ever. Minimally Tyson will earn more than twenty million dollars, Spinks more than ten. And it is the taste of money that has in recent days inspired *Time, Life, Sports Illustrated,* and *People* to devote covers to Tyson, and to his bride Robin Givens, an actress educated at Sarah Lawrence, hardly the typical silent and stoic fighter's wife."

By 10:30 p.m. Convention Hall in Atlantic City was buzzing, as reporters, cameramen, and spectators waited for the fighters to make their entrances. But neither Spinks nor Tyson had come out of his dressing room. The HBO commentators first attributed the delay to a problem with the wraps on Tyson's hands, and then to a standoff between Spinks and Tyson (ostensibly caused by Spinks's insistence that he was the real champion and, as such, should enter the ring last). Had the public been privy to the actual goings-on, the 4:1 odds might have swung even more in Tyson's favor.

Tyson cornerman Steve Lott remembers the scene. "Butch Lewis came running into the locker room saying, 'No one was here to watch the hands being wrapped. And I demand that the hand wraps be taken off Mike Tyson and put back on.' At that point the commissioner, Larry Hazzard, was called from ringside. There was a big brouhaha between Butch Lewis and Larry Hazzard."

As New Jersey boxing commissioner, Hazzard was responsible for restoring order. "[Tyson] was getting pissed off," Hazzard recalls. "They were doing some construction in the back of the dressing room, and there was a wall that had sheetrock and [Tyson] put his fist right through the fuckin' sheetrock."

According to Tyson, "Butch Lewis was trying to antagonize me before the fight and that wasn't gonna work. He was saying to unwrap the gloves, saying that nobody was here from his side [when my hands were wrapped]. He was trying to get me upset, get me frustrated. I may have said some foul words. He fed my fire. I'm a street guy, he's a street guy, so we were talking street stuff back and forth. Yes, I did [punch a hole in the wall]."

Why did Butch Lewis do it? Why enrage Tyson? The answer wasn't in Tyson's dressing room. It was in Michael's.

Emanuel Steward had flown to Atlantic City to see the fight and went to check on Michael. "I went into his dressing room; they couldn't even get him to come out, he was so scared. He was a nervous wreck, really freaking out. Leon wouldn't have given a damn. Leon was a free spirit. [Michael] didn't have the personality to come out."

Not until 11:20 did Michael finally make his way to the ring, snaking through a celebrity-studded audience that included Norman Mailer, Jack Nicholson, Warren Beatty, Sean Penn, Madonna, and, of course, Donald Trump. The fighter gave a hesitant wave to the crowd, acknowledging his family and friends. He entered the ring in a gleaming white robe as Kenny Loggins and Michael McDonald sang "This Is It" through the PA speakers. Sweat glistened on his cheeks and forehead. He had the look of a rabbit that had just spotted a hunter's rifle.

Boxing writer Royce Feour says, "I never saw a fighter entering the ring, and standing in the ring, that looked as scared as Michael Spinks. Never. And I've covered fights since 1965. Never. [Michael] was petrified."

Three minutes later Tyson entered, naked except for black trunks, black shoes, and red gloves. He charged through the crowd with all the elegance of a military tank. The overhead speakers blared music that was so dark and industrial, it sounded as though the audio man had opened a microphone in a prison sweatshop.

Once both fighters were inside the ropes, ring announcer Michael Buffer introduced Muhammad Ali, dressed impeccably in a dark-gray suit, pink tie, and oversize eyeglasses. Ali, presumably, still loved the spotlight, but his face was locked into a frozen stare as he inched his way to the center of the ring. He waved to the crowd with a jerking right hand that seemed to be controlled by an amateur puppeteer. His mouth, which once operated in only one mode—fast-forward—now struggled to get out of pause. He leaned into Michael's ear with some barely audible last-minute instructions.

"Stick and move," he mumbled.

Butch Lewis stood nearby, wearing what was now his trademark "chocolate tuxedo": white pants, white jacket, white bowtie, no shirt.

Next, Buffer introduced the fighters, a ritual that lasted more than two minutes.

Eventually, the bell rang.

Tyson, who had been in constant motion, galloped to the center of the ring like a bronco released at a rodeo. He met up with Michael and, predictably, began to swing for the fences. Unpredictably, Michael went toe-to-toe with the human wrecking ball. At about the forty-second mark, he threw an overhand right that missed Tyson by inches. At the one-minute mark, he paid the price for leaving his bicycle at home: Tyson threw a left to his head and a right to his body, and Michael dropped to one knee. It was the first time he'd been down in his career, aside from Hazzard's missed call in the Qawi fight.

Michael popped right back up.

Referee Frank Cappuccino gave him a standing eight, holding his fingers in the air as he ticked off the count.

"Six, seven, eight." The diminutive Cappuccino looked up into Michael's eyes. "You all right, Mike?"

Michael nodded. "I'm all right."

But he was far from all right. He was being gunned down by a pair of cannons wrapped in red boxing gloves.

He banged his fists together and marched back to the front line—fear seemingly replaced by courage. Two seconds later a Tyson right uppercut slammed him in the jaw.

Michael fell flat on his back. His head came to rest under the bottom rope. All he could do was stare blankly up at the klieg lights.

Jim Lampley announcing the fight. "And he's down again and in serious trouble. A right hand right on the chin."

Cappuccino, standing over Michael: "Three, four . . ."

Michael gamely tried to get up—he made it to one knee by the count of nine—but toppled back down between the bottom two ropes. When Cappuccino reached "ten," Michael's body was halfway out of the ring.

"He's not going to make it!" shouted HBO's Larry Merchant. "It's all over."

In less time than it took to buy a bucket of popcorn, Michael had slid from the peak of the mountain into Tyson's scrapheap.

"The fact that he went down and had never been down before was devastating to me," longtime friend James Caldwell says. "We were yelling from our seats, 'Box him! Box him!' Anything but stand in front of him. That was the killing point."

New York Times columnist Dave Anderson recalls, "Spinks was moving, boxing, dancing away from Tyson and I remember he kind of stopped and planted himself and I said, 'Oh my god.' I don't know anybody in those years who stood toe-to-toe with Tyson and lived to say it."

The Newark *Star-Ledger*'s Jerry Izenberg saw a ring strategist abandoning all strategy. "When Spinks went down the first time, he knew he was hurt. But Spinks is a fighter, he knows he's got two minutes to finish the round," Izenberg says. "He knows what he's supposed to do and he knows what he's not supposed to do. And what did he do? He did what he was not supposed to do. He should've grabbed Tyson and he should've danced like it was a bump and grind. He didn't get his head back. He didn't get his legs back. His thought process was totally paralyzed. You have to remember, he was in a place he had never been in his entire life. Michael absolutely froze in that fight. He was a brilliant tactician. He understood boxing. He understood what he could and couldn't do. And he forgot it all the night he fought Tyson."

Based on the way Tyson came charging out, referee Frank Cappucino had figured the fight wouldn't last two rounds. "I thought [Michael] would try to stay away from him, but I think he was too hesitant to try to get [Tyson] off his game. And that's why he got careless."

Michael's trainer Eddie Futch had said to Stan Hochman of the *Philadelphia Daily News,* "I told him, 'Go out and box this guy and move, let him wind down for five or six rounds and then we'll go after him.' I was as surprised as anyone in the house when he went out there and took him on like he did."

According to Rock Newman, the confusion had boiled down to two opposing plans. "There was a bone of contention that lasted to the end between Eddie [Futch] and Butch [Lewis]. Eddie thought Tyson was a bigger version of Qawi, a quicker version of Qawi, and a more powerful version of Qawi. And he had taught Michael to run, run, run. Eddie's strategy was to replicate the Qawi fight. Move, turn, dance, move, dance. In rounds one through four, Tyson was a truly great fighter. In five through eight, he became more ordinary, and after that he was subpar. So Eddie told Michael, 'Take him out in deep water and then we can drown him.' But Butch incessantly told Michael, 'Yeah, that's cool, but you gotta hit that motherfucker, hit 'im with the right hand like you did to Qawi in the first round. You gotta pop that motherfucker and get some respect.' And Eddie was always like, 'Take no early chances. Make Tyson chase you.'

"Well, Michael went out and tried to throw the big one and he got knocked out. And Eddie was, oh my god, he was so incredibly livid."

Michael defended his strategy to Dave Anderson of the *Times*. "I didn't think it was necessary to avoid getting hit," he said. "The boxer comes in and tries to nail you with a good right hand. I thought I'd exchange. Instead, he hit me with an uppercut. I just tried to do what I knew I had to do, and that was fight. Not that I stood toe-to-toe with him, but I tried to take the shot and I came up short."

The fight lasted all of ninety-one seconds, making it the fourth-quickest heavyweight title fight in history. (The fastest took place on April 6, 1900, when Jim Jeffries knocked out Jack Finnegan in fifty-five seconds.) In the end the ringside spectators had spent fifteen hundred bucks to see Tyson throw eight punches.

Some boxing fans questioned whether Michael could have gotten up and continued fighting. Perhaps they expected too much out of a man who'd been outrunning the odds for thirty-one years.

Steve Lott says, "When [Michael] went down it's not like he looked around and made a decision to stay down. His eyes were in a different country."

"I'm looking at his eyes," Frank Cappuccino recalls. "His eyes are way back in his head. I said, this guy is hurt."

Tyson's trainer Kevin Rooney remembers, "Boom, right uppercut. Spinks came right into it. Once he went down I knew the fight was over."

Former New Jersey Boxing Commissioner Larry Hazzard says, "The referee was counting over him, and when he got to, like, six and seven, Michael was still on his rear. I've given enough counts in my day to know that he's not going to make this one. I said, 'Un-fucking-believable.'"

There was no longer any question as to who owned the undisputed heavyweight title. Mike Tyson was, by all rights, king of the world.

And Michael Spinks, the kid from Pruitt-Igoe who'd lived the mythic journey to the far side of the rainbow, was now the former light-heavyweight champion and former heavyweight champion of the world.

Once his head cleared and he'd risen from the canvas, he walked down those three terrifying steps leading up to the ring and looked for the exit sign.

16

ON JULY 27, 1988, TWENTY-NINE DAYS AFTER SUFFERING THE ONLY loss of his career, Michael stood inside Tavern on the Green, New York's glitzy Central Park landmark, as waiters in sea-green uniforms served seafood and poured champagne. He was there to do what few other professional boxers had done: pull the plug on his career before it pulled the plug on him. He credited Butch Lewis with the decision, saying he'd always left his career in his promoter's hands.

"Twelve years is quite a while to be getting swung at and having to duck punches," Michael said to a gathering that included Lewis, Joe Frazier, and a roomful of boxing insiders and sportswriters. "It's been a tough twelve years, but it's been fun. I'm a happy young man today."

Who could blame him? He'd gone off to war and come back physically and mentally sound. And though he didn't understand Wall Street, he understood Butch Lewis, who managed his money and paid his bills, right down to doling out his spending allowances. Lewis told Michael he'd been investing his money, including the Tyson windfall, into conservative zero-coupon bonds. He said the stock market crash that had shaken the country eight months before the Tyson fight would have little effect on Michael's retirement. Improbable as it may have seemed back at Prutt-Igoe, the thirty-two-year-old would never have to work another day in his life.

During his retirement speech, Michael looked at Lewis and said, "I can't thank you and kiss you enough for all the wonderful things."

He wept when he said it. So did Lewis.

"There was no other team like us in boxing, ever," Lewis said. "Me and Slim, we're like family."

Lewis also made a point of injecting himself into Michael's greatest achievements—even ones that occurred before the two had met.

"We did it our way," he said. "We made history in Montreal when we won the gold medal. We became the first brother team to win gold medals and part of the first brother team to win world championships. We went on to be the first light-heavyweight to dethrone a heavyweight champion. Whatever it took to get the job done, we did it."

Michael's list of accomplishments was impressive, to say the least. He'd also been a dignified champion and a gentleman from start to finish. Yet, aside from the friends and newspapermen gathered at the Upper West Side restaurant, America had moved on. It had cast Michael aside the instant he'd walked into Tyson's whistling right uppercut. In the end Michael's retirement commanded about as much newspaper ink as the same-day passing of Frank Zamboni, the inventor of the ice-cleaning machine.

"Michael Spinks got a bad break in life," Mike Tyson now says. "He has legendary victories under his belt, but his legacy is being beaten by me in ninety-one seconds. That's not fair at all. He beat Larry Holmes twice, he beat Eddie Mustafa Muhammad, and he beat Qawi. He just got a bad break."

Top Rank promoter Bob Arum limits Michael's legacy to the light-heavyweight ranks. "Michael was heavyweight champion for a cup of coffee," he says, "and that all got blown away with the devastating knockout loss to Tyson. So nobody considered Michael a real heavyweight. He was a great light-heavyweight, he was a terrific fighter, a dedicated fighter—he knew how to fight—but nobody looked at Michael as a heavyweight."

Gerald Early, professor and author of *The Culture of Bruising*, says, "The public wasn't as clued in to the light-heavyweight division as they were to the heavyweight division. People don't pay much attention to it. The light-heavyweights are kind of like the Korean War, wherein the Vietnam War and World War II get all the attention, and nobody knows anything about the Korean War. I thought Michael was the greatest light-heavyweight champion of all time."

Carlo Rotella, author of *Cut Time: An Education at the Fights*, sympathizes with the plight of a light-heavyweight tactician expected to carry the aura of invincibility that comes with being heavyweight champion. "I don't know how you succeed in that climate, as a light-heavyweight champion who moves up to heavyweight, who isn't going to be knocking people's blocks off, who's not going to be physically terrifying. That's not the kind of thing people are incredibly impressed by. It's kind of lost on the lay fan."

In Tyson's view Michael didn't spend enough time creating a marketable persona. "He's a very dignified person, very kind person, very respectful person," Tyson says. "We don't think much about those guys in this business. . . . People want a guy with charismatic flair who can give 'em great excitement."

Douglas Hartmann, author of *Race, Culture and the Revolt of the Black Athlete*, agrees that Michael's personality wasn't the type to grab headlines. "Michael got lost in history," he says. "He didn't occupy our larger imaginations. He didn't want to have any kind of persona. . . . He didn't let himself be the all-American boy that he could have been, given his Olympic history and the story that you could have told around him."

Michael's ride in the ring was over. He had accomplished far more than he had set out to do. As he drove home to the quiet comfort of Greenville, Delaware, he wondered what lay ahead. One thing was certain: The days of Pruitt-Igoe were behind him. He had been one of the lucky ones. He had escaped and would never again be penniless.

Unfortunately, the same could not be said of Leon.

Leon hadn't made it to Michael's retirement luncheon, but the two brothers had been together five days earlier, on July 22, when Leon married his longtime girlfriend Betty Green. Michael paid for half the wedding, splitting it with Betty, and flew to Detroit for the celebration.

The newly christened Mr. and Mrs. Leon Spinks were making ends meet in a spare three-bedroom brick house in Franklin Park, which lay three miles south and a couple of socioeconomic rungs below Leon's former neighborhood of Rosedale Park. Cloned houses rimmed the streets, each fronted by a square patch of grass; the neighborhood conjured up images of little plastic houses on a Monopoly board. Leon's business manager, Al Low, struggled to impart to his client some basic financial horse sense, but Leon's portfolio failed to grow beyond his two main accounts: the few dollars in his pocket and the spare change he had sitting on the bar.

For three days the marriage went relatively smoothly. On the fourth day Leon was served with papers claiming he and his ex-wife Nova owed $187,000 in back taxes. Things went downhill from there: Betty would be in and out of her job on the assembly line at General Motors, and Leon would rarely be employed for more than a week or two at a time. He would spend most days in front of either a TV or a bar. He still made occasional headlines by smashing up cars—usually Betty's—but he had long since moved off the front page. By now, newspaper copy about the onetime heavyweight champion had grown shorter, the incidents more pathetic, his name less and less relevant.

Having vowed yet again to rebuild his life and his image, Leon took to spending Sunday mornings at church with Low, an active member of the Baptist church. Attending mass at various congregations in and around Detroit, Leon would penitently walk up to the front of the faithful and dedicate himself to God. But by the time the pews had emptied, Leon was back to being Leon.

Low scratched together whatever work he could find for his client. He had him signing autographs, competing in kickboxing events, and taking another turn at wrestling. At one match Low choreographed a scenario that culminated in Betty's getting in the ring and angrily swinging her purse around. The staged conflict wasn't all that far from the truth.

"I had many two- and three-o'clock-in-the-morning calls," Low remembers, "[usually] the result of partying and [heavy] drinking. Leon and Betty would drink pretty good. I'd get a call from Betty, 'Leon's doing this.' Then from Leon, 'Betty's trying to run me over with the car.' [One] night I went over. Leon was up on the porch and Betty had driven the car up onto the lawn. She was asleep and Leon was passed out."

Betty blamed the stormy marriage, her drained bank account, and her wrecked cars on Leon—particularly on his drinking, drugging, and philandering. For his part, Leon promised Betty she'd never see him drunk again, and in his defense, he spoke the near truth—because he would disappear for months. He'd go on prolonged binges, seen not by Betty but by his old St. Louis friends when he'd pop up in the bars and on the street corners he used to frequent. Every so often he'd pay a visit to his father, who was still in St. Louis and now dying of cancer. Although the two never reconciled, Leon had buried his anger in the rubble of Pruitt-Igoe.

Perhaps Leon had come to understand his father. He himself barely knew his own sons, Leon and Darrell, and had never met

Cory. All three of his boys had taken up boxing—lured into the ring by the famous Spinks name. Their mother, Zadie Mae, had seen what Leon and Michael had accomplished between the ropes and encouraged her sons to join the gym, hoping they too could punch their way to riches. On their journey into the ring, the boys had come under the wing of Charles Hamm, the plumber who had once trained Leon and Michael, and who still trained neighborhood kids out of his Northside Bombers Boxing Club. The storefront gym on West Florissant Avenue was so ramshackle it lacked a front door and indoor plumbing. But that didn't bother the kids who frequented it. The place may have been short on amenities, but it did have the kindhearted Hamm, who lived with his wife Jeridean one flight up from the gym. Hamm had turned many of his novices into competent boxers, and if the local legend is true, developed more than a handful of young plumbers in the process. He could still be found cruising north St. Louis in a rusted van, doling out boxing and life skills to the teenagers who had the smarts to listen.

For the younger generation of Spinkses—Leon, Darrell, and Cory—Hamm had stepped into the shadow their father had left behind.

"You would think they were my kids, I was around them so much," Hamm says. "I was a father figure to them, so they didn't miss having a father too much."

Darrell Spinks says, "Mr. Hamm was a coach-slash-father to me, Cory, and my brother Leon. He took care of me. I would walk around with busted shoes; he would buy me shoes. He would do everything. For a while Mr. Hamm didn't even know that Leon Spinks was our daddy 'cause we never did tell him. When he found out, he called my father and talked to him. My dad didn't know we was boxing."

Cory also found a substitute father in Hamm. "Charles Hamm did so much for me. I love him to death," he says. "I looked up to him as being a dad. He's a terrific man."

In the mid-1980s, upon Betty's urging, Leon invited his three sons to Detroit for the summer. Zadie Mae agreed to let the two older boys go, but said that Cory, who wasn't yet ten, was too young.

"It was supposed to be two months but it ended up being one month," Darrell remembers. "My brother Leon didn't talk to my father. He stayed out of his way. He was angry. He say, 'We stay in the ghetto and we got a rich father.' My brother never did forgive him."

At one point during the visit, the two Leons went into the backyard for an impromptu sparring session and the young Leon held his own against the ex-champ. Later that day the two got into it when the youngster asked his father for money for gym shoes. The argument spilled onto the windowed front porch.

"The next thing, I heard the glass break," Betty recalls. "I jumped up and ran to the porch to see what was going on. Big Leon had pushed Little Leon in the chest, and he fell against the glass. Big Leon started saying, 'Don't let that sparring session go to your head thinking you can whip my ass.'"

The wedge between the two Leons was deeper than ever.

⌐•—•¬

What makes Leon's case especially frustrating is that he blew opportunity after opportunity. There was never a shortage of people willing to help him get back on his feet.

"[Managing Leon] sometimes felt more like a babysitting job than it did anything else," Al Low explains. "It was a daunting task, but it was one that you really wanted to do 'cause you wanted to help him so much. Leon was a good guy with such a good heart.

"He wanted to please people and he wanted people to love him. I remember we were in Vegas one time and he handed the fellow who took us up in the elevator a hundred dollar bill. So I said, 'Lee, why did you give him a hundred dollar bill for taking us up?' He said, 'Oh, I just wanted him to remember me and think good of me.' I said, 'Well, Lee, he knows that you were the heavyweight champion of the world. He's not going to forget that.'

"He went through a lot of money in a very short time. He was just handing it out to entourages, and for parties. But he would just smile and go on. It just didn't make any difference how much he lost as long as he was OK tonight. If he had enough money in his pocket for that evening's activity, then life was good and everything was fine."

Boxing manager Jackie Kallen said she "wanted to help Leon out any way she could." She convinced her dentist to replace Leon's missing front teeth for free. She also worked with Al Low to find Leon a steady job. Kallen and Low approached Al Balooly, the owner of Jovans, a restaurant in the upscale Detroit suburb of Birmingham. They thought Leon could make money simply by shaking hands and telling stories.

The value of employing retired sports celebrities wasn't lost on Balooly, who had already hired former Tigers pitcher Denny McLain to entertain patrons at the electronic keyboard. McLain, too, was down on his luck. Two decades past his baseball prime, he had served prison time for an assortment of federal offenses. McLain had shed many of the 330 pounds he'd weighed only a few years earlier, and at Jacques, the bar side of Jovans, he earned a thousand dollars a week playing such pop standards as *Misty* and *Yesterday*. Balooly offered Leon far less, and Leon took it gladly.

For Balooly, the experiment proved to be an instant success. The place was jammed nightly with customers eager to share a drink with a couple of former sports stars.

For Leon the job was a dream come true. He'd gone to bartending school in the vague hope of someday setting up his own joint, and when the chance came to pour drinks at Jacques, he took to the job with gusto. He'd show up on time, flashing his gleaming new front teeth, and sporting the last vestige of his glory days: a full-length mink coat. He would shake hands, pose for pictures, and on request pop out his dentures to reveal his famous toothless smile. For three months Jacques was the hottest spot in town. *Newsweek* and *Time* showed up. So did local television and radio stations. Everyone wanted to celebrate Leon's latest comeback.

Denny McLain remembers, "Anybody could talk to [Leon]. He'd sign autographs all night. [And he'd] tell the same stories every night, one after the other. I never heard him get mad; I never heard him wallow in self-pity.

"One night, Leon lost his teeth for a couple of hours. Everybody in the place was on their hands and knees trying to find the damned teeth, like looking for a contact lens. Eventually, I think, it had fallen behind one of the bottles in the well and when they went to use that bottle of liquor or whatever, they found the teeth."

The problem was that Leon's job came with temptation. McLain recalls, "Every person he signed an autograph for bought him a drink, then another drink, and another drink."

Emanuel Steward remembered stopping in one night, "I go in there. *Hey, look at that. It's Leon.* 'What in the fuck are you doing?' He's behind the bar all dressed up. So I ask for a Chardonnay and I get a glass filled [to the rim].

"I said, 'What's this?'

"He said, 'Go, go, enjoy yourself.'

"Then he grabs another glass and says, 'That looks so good I gotta have a fuckin' glass too.'"

The customers, many of whom shared a glass with Leon, loved him. Yet he and Balooly parted ways after a few short months.

When asked why he let Leon go, Balooly says the novelty had run its course. McLain backs the story. But Al Low doesn't.

"The night Leon was let go, Denny called me," Low remembers. "I picked [Leon] up and took him to dinner down the road and talked to him. He'd been sampling some of the steaks, and I think he was going to take a couple home with him. He was very embarrassed and sad. I told him that the job wasn't his niche and that we needed to find another direction to go."

But Low soon realized that Leon was running out of options.

17

IN FEBRUARY 1990 ALL HELL BROKE LOOSE IN THE HEAVYWEIGHT division. The seemingly indomitable Mike Tyson was brought down by the 42–1 underdog Buster Douglas. In a quasi-replay of Leon's reign, Douglas upset the underprepared champion and then spent more time celebrating his victory than staying in shape. Eight months later, after ballooning to 246 pounds from 231, Douglas took on former cruiserweight Evander Holyfield for his first defense— and got nailed in the third round by an evening-ending right hand. Holyfield walked away with the undisputed title, but in two years he would lose it to Riddick Bowe. A month after that Bowe would refuse to defend against Lennox Lewis and be stripped of the WBC belt. Once again the heavyweight division would be splintered and America would be denied a unified champion.

While all this was going on, Leon and Michael were continuing down their divergent paths. Michael was happily retired from the ring and working with Lewis in repping young fighters. Leon, at age thirty-eight, had questionable mental faculties and fewer skills than a dime-a-dozen bar fighter, yet he pushed to get back in the ring. He and Betty moved to Chicago, where he found a manager in John Caluwaert. A local business and real estate attorney, Caluwaert got together a group of investors to pay off Leon's debts and launch his comeback.

"I took a heavy look at what would be involved," Caluwaert told the *Chicago Tribune.* "It's a major investment in your life, not to mention money. We had a couple of sports psychologists sit down with Leon and his wife in my office. I was very much aware of his background; it's no secret he comes from a very difficult past. But I became aware of his phenomenal strengths as an individual, much of which has been blurred by media attention. The psychologists gave a very positive report."

Leon's comeback became official on November 15, 1991, in Gary, Indiana. His opponent was Lupe Guerra—the same Lupe Guerra he'd kayoed in four rounds six years earlier. Guerra, a used-up journeyman with a 23–24–2 record, had lost four of his previous six fights. What's more, he hadn't won more than two fights in a row in eleven years.

Leon kayoed Guerra in three rounds and then beat Andre Crowder, Rick Myers, Rocky Bentley, and Jack Jackson—four palookas with a combined record of 27–75–3. It's fair to say the division's top heavyweights weren't looking over their shoulders.

In September 1992, two months after beating Jackson, Leon was matched against Kevin P. Porter at the Lansing Civic Center in Michigan. The fight didn't get much press—Leon's mythic status had eroded along with his reflexes.

"[At the weigh-in] Leon wasn't dressed too good," Porter recalls. "He had on some wrinkled pants and an old sweater with the sleeves cut off it. And a shoe with a hole. I really felt sorry for him. The shoe was worn out on the side and there was a big hole. I'm like, man, my god, former world champion. I've been poor all my life, money comes and money goes, but I don't think I've ever had a hole [like that] in my shoe."

It turned out that Porter—who'd lost his previous nine fights—was too much for Leon. Porter remembers being surprised at how easy it was to outpoint the former champ. "I did a couple of windmills with the right hand and hit him with the left hook. I did a couple of windmills with the left and hit him with the right. I tricked him a lot. I saw blood coming out of his mouthpiece. He was pissed."

Those who cared about Leon begged him to quit, but he kept fighting. He kayoed Kevin Poindexter, a professional leather-eater who'd lost eleven of fourteen fights, and then couldn't get by James Wilder, another perpetual loser with a 2–34–1 record. Leon's friends argued that the boxing authorities should not have sanctioned the fights. Leon's managers and promoters countered that Leon had passed every physical and neurological exam in the book—and that he needed the paydays to survive.

Jackie Kallen, who witnessed it all as a friend to Leon, says, "[Leon] is an example of boxing when they use and abuse a fighter for his name and he's not in any shape to be really fighting. You didn't have to be a licensed psychiatrist, psychologist, or neurologist to know that this man should not be in the boxing ring. All they had to do was have him count backwards from one hundred or ask him to do patty-cake, patty-cake, baker's man, and they'd see that there was something not quite right."

In 1994, after Caluwaert hopped off Leon's caravan of managers, Charles Farrell hopped on. The ex-gambler from Boston figured he could do what his predecessors couldn't: reestablish Leon as a marketable entity. Farrell put Leon in against Eddie Curry, a ring veteran who'd managed only four wins in his previous eighteen matches.

Farrell says, "Eddie Curry was a kind of dive artist, so you could expect him to lose if you paid him to lose. [I didn't pay him because] it didn't occur to me that Leon would lose. I didn't realize how diminished Leon was. Leon got banged around and I wound up engineering a win for him, making a deal that got him a win out of a loss."

Here's how it happened: After beating Leon for eight rounds in sweltering heat in Raleigh, North Carolina, Curry was awarded a lopsided decision—but Farrell knew Leon needed the victory. Earlier in the evening, he had noticed a typo on the posters in the arena—the signs were mistakenly promoting the eight-round fight as a ten-rounder. He approached Curry's cornerman, Bobby Mitchell. (Mitchell was later sentenced to thirty-seven months in prison for bribing opponents of Richie Melito Jr.)

"I had done business with Mitchell before," Farrell explains, "so I said, 'Look, it's a ten-round fight and it has to keep going to ten rounds. That's what people paid for.' But Eddie Curry wouldn't fight. He's one of these guys that gets paid by the round, so he cut off his gloves. I kept saying, 'You got one minute, this is a ten-round fight.'

"Finally, Mitchell says, 'I see what you're doing here. Can we take care of this in the back?'

"I said, 'Sure, we can take care of it anywhere you want.'

"And someone said, 'The decision's [already] been announced.'

"I said it's been announced to three hundred people. It's nothing. So let's fix it. So we did. [We agreed on] a TKO win for Leon in the ninth. And that's what I was told would go into the record books."

The fight actually shows up in most record books as a win via disqualification, but regardless of how it's registered, the added victory did nothing to advance Leon's cause.

Leon then chose to take a fight with Shane Sutcliffe, a matchup strongly opposed by Farrell. According to Farrell, once he saw Leon's performance against Curry, he'd never have "willingly put Leon in with anybody that could punch back."

Farrell's instincts proved to be correct. Leon kissed Sutcliffe's fists for eight rounds and lost a lopsided decision.

Farrell figured he could undo the loss by setting up an easy victory against John Carlo, a gym rat who'd never set foot in a professional boxing ring. In Farrell's view Carlo was an ideal opponent for Leon. Not only was the thirty-three-year-old willing to risk getting in the ring with the ex-champ, but he also looked the part of a legit boxer. He stood just under six-two and weighed a convincing 210. The only issue was sanctioning the mismatch, but Farrell got it by the lax D.C. commission by fabricating a record of 11–2–1 for Carlo.

"I figured I had nothing to lose," Carlo says. "If I lost to Leon Spinks, who was an ex–world champ, it would be more of an honor just to fight him."

The night before the fight, Farrell told a jittery Carlo not to worry about getting hurt because he'd never know what hit him.

Farrell recalls, "I said, 'The bell is gonna ring and there's gonna be a rush of adrenalin and within about thirty seconds you're gonna be exhausted. And Leon's gonna knock you out.' And then I said, 'If you can beat him, beat him, because it means he shouldn't be in the ring with anybody.' Famous last words."

One minute and nine seconds into the fight, Leon was flat on his back. The former champ hadn't fired off a single punch.

"I went out and jabbed," Carlo says, "and I noticed that he went to block it. So I faked the jab and threw a hook and it landed right on his jaw. It was so quick. He went down right away. I only threw three punches."

Farrell now admits to some regret. "I guess you would have to say I'm sorry I put him in [against Carlo] because, as his manager, my primary responsibility is to keep the fighter safe," he says, "and my secondary responsibility is to get him paid. It was bad judgment on my part because I didn't know how far gone he was.

"[If I had it to do again,] I would have fixed the fight. I would have not have missed that last step. Because I could have then put him in a fight where he wouldn't have gotten hurt, where he would actually have gotten paid. It might have helped his life a little bit. He was beyond being trained. He was way beyond doing real gym work."

It was true that Leon needed a payday, but at the rate he burned through money, he would have had to fight every twenty-four hours. It took him only one evening to go through the fifteen hundred dollars he'd earned against Carlo.

"One of the truisms about fighters is that they always have their hand out," Farrell claims. "I do not blame them for that. They're an incredibly disenfranchised group. If they don't look out for themselves, there's a very good chance that nobody will look out for them.

"[After the Carlo fight,] I'm sitting in the lobby of the hotel where Leon is staying and I'm taking care of some business. And Leon came up to us—he's a very shy person—and he wanted to know if he could enter our space. We talked alone for a couple of minutes, and as he's leaving, he says, 'Can I get some money?' And I said, 'Sure, what do you need?' I'm thinking a couple hundred dollars, maybe five hundred. And he says, 'Can I get five dollars for a sandwich?'

"He talks about what he needs. That's it. He needed to get something to eat; he didn't have the money. That's what he wanted. It doesn't occur to him to make more of his situation than he perceives it to be."

Leon felt Carlo had gotten lucky and asked Farrell to pursue a rematch, but Farrell refused, advising Leon to retire. "He had no business fighting anybody," Farrell says. "He was knocked out, essentially, by one punch. He should not have been in the ring."

But that didn't stop Leon. Eight months later St. Louis attorney and boxing promoter Steve Frank arranged a bout at a country-and-western bar called Little Bit of Texas. It was a far cry from Vegas. The ring was set up on a dance floor usually occupied by line-dancers and two-steppers. The mechanical bull rested silently in the corner. The sign over the ring read No Spurs Allowed.

In the hopes of protecting Leon, Frank had scoured the town for an über-unworthy opponent. He'd decided on the bar's bouncer, a blond-haired, mullet-wearing thirty-three-year-old lug named Ray Kipping. Like Carlo, Kipping fit the bill—he stood six-four, weighed 220, and couldn't fight a lick. His pro record, if you could call it that, was 1–2–1.

Steve Frank recalls, "I want to promote my fight, so I call up [Tom Wheatley, boxing writer for the *St. Louis Post-Dispatch*] and I say, 'Leon's gonna fight Ray Kipping for the IBA championship, the International Boxing Association. Kipping's record is 32–2 with twenty-eight KOs.' I made [the whole thing] up. So Jon Saraceno stopped off at the airport, bought a *Post-Dispatch,* and reads about the fight. So he puts it in his column in *USA Today.* So I had a belt made and Leon [fought for] the belt."

Knowing Leon's appetite for booze, drugs, and self-destruction, Frank tried his best to keep Leon on the straight and narrow. He put Leon's son Darrell on the undercard, matching him up against the eminently beatable Earl Abernathy. It would be Darrell's third pro fight, the first of which had been a four-round decision over the same Earl Abernathy.

Frank figured he was handing Darrell an easy victory and hoping, in exchange, that the younger Spinks would keep an eye on his wayward father. This soon proved to be a farcical plan when, according to Frank (but denied by Darrell), Frank brought his promoter-friend Ray Sepulveda to Darrell's hotel room to introduce the two before the fight.

"It's four-thirty and we go to Darrell's room," Frank recalls. "The door was partly open. There's no answer but we hear someone in there. So I push the door open. [Darrell's] having sex with a girl, and, I mean, slamming this girl. I said, 'Darrell, what the fuck are you doing?'

"And he doesn't break stride. 'What's up, Steve?'

"Ray Sepulveda's jaw is on the ground. He's like, 'What the hell?!'

"I say, 'Darrell, I want you to meet Ray Sepulveda.' Then Ray says, 'Excuse me if I don't want to shake your hand.'

"It's awkward, so I say, 'Is there anything I can get you?'

"He orders a cheeseburger. *And he's still having sex.* And then he asks [the girl] if *she* wants anything. *And she orders fries.*"

According to Frank, the incident was merely the beginning of his troubles that evening. A half hour later he learned that the Spinks-Kipping fight was in jeopardy.

"At five o'clock somebody called [the state commission] and said Leon's punch drunk," Frank remembers. "So Butch Wilkinson from the commission says, 'I'm told Leon can't fight.'

"I said, 'My brother [neurophysiologist Bennett Frank] examined him.' So Wilkinson says, 'We need a written statement notarized.' But my brother was at my cousin's funeral.

"We reached an agreement. The fight was [shortened] to eight rounds and fought with sixteen-ounce gloves. Sparring gloves."

That doesn't sway Jackie Kallen. "They put him out like a circus performer," she says, "and I thought it was so cruel, because if there's any doubt, the man's over forty years old. Look at his record—he's been knocked out nine or ten times. For what reason? Your brother's the doctor? He approved it? The whole thing was shameful."

"I'll put my brother's credentials against anybody's in the country," Frank responds. "He gave Leon an extremely thorough exam. He said there's a slight tremor in his hand that's probably related to boxing, but he's fine. Leon's problem at the time was his drinking. I truly, truly believed that Leon was not in any danger. I think the damage was already done with all those years of drinking and drugs, and taking fights without training against really good fighters."

Leon beat Kipping in a unanimous decision. According to Marty Bickle, who judged the fight, it was a "typical Leon maul-and-brawl fight," and the norm for "somebody at the end of their career."

"Let's put it this way," Bickle says now, "when the fight was over, both fighters were *verrrry* tired."

Ray Kipping says, "Physically, [Leon's] body was OK, but his head wasn't. Even before the fight, he talked funny. I wanted a rematch but I was told he was too sick."

After the fight Steve Frank paid Leon five thousand dollars— the $2,500 purse plus an additional $2,500 in cash.

"I bet you that money was gone before I left the building," Frank says. "[Leon] would just give his money away."

Six months later, on December 4, 1995, Frank promoted Leon's final bout, an eight-round slopfest against Fred Houpe, a onetime hopeful who'd been away from the ring for seventeen years. Again, the fight was held at Little Bit of Texas, and again Frank wasn't able to stop Leon from being Leon.

Frank recalls, "I put him up at the Harley Hotel a few days before the fight. The area was foreign to Leon and I knew that if I cut off the phone, there was no way he would escape. At four o'clock I went into his room. It smelled like marijuana and he was drinking a beer. I'm 99 percent sure that in both of the fights I promoted, Leon went into the ring messed up. He'd had something to drink and I know that he was smoking."

An impaired Leon had no chance against Houpe and lost a unanimous decision.

"At the end there, he could be knocked out fairly easily," Jackie Kallen remembers. "I think a lot of it was the alcohol too. His balance was gone and his reflexes were shot. I cringed anytime I saw his name on a list of fights. I think if the promoter was a kind guy, he would've had him sign autographs and make an appearance and give him a thousand dollars rather than put him in the ring. What kinds of ethics does a person display?"

Many boxing insiders agree that Kallen makes some valid points—there's no doubt that aging fighters are pushing their luck any time they step into the ring. But the same insiders say that all managers, Kallen included, will continue to put fighters in the ring well past their prime, especially if the fighter has passed a neurological exam and the fight appears to be evenly matched. It is, after all, what they do for a living.

In Leon's case his small circle of friends and family had tried telling him that his skills were gone and that taking beatings from the likes of Eddie Curry and Fred Houpe was a sure sign to retire. He ignored them. And he wound up paying the price.

After Leon's last fight his health deteriorated so badly that it became evident on neurological exams, in physical tests, and to the naked eye.

Betty Spinks says, "Lee was dragging his leg, falling, and getting lost. His father called and asked me if Lee had a stroke. I took him to the doctor and had tests done. He'd had no stroke. They said he had memory loss. They said it's from the boxing, but the alcohol is making it worse. Dementia is setting in. So my son and I bought boots to support his ankle. We couldn't even leave him home by himself. He'd fall through glass tables. He'd lose his keys."

Two years later, in 1997, while still married to Betty and maintaining an apartment in Chicago, Leon wandered back to his old neighborhood in St. Louis. At the age of forty-three, he was back where he'd started: a short walk from Kenny Loehr's gym—and a shorter walk to the overgrown lot where Pruitt-Igoe once stood.

There, New York *Daily News* reporter Wayne Coffey found him living in a homeless shelter. Leon explained his situation by saying that he preferred to stay in St. Louis.

Leon told Coffey, "Everybody [in Chicago] is too busy criticizing me for what I've been through and what I did. They tear you down about what you should have been."

For $4.75 an hour, Leon was sweeping the aisles of Kiel Auditorium, the downtown arena where boxing fans had stood on a spring night in 1977 cheering their young hometown hero as he raised his arms in triumph over the fallen Pedro Agosto one minute and fifty-five seconds after the opening bell.

Jesse Davison, Leon's boyhood pal, spotted him one day in June. "I saw him sweeping the floor. He looked at me and said, 'Hey Jesse, what's goin' on?' I said, 'Leon, you made millions and you sweepin' the floor?' I had tears in my eyes when I saw that. It shocked me. I thought, *damn, he's come a long way.* Amazing. God can bring you up and bring you back down if you don't do it right."

Michael, on the other hand, couldn't have been farther from the war zone that had led him to God, boxing, and ultimately, riches. He was halfway across the country, partying with Denzel Washington, Joe Frazier, and three hundred other VIPs at Butch Lewis's oceanfront mansion in the Delaware resort of Bethany Beach. It was the start of a three-day bash celebrating Lewis's fiftieth birthday. James Brown sang. Bobby Womack followed. A "Big 50" birthday message streaked across the soft evening sky, courtesy of BET founder Robert L. Johnson. Delaware Governor Thomas Carper signed a proclamation declaring a statewide Butch Lewis Day. Rumor was that the party cost more than half a million dollars.

It was hard to look at Michael without comparing his and Leon's journeys.

Butch Lewis told the New Orleans *Times-Picayune,* "I know I could have made Leon upwards of fifty million [dollars] if he had disciplined himself and done the right things for four or five years. A lot of people felt that [Michael] had less talent. One took one fork in the road; one took the other."

But while Lewis spoke of the riches Leon might have earned at the top of the fight game, the bigger question may be whether Leon would have been better off if he'd never climbed the mountain at all—if he would have had a happier life just being Leon, instead of "the guy who beat Muhammad Ali."

"He got lucky with the one fight with Ali," Jackie Kallen says, "and I think it turned out to be the worst thing that ever happened to him. You beat the greatest. People expect that you're the greatest now, and he could never fill those shoes. When you've been to the top of the mountain and the whole rest of your life you're sliding down, that's really difficult."

In the end the heavyweight title had broken its promise to Leon—much as it had to Joe Louis and, yes, even Muhammad Ali. It made him rich for a while, but it's hard to say that a forty-three-year-old ex-fighter with nothing to show for his career other than dementia and a minimum-wage job could look at his rusty championship belt and say thank you.

18

BOXING HAS SPIT OUT A LONG LIST OF FIGHTERS THAT HAVE STUCK around too long. Michael Spinks wasn't one of them. At thirty-two he walked out of the ring—and stayed out.

On June 12, 1994, when Michael was inducted into the Boxing Hall of Fame in Canastota, New York, he became the youngest fighter in history to earn boxing immortality. Addressing the more than two thousand fans who attended the ceremony, he was, as always, a man of few words. Many of them were directed at Butch Lewis.

"Thank you," he told the crowd, which included Lewis and Leon. "I'd just like to say that it's been one heck of a weekend, a very special weekend for me and a very special weekend for my crew that I shared my career with. I take into the Boxing Hall of Fame Butch Lewis and Butch Lewis Productions. I take into the Boxing Hall of Fame with me all the people all over the world that prayed for my well-being. I thank God for everything that he has allowed to happen in my life. And I also thank you beautiful people of Canastota. May God bless you all."

The bond between Michael and Lewis extended through July 23, 2011, when Michael received word that his friend, partner, and surrogate father was gone. Butch Lewis had died of a heart attack at his home in Bethany Beach. With the death of his mother Kay thirteen years earlier, Michael had now lost the two people he trusted the most.

A memorial for Lewis was held at the Chase Center in Wilmington, Delaware, drawing a standing-room-only crowd of more than a thousand grieving friends and family members. The lineup of mourners was a testament to Lewis's influence. Denzel Washington paid his respects, as did Morgan Freeman, Queen Latifah, Mike Tyson, Robert L. Johnson, and a roster of Delaware businessmen and politicians. The service lasted three and a half hours and ended with a twenty-five-minute performance by Stevie Wonder, who tweaked his famous hit and sang, "Here he is, Father. Signed, sealed, delivered, he's yours."

Michael wept as Lewis's body was loaded into a horse-drawn carriage to be brought to its final resting place.

"He helped me stay in the game," Michael told the Wilmington *News Journal*. "I wouldn't have been able to do it without him. He was a very unique individual and very special to me. We got together; it was like a marriage. We were both married to our jobs, but we were together."

Less than two weeks after Lewis's death, Michael's health coverage lapsed. He soon discovered that none of his monthly bills were being paid. For more than two decades, Lewis had lived up to his side of their agreement and managed Michael's finances. Now, with Lewis gone, Michael's money appeared to be gone, as well.

Confused, Michael made a desperate call to the one person he thought would have some answers: his friend from Butch Lewis Productions, Amelia Patterson.

"What happened to my money?" he asked in quiet desperation.

It was the middle of the night, but Patterson wasn't put off by the call. In fact, she'd been expecting it.

"Butch must've spent it all," she told him.

Michael didn't say a word. But he also didn't hang up. He just stayed on the open line, processing Patterson's response in silence.

Understandably, he was shell-shocked. But it was all coming together. How else had Lewis paid for a mansion, oceanfront property, a purple Bentley, and extravagant birthday bashes?

"[Butch] did not have the kind of resources or money to afford his type of lifestyle," Patterson explains. "He was wining and dining Bob Johnson of BET, hanging out with Denzel Washington, presidents of banks. He had some other businesses—he produced a show on BET, he had invested in BET—but I really don't believe that he was generating the kind of income that afforded him his grandiose lifestyle. I knew one day it was gonna happen. Sooner or later it would reveal itself."

Lewis's friends, including the co-executor of his estate, Robert L. Johnson, insist that Lewis always had Michael's best interests in mind. Yet Michael had earned more than $25 million in his career, and Lewis's entire estate was worth only $8.5 million. To Michael, it seemed that his fortune was no more real than the bogus rings Lewis had once sold on Market Street. Except for a single retirement account worth about $2.5 million, none of Michael's earnings had been earmarked for his old age.

Apparently, as wary as Michael had been, he'd still wound up wearing the same shoes as the parade of champions who'd come before him. Lewis's betrayal stung even more because Michael had trusted him with everything.

Patterson says, "I used to wonder if I [should tell] Slim, 'You're gonna have to do x, y, and z. You're gonna have to file a suit against the estate, as much as you probably don't want to.' The kind of loyalty that Slim had with Butch is unheard of. Even talking to [Slim] on the phone when he's questioning me about his money, he still couldn't believe that Butch did this. And he still couldn't say anything bad about Butch. That's incredible love and loyalty."

But even Michael's loyalty had its limits. On October 13, 2011, he went ahead and filed a lawsuit against Lewis's estate. The promoter's will provided a minimum of one million dollars to each of his three children, Sita, Brandon, and Ronald Jr.; $104,000 to a fourth child, Kevin Mosley; $50,000 to each of his four grandchildren; and $52,000 to each of five other relatives. But it contained no provision for Michael.

The lawsuit charged that Lewis had engaged in "fraudulent, unfair, and unconscionable" conduct by "commingling and mishandling" Michael's earnings; it also charged that Lewis had taken custody of four hundred tapes of Michael's fights, six championship belts, and a full-length mink coat.

More than a year later, in November 2012, Michael's attorney reached a settlement with Lewis's estate. Although the terms of the agreement were confidential, it was made public that Michael would be able to meet his monthly bills and continue to live in his home.

"It was unfortunate that Butch's early death took place. It prevented him from doing everything he would've done for Michael had he lived," Robert L. Johnson says. "And he always, as far as I was concerned, always had Michael's well-being forefront in his mind."

If Lewis could speak from the hereafter, he'd probably say he had every intention of continuing to pay Michael's bills, and if the money ran out, he would have found a way to continue fulfilling his obligation to Michael.

He'd probably also say that he left his fighter in better financial shape than most ex-champions find themselves. And in that he'd be right. Especially if one were to compare Michael to his brother.

＊～＊

Nevada, 2013. At age fifty-nine Leon struggles through daily life. Dementia has dulled his memory, garbled his gravelly speech, and reduced his gait to a rickety, lopsided hobble.

He is part of an ongoing study at the Cleveland Clinic Lou Ruvo Center in Las Vegas. There, doctors are examining the brains of boxers and mixed-martial-arts fighters. There's no shortage of irony in the fact that the Nevada State Athletic Commission and Top Rank Boxing—two entities that could be considered complicit in Leon's demise—are championing the study. Charles Bernick, the neurologist heading up the study, has been quoted as saying that science "has known for years that boxers—perhaps twenty to fifty percent of boxers who've fought professionally—will develop longterm brain complications." Those complications include early-onset dementia, Alzheimer's, and Muhammad Ali's insidious opponent, Parkinson's disease. Bernick and his team can no longer help Leon, Ali, or their contemporaries, although they hope to identify early warning signs that could benefit young fighters before it's too late.

But all is not lost for Leon. He has stumbled upon something more important to him than the alcohol-dazed stupors he spent his life chasing. He has found a family.

In 2000, while separated from Betty and doing autograph shows in Branson, Missouri, he met Brenda Glur, a petite, white-skinned, blonde-haired dresser for the touring company of the Radio City Rockettes. Brenda fell for Leon and brought him back to her hometown of Columbus, Nebraska, which boasted a population of 22,000, and, until Leon showed up, virtually no black residents. But Leon pulled off the biggest upset of his career, winning over the town and assuming the role of mini-celebrity. The locals called him "Champ," and despite his obvious physical and mental difficulties, Brenda managed to set him up with a series of odd jobs. He swept floors at the local YMCA, worked as a school bus monitor, and unloaded trucks at McDonald's.

In 2011 Leon and Brenda moved to Henderson, Nevada, and married in a small, private ceremony in nearby Las Vegas. Pop singer

Tony Orlando, a close friend of the couple, was the best man. Toni Wine played keyboard and sang her composition "A Groovy Kind of Love" as the bride walked down the aisle.

"It was wonderful, because they had it where Elvis Presley had his marriage in Vegas; and there was Kenny Norton and Earnie Shavers—they were there with their families," Orlando remembers. "Brenda was with her kids from another marriage. And Leon came dressed up in his white shirt and tuxedo, and I just got a kick out of it because you could see he was uncomfortable wearing that stuff. You could see when he gave the vows he did it with such seriousness and such intent that he didn't want to make a mistake. I thought that was such a loving, wonderful, typical Leon Spinks."

Leon and Brenda get by on money earned from occasional autograph signings. Leon can't erase the past, nor does he express any desire to, but he has made an effort to reconnect with Darrell and Cory. Sadly, he'll never be able to make amends with his oldest son, Leon, who was gunned down in St. Louis in the summer of 1990.

Six days before the shooting, *Sports Illustrated* had heralded the promising light-heavyweight, who, like his father, was more vulnerable outside the ring than in it. He liked to drink, loved to party, and lived on the edge. He had been born with his mother's last name, Calvin but fought under the name Spinks, as did his younger brothers. Leon Calvin was buried two months shy of his twentieth birthday and left behind two children, Little Leon and Irene.

Darrell and Cory escaped a similar fate but not the constant dangers that threatened them while growing up on East John Avenue. The neighborhood was three miles north of Pruitt-Igoe, but just as neglected and nearly as violent. Darrell has been shot three times, and Cory survived a stabbing by his ex-wife.

"It was real tough," Cory says. "You either had to learn how to fight to protect yourself or you got ran over on. There was a lot of shootings, a lot of killings. Most of us that grew up in that neighborhood were blessed to get out. I saw my friends get killed. It was everyday life."

Like his brothers, Cory also had a professional boxing career. From 2003 to 2005, he was the undisputed welterweight champion; he also went on to win the IBF light-middleweight title. He and Darrell have opened their gloved arms to their father, forgiving him for his years of neglect.

"Now, when my daddy comes to St. Louis," Darrell says, "I'm the one he stays with. I mean, he stays in a hotel, but he likes to hang around me and my friends. They show him so much love."

Cory says, "Our relationship is phenomenal. The old guy has stepped up to the plate. He's a terrific granddad to my daughter. He never misses anything. He embraces her and plays with her. He sends her something if it's her birthday. He comes to my fights. He's around more. He's in my life.

"I feel so blessed to be Leon's son. Leon has accomplished so much. Some people will never accomplish that much in their life. I praise him for doing that. Someday I want to train fighters and have my own gym and bring my father into it."

In the end Leon's greatest liability has become his strongest asset. The naive, devil-may-care attitude that caused so many problems in his younger years is saving his life now.

Leon's friend Tony Orlando says, "I have a very special love for Leon. It's not difficult to love him. He's a kindhearted, gentle man. So many fighters find disappointment at the end of the road. Here they've had the glory of a championship and they've worked hard to be who they became, and then they run into rough times. The rough times that [Leon] has gotten into, I never heard him crybaby or beg for anything. He's a man who stood up to whatever came his way."

Leon's late-career manager Charles Farrell says, "[Leon's] is a life that can be seen in very, very sad terms. [Leon] doesn't do that. He is alive in the moment that he is living, and I've got great respect for that. I believe that Leon doesn't dwell on what he deserves or doesn't deserve. I don't believe that enters into his psychological orbit at all. One day he's a guy with eight pro fights, and the next day he's the heavyweight champion and a multimillionaire. Eight months later he's an ex-champion and he's broke. Those are just the things that happened. And there's not this connecting component where he thinks, my God, what a strange trip this has been."

Leon has finally broken free of the same hellhole that Michael left so many years ago. Leon traveled like a racecar and Michael like a dependable sedan, but both have achieved what they dreamed of when they donned their gloves back at the DeSoto.

They escaped Pruitt-Igoe.

❧

St. Louis, 2013. Nearly four decades after the last brick of the Pruitt-Igoe housing disaster fell to the ground, most of the fifty-seven-acre site lies vacant, a rocky expanse of discarded junk, broken glass, and contaminated soil—an unmarked burial ground for the dreams of the city's have-nots. Only weeds survive.

As for the rest of the city, St. Louis continues to outpace the country's homicide rate. It is still consistently ranked among the most dangerous cities in the United States, and in 2012, ranked second, behind only Detroit. The General Motors plant has closed. The Brown Shoe Company has moved. Vashon High School has been torn down and relocated a mile away. The school is still 99.9 percent black and shows no plans of diversification. Less than half of its student body graduates.

Throughout St. Louis there is little acknowledgement of Leon or Michael—there are no plaques at the site of the DeSoto the way statues honor Bob Gibson and Lou Brock outside Busch Stadium. There are no busts at Kiener Square, where St. Louis officials stood in 1976, gushing over the Spinks boys and their newly minted Olympic gold, proclaiming Michael and Leon Spinks Day, preaching city pride, and promising bright futures. Along the St. Louis Walk of Fame, on Delmar Boulevard, visitors track 116 of St. Louis's most notable alumni. Leon and Michael are not included.

The roads out of north St. Louis are few, so amateur boxing continues to thrive. Kenny Loehr, now eighty-one, can still be found training the local kids, teaching them to defend themselves while preaching character and discipline—only now he does so out of the 12th and Park Recreation Center. He's there every afternoon, Monday through Friday, calling the kids "freaks" and buying the occasional pizza. And he still warns them against turning pro. If they do, he says, they'll be eaten up and spit out.

But across the room, at the speed bag, is a young kid with no other choice. His father is gone, his mother is hungry, his brother is in prison. And so he perfects his footwork, polishes his jab, strengthens his hook. He tells himself he'll be different. He'll retire young, rich, famous, and sharp.

All he needs is the heavyweight title.

Acknowledgments

We owe a debt of gratitude to the many people who have made this book possible, most notably Leon and Michael Spinks. Throughout their lives they repeatedly stood up against outsized opponents, both in and out of the ring. And for that, their story needed to be told.

During the two years spent researching and writing this book, we made repeated efforts to interview both Spinks brothers. We caught up with Leon at the Hall of Fame in the summer of 2011. Unfortunately, after a short interview, he proved to be an unreliable witness to his own story. Perhaps it was the many drinks that well-intentioned fans passed his way, or the memory issues that have begun to plague him. It may have been both.

We contacted Michael through his attorney, Vincent Sarubbi, who'd kept Michael out of circulation until his lawsuit against the estate of Butch Lewis was resolved. The long wait finally ended in late November 2012, at which point Mr. Sarubbi, perhaps protecting his client, attached several unrealistic demands (including a sizable interview fee) to a meeting with Michael. In the interest of maintaining objectivity, we declined.

Thanks go to a long list of interview subjects who gave their time and insight to the project, particularly Leon's surviving children, Darrell and Cory, who spoke as openly about the low times as the high ones.

Jerry Izenberg certainly had better things to do than spend hours on the phone with us. Yet he was always ready to chat, answer a question, share an anecdote, or give advice. For that, we owe him one. We hope he calls and collects.

This book is credited to two authors, but it is very much the work of three people. Our uncredited secret weapon was Justin

Davidson—a thorough researcher, probing interviewer, and diligent fact-checker. Remember the name. He'll be writing his own books someday, and they'll be good ones.

Speaking of book releases, a special thank-you goes to our editor, Keith Wallman, and our agent, Elizabeth Evans. They did more than champion the story. They believed we were the ones to tell it.

Interview Subjects

Abraham, Seth—July 31, 2012

Anderson, Dave—October 8, 2012

Armstrong, Davey—August 23, 2011

Arum, Bob—July 18, 2012

Arzt, Sydney—September 22, 2012

Balooly, Al—August 19, 2011

Bickle, Marty—August 24, 2011

Boyd, Luther—February 6, 2012

Brown, Ed—May 15, 2012

Caldwell, James—February 6, 2012; February 27, 2012

Cappuccino, Frank—August 6, 2011

Carlo, John—July 19, 2012

Carter, Helene—June 19, 2012

Conforti, Michael—June 20, 2012

Cooney, Gerry—June 24, 2011

Crittenden, John—August 23, 2012

Cross, Mike—July 10, 2011

Darrow, Bill—May 6, 2012

Davis, Howard—January 21, 2012; April 22, 2012

Davison, Jesse—July 8, 2011

DiNicola, Ron—August 27, 2011

Drayton, Buster—September 10, 2011

Dundee, Angelo—June 11, 2011

Early, Gerald—March 2, 2012

Farrell, Charles—July 9, 2012

Feour, Royce—June 21, 2012

Frank, Steve—July 10, 2011; September 19, 2011; February 27, 2012

Giachetti, Richie—February 4, 2012

Gibson, Alma—May 15, 2012

Greenburg, Ross—January 23, 2012

Guy, Rick—May 6, 2012

Hamm, Charles—July 10, 2011

Hartman, Karen—June 20, 2012

Hartmann, Douglas—June 18, 2012

Hauser, Thomas—May 28, 2012

Hazzard, Larry—July 5, 2012; July 17, 2012

Hefton, Brad—September 4, 2012

Holley, Steve—March 20, 2012

Howell, Jim—January 30, 2012

Izenberg, Jerry—August 18, 2012; August 23, 2012;
    September 11, 2012

Jastrow, Terry—June 14, 2012

Johnson, Robert L.—December 11, 2012

Kallen, Jackie—August 22, 2011

Kane, Kip—July 25, 2012

Kilroy, Gene—August 24, 2012

Kipping, Ray—August 23, 2011

Kunkle, Bill—September 15, 2011

Lafata, Sam—September 29, 2011; February 21, 2012

Lampley, Jim—February 24, 2012

Lederman, Harold—June 21, 2011

Lipsyte, Robert—June 5, 2012

Loehr, Kenny—July 8, 2011

Lotierzo, Frank—July 16, 2012; November 13, 2012

Lott, Steve—August 11, 2011

Low, Al—February 12, 2012

Lueckenhoff, Tim—September 2, 2011

Marks, Cozy—September 3, 2011; August 26, 2012

Martorelli, Jack—March 28, 2012

Mason, Mark—April 18, 2012

Matthews, Wallace—August 30, 2012

Mayweather, Floyd, Sr.—March 18, 2012; March 20, 2012

McLain, Denny—August 17, 2011

Mooney, Charles—February 21, 2012; April 22, 2012

Mustafa Muhammad, Eddie—July 21, 2011

Newman, Rock—July 15, 2012; July 29, 2012

Orlando, Tony—October 17, 2012

Patterson, Amelia—July 15, 2012

Petty, Harold—July 8, 2011

Porter, Kevin P.—August 17, 2011

Qawi, Dwight—August 6, 2011; February 12, 2012

Randolph, Leo—August 22, 2011

Rooney, Kevin—June 11, 2011

Rotella, Carlo—July 12, 2012

Roth, Jerry—July 21, 2011

Sammons, Jeffrey—June 5, 2012

Santana, Tony—January 22, 2012

Shabazz, Omar—July 20, 2012

Shilstone, Mackie—March 8, 2012; March 9, 2012; March 24, 2012

Spinks, Betty—July 9, 2011; August 21, 2011

Spinks, Cory—May 23, 2012; September 6, 2012

Spinks, Darrell—July 10, 2011; July 11, 2011; October 5, 2011; October 8, 2011; September 19, 2012

Spinks, Leon—June 11, 2011

Stafford, Roger—August 30, 2011

Steward, Emanuel—September 9, 2011

Tangstad, Steffen—August 12, 2012

Tearney, Greg—August 30, 2012

Tompkins, Barry—May 10, 2012
Tyson, Mike—February 17, 2012
West, Doc—March 28, 2012
Wheatley, Suzanne (aka S. J. Stockhausen)—January 19, 2012
Wilkinson, Butch—August 26, 2011

BIBLIOGRAPHY

Books

Brunt, Stephen. *Facing Ali: 15 Fighters/15 Stories.* Guilford, CT: The Lyons Press, 2004.

Dundee, Angelo, and Bert Sugar. *My View from the Corner: A Life in Boxing.* New York: McGraw-Hill, 2009.

Early, Gerald. *The Culture of Bruising: Essays on Prizefighting, Literature, and Modern American Culture.* New York: Ecco Press, 1995.

Hartmann, Douglas. *Race, Culture and the Revolt of the Black Athlete.* Chicago: University of Chicago Press, 2004.

Hauser, Thomas. *Muhammad Ali: His Life and Times.* New York: Simon & Schuster, 1992.

Heller, Peter. *Bad Intentions: The Mike Tyson Story.* Cambridge, MA: Da Capo Press, 1995.

Holmes, Larry, and Phil Berger. *Larry Holmes: Against the Odds.* New York: St. Martin's Press, 1998.

Marsh, Irving T., and Edward Ehre, eds. *Best Sports Stories 1979.* New York: E.P. Dutton & Co., 1979.

Mr. T. *Mr. T: The Man with the Gold: An Autobiography.* New York: St. Martin's Press, 1985.

Norrell, Robert J. *The House I Live In: Race in the American Century.* New York: Oxford University Press, USA, 2006.

Rotella, Carlo. *Cut Time: An Education at the Fights.* Chicago: University of Chicago Press, 2005.

Magazines

Boyle, Robert H. "Man, It Was a Rumble in the Riverfront." *Sports Illustrated*, June 14, 1976.

Coffey, Wayne. "Leon Spinks Looking for Big Comeback in Life." New York *Daily News*, March 7, 1997.

Cormier, Ryan, and Sean O'Sullivan. "Last Goodbye for Butch Lewis." *News Journal* (Wilmington), August 2, 2011.

Ebony. "Leon Spinks: The 'Boy' Who Did a Man's Job on Muhammad Ali." May 1978.

Friedman, Jack. "Stripped of His Title, Not of His Heart, Michael Spinks Fights Gerry Cooney, but Looks Out for Leon." *People*, June 19, 1987.

Fussman, Calvin. "A Yawning Gap in His Life." *Sports Illustrated*, March 14, 1983.

Hoffer, Richard. "Court Ruling Excites Butch Lewis." *Los Angeles Times*, March 21, 1987.

———. "Fists Full of Dollars." *Sports Illustrated*, January 15, 1990.

Kanew, Evan. "The Dream Team." *Sports Illustrated*, August 3, 1996.

Killeen, Austin. "Leo Randolph: The Golden Prodigy." *International Boxing Research Organization Journal*, September 2009.

Leavy, Walter. "The New King of the Ring." *Ebony*, March 1986.

Leerhsen, Charles. "Spinks Stands Tall in Brawl." *Newsweek*, March 28, 1983.

McCallum, Jack. "A Golden Moment for Leon's Little Brother." *Sports Illustrated*, July 27, 1981.

McMurran, Kristin, Jim Forbes, and Cynthia Mitchell. "His Wife Calls Leon Spinks a 'Man-Child,' but the Title Has Been No Promised Land." *People*, May 1, 1978.

Nack, William. "A Crowning Achievement." *Sports Illustrated*, March 28, 1983.

———. "Dark Days for Neon Leon." *Sports Illustrated*, March 31, 1986.

———. "Spinks Was No Sphinx." *Sports Illustrated*, January 21, 1980.

Newman, Bruce. "Sometimes a Guy's Gotta Swoop." *Sports Illustrated*, July 24, 1978.

Putnam, Pat. "Battle of the Ballot." *Sports Illustrated*, April 28, 1986.

———. "The Big Showdown." *Sports Illustrated*, June 27, 1988.

———. "The Day the Gold Turned Green." *Sports Illustrated*, February 14, 1977.

———. "He's the Greatest, I'm the Best." *Sports Illustrated*, February 27, 1978.

———. "The Iron Ball and the Bible." *Sports Illustrated*, March 13, 1978.

———. "The Louisiana Purchase." *Sports Illustrated*, October 2, 1978.

———. "Michael Played the Heavy." *Sports Illustrated*, September 30, 1985.

———. "Oh Brothers—They Put Punch Into It." *Sports Illustrated*, August 9, 1976.

———. "One More Time to the Top." *Sports Illustrated*, September 25, 1978.

———. "They Got Leon All Messed Up." *Sports Illustrated*, March 27, 1978.

Saraceno, Jon. "Ali, Spinks Cross Unsteady Paths to Help Support Brain Study." *USA Today*, February 18, 2012.

Simms, Gregory. "The Other Side of Leon Spinks." *Jet*, June 8, 1978.

"Spinks' Girlfriend Killed in Philly Auto Collision." *Jet*, January 24, 1983.

Newspapers and Wire Services

Abel, Allen. "It's So Tough That the Cops Don't Dare Come in the Buildings." *Globe and Mail* (Toronto), February 17, 1978.

———. "Spinks Wasn't Ready Second Time." *Globe and Mail* (Toronto), September 18, 1978.

Anderson, Dave. "Ali! Ali!" *New York Times,* February 16, 1978.

———. "'Don't Stop,' but He Did." *New York Times,* April 21, 1986.

———. "A Reign Is Ended as Face Shows Stings of Defeat." *New York Times,* February 16, 1978.

———. "Sports of the Times: Loss to Age Not Candles." *New York Times,* September 22, 1985.

———. "Sports of the Times: The Other Larry Holmes." *New York Times,* April 19, 1986.

———. "They're Trying to Steal Leon." *New York Times,* February 28, 1978.

Archdeacon, Tom. "Michael Spinks' Lessons Beyond Boxing." *Miami News,* June 12, 1987.

"Armstrong Punches Out Olympic Ticket." The Associated Press, June 6, 1976.

Aschburner, Steve. "He Would Rather Switch Than Fight." *Star Tribune* (Minneapolis), June 26, 1988.

Barnes, Bart. "Promoter Lewis Is No. 3, and Trying Harder." *Washington Post,* July 3, 1983.

Barrish, Chris, and Sean O'Sullivan. "Estate of Promoter Butch Lewis Hit With Lawsuits." *News Journal* (Wilmington), October 30, 2011.

Berger, Phil. "Ali's Made-for-TV Challenger." *New York Times,* January 29, 1978.

———. "Boxing: Death at Hands of Elusive Foe." *New York Times,* July 29, 1990.

———. "Cash Fight Snarls Unification Series; King, Lewis Trade Verbal Punches." *New York Times,* January 26, 1987.

———. "Lewis Promotes Himself as Well as the Fighters." *New York Times,* May 30, 1983.

———. "Spinks Learns Value of His Work." *New York Times,* April 14, 1986.

Boswell, Thomas. "A Champion's Roots Spinks; Champ Now Prey of Ring Sharpies." *Washington Post,* February 19, 1978.

Bradley, John Ed. "Spinks: Alone for the Ride." *Washington Post,* July 10, 1983.

———. "Spinks Believes 'Anything's Possible'; Holmes' Challenger Already Has Proved He Can Survive St. Louis Ghetto. *Washington Post,* September 18, 1985.

Brady, Dave. "King, Arum Swap Slurs as Boxing Heads for Courts; King, Arum Trade Slurs Over Spinks." *Washington Post,* March 29, 1978.

Broeg, Bob. "Spinks Brothers Fight for a Future." *St. Louis Post-Dispatch,* August 4, 1976.

Brown, Sylvester, Jr. "At Pruitt-Igoe, Crime Moved in Fast, Doomed Experiment." *St. Louis Post-Dispatch*, November 6, 2005.

———. "Monument to Failure Lies Fallow Amid Ghosts of Danger and Decay." *St. Louis Post-Dispatch,* January 2, 2005.

Bruton, Mike. "A Weighty Decision for Spinks." *Philadelphia Inquirer,* June 8, 1985.

Burns, Robert. "Today's Focus: St. Louis Tops the Murder Heap." The Associated Press, April 3, 1980.

Cady, Steve. "U.S. Is Assured 7 Boxing Medals." *New York Times,* July 28, 1976.

Carnicelli, Joe. "Spinks Feels He Won't Be a Pushover for Holmes." United Press International, June 11, 1981.

Cipriano, Ralph. "A Cutman Who's Above All the Rest." *Philadelphia Inquirer,* June 27, 1991.

"Close-Knit American Boxers Seek Six Gold Medals Tonight." The Associated Press, July 31, 1976.

Cooper, Richard T. "Anatomy of a Housing Failure." *Spokesman-Review* (Spokane), September 1, 1971.

Dahlberg, Tim. "Former Heavyweight Champion Spinks Reflects on His Rise to Top and His Decline." The Associated Press, February 16, 2003.

Doogan, Brian. "The Big Interview: Leon Spinks." *Sunday Times* (London), October 3, 2006.

Dorr, Dave. "Boxers Play Cinderella." *St. Louis Post-Dispatch,* July 30, 1976.

———. "Leon Steals Spotlight from Cosell." *St. Louis Post-Dispatch,* July 20, 1976.

———. "Michael Watches Leon Strike Closer to Gold." *St. Louis Post-Dispatch,* July 27, 1976.

———. "Wanted Preachers: Boxers' Mother Credits the Lord." *St. Louis Post-Dispatch,* July 29, 1976.

"Fight Night for Spinks, Cooney." The Associated Press, June 15, 1987.

Finney, Peter. "Auditorium Makeover Sweeps Away Memories." *Times Picayune* (New Orleans), May 2, 1995.

Fiske, Jack. "Spinks at 200 for Holmes Fight." *San Francisco Chronicle,* September 21, 1985.

Giegerich, Steve. "Loss of Corvette a Turning Point for St. Louis Manufacturing." *St. Louis Post-Dispatch,* July 10, 2011.

Gildea, William. "*Confronting the Riddle of Spinks; In the Mountains, Waiting for the Bell.*" *Washington Post,* May 29, 1988.

———. "Leon Spinks Looks to Answer the Bell; Former Champ, 41, Fights Here Saturday." *Washington Post,* October 19, 1994.

Goldstein, Alan. "Spinks Trying to Shake Obscurity." *Baltimore Sun*, October 22, 1994.

Gordon, Jeff. "Leon Spinks Should Punt Latest Idea." *St. Louis Post-Dispatch*, August 3, 1988.

Gordon, Randy. "Michael Spinks Now Stands Tallest Among the Light Heavyweights." *The Ring*, May 1983.

Greer, T. "Spinks' Choice: Daughter or the Ring." *Philadelphia Inquirer*, July 14, 1983.

Grossfield, Stan. "Riches to Rags; Years After Gaining World Fame and Fortune, It's Been a Hard Fall from Glory for Leon Spinks." *Boston Globe*, December 21, 2005.

Gustkey, Earl. "A Longshot: Once Again, the Odds Are Against Him, but Don't Ever Count Out Michael Spinks." *Los Angeles Times*, June 26, 1988.

———. "Tyson Does a Minute-and-a-Half Waltz; It Takes 1:31 to Make Spinks a Lightweight." *Los Angeles Times*, June 28, 1988.

Haas, Al. "Spinks Finds Peace in his Big Rural Home." *Philadelphia Inquirer*, November 24, 1985.

Hanson, Lloyd. "Spinks' Downfall Retold by Camp Lejeune Trainer." *Wilmington Star–News*, July 13, 1980.

Hasen, Jeff. "Spinks Belts Cooney in Fifth." United Press International, June 16, 1987.

Hinman, Kristen. "Prized Fighter: Boxing in St. Louis Will Never Die—Not as Long as Kenny Loehr Has a Kid in the Ring." *Riverfront Times* (St. Louis), December 3, 2008.

Hoffer, Richard. "Leon Sinks Teeth Into a Comeback: Bark May Be Worse Than Bite, but Tell Johnny, He's Back." *Los Angeles Times*, February 6, 1985.

———. "Maybe Michael Spinks Is Taken Too Lightly; After All, There's Leon." *Los Angeles Times*, September 21, 1985.

———. "It's Spinks vs. Cooney Tonight, and Non-Title Bout Leaves Fans Cold." *Los Angeles Times,* June 15, 1987.

———. "Spinks' Toughest Opponent: Self-Doubt Still Getting the Better of Fighter Despite His 30-0 Record." *Los Angeles Times,* June 14, 1987.

"Holmes Wants Loss to Spinks Reversed." The Associated Press, June 25, 1986.

Izenberg, Jerry. "The Champion." *Star-Ledger* (Newark), September 19, 1985.

———. "Down & Sloppy." *Star-Ledger* (Newark), April 20, 1986.

———. "E pluribus Unum." *Star-Ledger* (Newark), March 19, 1983.

———. "El Dorado." *Star-Ledger* (Newark), June 24, 1988.

———. "Emotional Tug of War Rages to Tear Spinks Brothers from Nest." *Star-Ledger* (Newark), March 16, 1978.

———. "Of Fallen Idols." *Star-Ledger* (Newark), April 17, 1986.

———. "The Long Shot." *Star-Ledger* (Newark), September 20, 1985.

———. "Miracle of Miracles." *Star-Ledger* (Newark), September 16, 1978.

———. "Spinks, Futch a Perfect Match." *Star-Ledger* (Newark), June 13, 1987.

Katz, Michael. "Ali: Ready, Willing, but Is He Able?" *New York Times,* September 29, 1980.

———. "Holmes Aims to Stop Spinks but Sets His Sights on Retirement." *New York Times,* June 10, 1981.

———. "Leon Spinks Fights to Pay the Bills." *New York Times,* March 5, 1983.

———. "Leon Spinks in Search of Himself and Title." *New York Times,* June 8, 1981.

———. "Michael Spinks Finds He's Too Good for His Own Good." *New York Times,* February 23, 1985.

———. "Michael Spinks Is Under Pressure." *New York Times,* July 13, 1981.

———. "Spinks Blows Up a Storm in Training." *New York Times,* January 11, 1978.

———. "Spinks Facing 'Ol What's His Name." New York *Daily News,* September 5, 1986.

Kindred, Dave. "World Moves, Champ Spins; Despite Public Statements, Ali Admires His Conqueror." *Washington Post,* August 27, 1978.

Kriegel, Mark. "True Champ Michael Spinks Survives Boxing, Retirement with Grace." New York *Daily News,* July 26, 1998.

Krupa, Gregg. "Legendary Boxing Trainer Emanuel Steward Dies." *Detroit News,* October 25, 2012.

Kunda, John. "A 200-Pound Surprise for Holmes." *Morning Call* (Lehigh Valley), September 21, 1985.

Lader, Martin. "Boxers Are U.S. Hope." United Press International, July 30, 1976.

"Leon Spinks' Career May Be Nearing End." The Associated Press, June 1, 1988.

Lincicome, Bernie. "Boxing Finally Meets Its Match." *Chicago Tribune,* February 18, 1985.

———. "Holmes Went a Fight Too Far." *Chicago Tribune,* September 22, 1985.

———. "Little Doubt of Spinks' Fate." *Chicago Tribune,* September 20, 1985.

Litsky, Frank. "Roland Schwartz, 85, Coach of Prominent Amateur Boxers." *New York Times,* April 8, 1998.

Logan, Greg. "Spinks' Man; Gambling, Scrambling Butch Lewis Plays His Ace for Boxing's Biggest Pot." *Newsday* (New York), June 26, 1988.

———. "Spinks Still Feels the Pain from a Year-Old Tragedy." *Newsday* (New York), February 25, 1984.

Macdonald, Bob. "Leon Spinks 'Born Again.'" *Daily Telegraph* (London), February 1, 1985.

Malone, Ray. "Romney Looks Over High-Rise Complex." The Associated Press, May 15, 1971.

Marantz, Steve. "Spinks Faces Biggest Test Alone." *Boston Globe,* March 16, 1983.

Markus, Robert. "Leon Spinks Lands With 'No Regrets.'" *Chicago Tribune,* July 30, 1989.

Matthews, Wallace. "Kicking Leon When He's Down." *Newsday* (New York), July 11, 1988.

———. "Spinks' Farewell to Fists; Occasional Tears During Speech." *Newsday* (New York), July 28, 1988.

———. "Spinks and Tyson? Not Soon." *Newsday* (New York). January 21, 1988.

———. "Tyson Is Skimping on Prep for Spinks." *Newsday* (New York), May 5, 1988.

———. "Underdog and Loving It; Spinks Says He Is Typically 'Scared' and 'Worried' Before a Fight, but Tyson Isn't Buying the Modesty." *Newsday* (New York), June 20, 1988.

"Michael Spinks Arrested on Gun Charge." The Associated Press, January 6, 1983.

"Michael Wears Smile; Mamma Wears Medal." United Press International, August 3, 1976.

"Mike Spinks Wins Easily." United Press International, July 28, 1976.

Miller, Ira. "Cuba Mastery: Double Gold, Stevenson KO." United Press International, July 30, 1976.

Moore, Shelley. "The Making of a Fight Promoter." *New York Amsterdam News*, September 8, 1979.

Moore, Terence. "Jones Should See Spinks' Precedent." *Atlanta Journal–Constitution,* March 1, 2003.

"Mrs. Spinks, Sons Are Jubilant at Montreal Reunion for Bouts." United Press International, July 31, 1976.

Murray, Jim. "The Other Spinks Lives in Slow Lane." *Los Angeles Times,* September 27, 1987.

———. "When Little Champs Fight the Big Champs, It's Lights-Out Time." *Los Angeles Times,* September 6, 1985.

"Olympic Boxing Official Picks Ali Over Spinks." United Press International, February 12, 1978.

Pepe, Phil. "Will Braxton-Spinks Be Like Arguello-Pryor?" New York *Daily News,* March 18, 1983.

Phillips, Angus. "'New' Spinks Still Lights Up the Ring; Neither Time nor Smile Has Changed for the 'New' Leon Spinks." *Washington Post,* June 11, 1981.

Povich, Shirley. "Heavyweight Fight Picture Is Fuzzy and a Counterfeit." *Miami Herald*, November 4, 1984.

"Prayers Answered for U.S. Boxers." United Press International, July 28, 1976.

Richmond, Peter. "Spinks Has Small Ego in His Corner; No-Brag Attitude Isn't Nonchalance, He Warns." *Miami Herald,* June 23, 1988.

Roberts, Randall. "It Was Just Like Beverly Hills." *Riverfront Times* (St. Louis), June 1, 2005.

Rogal, James C. "'God Bless' Anonymous Trip Donor." *St. Louis Post-Dispatch,* July 30, 1976.

Rule, Sheila. "Boxers' Mother Credits the Lord." *St. Louis Post-Dispatch,* July 29, 1976.

———. "Missing Spinks Link Springs Up in Time." *St. Louis Post-Dispatch*, August 5, 1976.

Schmitz, Brian. "Tyson-Spinks Weigh-In an Exercise in Boredom." *Orlando Sentinel,* June 26, 1988.

Schuyler, Ed. "An AP Sports Analysis." The Associated Press, September 24, 1985.

———. "Michael Spinks Fights with Fear." The Associated Press, June 26, 1988.

Seltzer, Robert. "Outside the Ring, He Fights Stereotypes—and He Wins." *Philadelphia Inquirer,* May 22, 1988.

Seymour, Gene. "The Facts of Her Life—She Was a Champ's Girlfriend . . . but There Was More to Sandra." *Philadelphia Daily News,* January 10, 1983.

Shales, Tom. "Flying with Spinks; After the Big Fight, Reaping the Hypothon Harvest at CBS." *Washington Post,* February 17, 1978.

"Since Turning Professional, Michael Spinks Has Been Best Known as Leon's Little Brother." United Press International, July 17, 1981.

Smith, Elmer. "On Floor at the Shore Spinks Drops Cooney, Wins by TKO in 5th." *Philadelphia Inquirer,* June 16, 1987.

Smith, Red. "On Viewing the Fight from Boston." *New York Times,* October 5, 1980.

Smith, Sam. "Breathless Cooney Defenseless." *Chicago Tribune,* June 17, 1987.

———. "Fame Eludes 'Other' Spinks." *Chicago Tribune,* June 5, 1985.

———. "Leon Spinks Finds His Way; Errant Fighter Returns With 'God On My Side.'" *Chicago Tribune,* March 31, 1985.

Sons, Ray. "Boxers Step into the Lion's Cage." *Chicago Daily News,* July 31, 1976.

"Spinks Brothers Head Boxing Team." The Associated Press, June 7, 1976.

"Spinks Starts Fast, Flattens Foe in First." *Boston Globe,* July 20, 1976.

Taylor, Leon. "Guilty Plea on Gun Is Fine with Spinks." *Philadelphia Daily News,* April 5, 1983.

Timmermann, Tim. "Becoming a Champion Has Been Cory's Destiny; Road to Title Is Filled With Pain." *St. Louis Post-Dispatch,* May 14, 2004.

Tuite, James. "Spinks Defeats Ali to Capture Title." *New York Times,* February 16, 1978.

Waters, Mike. "Holmes Gets Overdue Respect; Hall of Fame Inductee Larry Holmes Dominated His Era with Little Fanfare." *Post-Standard* (Syracuse), June 8, 2008.

———. "Young U.S. Boxers in '76 Overcame Hardship, Doubt." *Post-Standard* (Syracuse), June 9, 2006.

Weich, Susan. "Boxing Legend Kenny Loehr Still Ringside at 80." *St. Louis Post-Dispatch,* May 13, 2012.

Wheatley, Tom. "After the Gold Rush, Work Ethic Pushes Michael to the Top." *St. Louis Post-Dispatch,* June 26, 1988.

———. "Marine Corps Couldn't Handle Leon Spinks." *St. Louis Post-Dispatch,* June 23, 1988.

———. "Spinks' Left Uppercut Could Stop Heavily Favored Tyson." *St. Louis Post-Dispatch,* June 27, 1988.

White, M. J. "Round 1: It's a Draw in the War of Insults." *Miami Herald,* July 14, 1983.

Whiteside, Larry. "Holmes TKOs Spinks in 3." *Boston Globe,* June 13, 1981.

Winderman, Ira. "Leon Spinks Back in Ring Today; Ex-champ Has Nothing to Lose, Title Shot to Gain, He Hopes." *Fort Lauderdale News & Sun-Sentinel,* January 17, 1987.

Ziegel, Vic. "Saturday Night Is Latest Leon Spinks Comeback." New York *Daily News,* October 23, 1994.

Websites/Films/Miscellaneous

"Factsheet; The Games of the Olympiad." Olympic.org, May 2012.

Friedrichs, Chad. *The Pruitt-Igoe Myth.* Directed by Chad Friedrichs. New York: First Run Features, 2011.

HUD. "Pruitt Homes and Igoe Apartments Public Housing Complex: Final Environmental Impact Statement." September 1974.

"Induction Statistics." sss.gov/induct.htm.

Johnson, Lyndon B. "Special Message to the Congress Proposing a Nationwide War on the Sources of Poverty." March 16, 1964.

Linder, Doveed. "An Interview with Leon Spinks." BoxingTalk. com, May 1, 2004.

Maysles, Albert. *Muhammad and Ali.* Directed by Albert Maysles. ESPN, 2009.

Mladinich, Robert. "Charles Mooney, Money and What Might Have Been." TheSweetScience.com, February 1, 2006.

———. "Where Are They Now? Michael Spinks." TheSweet Science.com, November 4, 2007.

Tallent, Aaron. "The Joke That Almost Ended Ali's Career." TheSweetScience.com, February 20, 2005.

Index

About the Authors

John Florio's work has appeared in print, on the web, and on television. He is also the author of the Jersey Leo crime novels, *Sugar Pop Moon* and the forthcoming *Blind Moon Alley*. He lives in Brooklyn, New York. You can visit him at johnfloriowriter.com.

Ouisie Shapiro is a five-time Emmy-winning writer and producer of sports documentaries. Her writing credits include HBO's *Joe Louis: America's Hero Betrayed*; *Namath: Beaver Falls to Broadway;* and *Lombardi*. She has also produced ESPN SportsCentury documentaries on Jack Dempsey, Sonny Liston, and Rocky Marciano, among others.